C000131801

RUSSIAN VILLAGE PROSE

RUSSIAN VILLAGE PROSE

THE RADIANT PAST

Kathleen F. Parthé

PRINCETON UNIVERSITY PRESS

PRINCETON, NEW JERSEY

COPYRIGHT © 1992 BY PRINCETON UNIVERSITY PRESS
PUBLISHED BY PRINCETON UNIVERSITY PRESS, 41 WILLIAM STREET,
PRINCETON, NEW JERSEY 08540
IN THE UNITED KINGDOM: PRINCETON UNIVERSITY PRESS, OXFORD
ALL RIGHTS RESERVED

LIBRARY OF CONGRESS CATALOGING-IN-PUBLICATION DATA

PARTHÉ, KATHLEEN

RUSSIAN VILLAGE PROSE : THE RADIANT PAST / KATHLEEN F. PARTHÉ

P. CM.

INCLUDES BIBLIOGRAPHICAL REFERENCES AND INDEX.

ISBN 0-691-06889-5 — ISBN 0-691-01534-1 (PBK.)

1. RUSSIAN FICTION—20TH CENTURY—HISTORY AND CRITICISM.

2. COUNTRY LIFE IN LITERATURE.   I. TITLE.

PG3096.C68P37   1992

891.73′4409321734—DC20   91-45226   CIP

THIS BOOK HAS BEEN COMPOSED IN LINOTRON BASKERVILLE

PRINCETON UNIVERSITY PRESS BOOKS ARE PRINTED ON ACID-FREE PAPER
AND MEET THE GUIDELINES FOR PERMANENCE AND DURABILITY OF THE
COMMITTEE ON PRODUCTION GUIDELINES FOR BOOK LONGEVITY OF THE
COUNCIL ON LIBRARY RESOURCES

PRINTED IN THE UNITED STATES OF AMERICA

1 3 5 7 9 10 8 6 4 2

1 3 5 7 9 10 8 6 4 2
(PBK)

THIS BOOK IS DEDICATED

TO MY MOTHER

Frances Nagengast Parthé

AND TO THE MEMORY

OF MY FATHER

Arthur Charles Parthé

CONTENTS

PREFACE

Forests shed their crowns of leaves,
But powerfully underground
Roots twist and thrust
Like a gnarled hand.
(Andrei Voznesensky)[1]

D URING what is now called the "period of stagnation" in the
Soviet Union, that is, the years between the ouster of Nikita
Khrushchev in 1964 and the advent of glasnost in the mid-
1980s, millions of copies of novels, story collections, and literary periodicals were published, thousands of reviews were written, and writers, critics, and scholars regularly gathered together at conferences to
discuss literary matters. Yet few people would now say that what was
going on was a naturally functioning "literary life"; it seems more like
a carefully controlled simulation of life, with overt censorship, the internal censor of experienced authors and critics, the carrot-and-stick
approach of the Writers' Union, and abundant evidence of what could
happen to a writer who broke the rules.

Scholarship and journalism in the West during these years focused
to a large degree on what lay outside the official system—on *samizdat*
(literature circulated underground), *tamizdat* (literature written in the
USSR but published abroad), and, to some extent, on émigré literature. In the glasnost years, the emphasis—both East and West—has
been on the return of works and writers to the Soviet Russian literary
process, that is, on the unification of post-Revolutionary Russian-
language literature. The underlying assumptions are that "delayed"
literature (*zaderzhannaia literatura*), by virtue of its having been delayed, carries a uniformly higher value than anything that was officially published in the USSR, and that those who did publish through
official channels necessarily compromised the truth and even the
artistic quality of their works.

This gloomy picture is a simplification of what was—and still remains—a complex and fascinating literary process. As a number of
leading émigré writers themselves have said, Russian literature was
never fully alive outside of Russia, nor completely dead within its borders. And a commonly offered proof of the survival of Russian literature within the USSR during those "stagnant" years is Village Prose
(*derevenskaia proza*), the most aesthetically coherent and ideologically

important body of published literature to appear in the Soviet Union between the death of Stalin and Gorbachev's ascendancy. What Russian structuralists have said of pre-Petrine literature is true of the Soviet period; there was a "cultural canon," but there was also a "zone of permitted anomalies, exceptions to the rules."[2] Village Prose is not the only literature that moved far beyond the Socialist Realist canon and yet somehow prospered under censorship, but it is a much larger, more influential, and longer-lasting movement than either Youth or Urban Prose. But Village Prose is not simply good by default; it is literature with its own intrinsic value.

The main purpose of this book is to characterize the Village Prose movement as a whole through the identification of those parameters which make up its "code of reading." I drew up this "code of reading" for *derevenskaia proza* after examining a considerable amount of literature on rural themes in the Soviet period as well as the criticism of that literature. The criterial properties of Village Prose are articulated in the first chapter; chapters 2 through 5 analyze in detail core characteristics such as CHILDHOOD, attention to LANGUAGE, GENERATIONAL and CYCLICAL TIME, MEMORY, and LOSS. Chapter 6 covers critical reactions, and the ways in which Village Prose and the criticism it stimulated came to occupy what Rosalind Krauss has elsewhere called a "paraliterary space." Chapter 7, which at first glance appears to be a digression on the use of the detective story format for rural themes, leads naturally into a discussion of the end of the Village Prose movement and the kinds of works that evolved from Village Prose in the mid-1980s. Chapter 8 completes this discussion first by demonstrating ways in which Village Prose writers (*derevenshchiki*) were constantly "rereading" the literary landscape; I then explain the various—and at times contradictory—views of the legacy of Village Prose. The two appendixes contain my translation of a particularly fine example of canonical Village Prose—Aleksei Leonov's "Kondyr"—followed by a parametric analysis of that story.

Because the main goal of this book is an elaboration of the constitutent elements of Village Prose, there may appear to be gaps in the presentation, that is, certain well-known writers and works are not mentioned or not emphasized while lesser-known figures are foregrounded. It was simply not feasible to include all authors and works without losing sight of the focus of discussion. Also, I have chosen for reasons of space and coherence of argument not to discuss in any detail the nineteenth- and twentieth-century antecedents of Village Prose, "village poetry" (Fokkina, Rubtsov), adaptations of Village Prose works for the stage or screen, and non-Russian Soviet rural prose (Moldavian, Estonian, Belorussian, and so forth). And, while

women are central to this literary movement as characters and as critics, there are to my knowledge no important women writers of Village
Prose itself. My goal—which is typological rather than taxonomic—
has been to provide a comprehensive characterization of Russian Village Prose, illustrated by numerous examples from specific works.
There has been a great deal of critical and scholarly work in the Soviet
Union analyzing rural literature from the level of specific works and
authors to more wide-ranging discussions of genres, decades, and literary style. Western scholars have themselves provided basic chronol-
ogies of the movement, and characterizations of a number of its leading themes, works, and authors. This book does not seek to replicate
their often fruitful work, but to systematize it, and for the first time to
present Village Prose as a coherent whole, which is possible now that
the movement is over.

The immensely popular and talented Vasilii Shukshin is the figure
whose virtual absence from this book will most likely stimulate comment. While he is of rural origin, and while some of his stories fall
within the parameters of Village Prose, he could not accurately be
called a *derevenshchik*; Geoffrey Hosking rightly speaks of him as
standing "rather to one side of the 'village prose' school."[3] Shukshin
views the village and its inhabitants with an affection that has a very
ironic resonance; what interests him are not the righteous people
(*pravedniki*) of Village Prose, but cranks and eccentrics (*chudiki*), and
while Village Prose likes a village well-regulated by tradition, Shukshin's favorite situation is the *skandal*.[4] He has one of those utterly
distinctive voices in literature that defies the efforts of scholars and
critics to place it within any other context than its own; this includes
efforts in the late 1980s to turn him posthumously into a religious
nationalist. His characters are in transit between town and country,
seeking ways not to return to their highly structured village past, but
rather to find some measure of personal freedom in the present.

The omission of a particular writer or story should not alarm readers; the system of parameters provided in this book can be applied to
other works on rural themes. However, if the picture of Village Prose
is to be complete, what cannot be omitted from this study is a discussion of the possible connections between Village Prose and the rise of
Russian chauvinism.

The political immediacy of extreme Russian nationalism with its
predictable anti-Semitic overtones touched many scholars in the field
in the late 1980s. The links between Village Prose and this potentially
destructive development polarized readers of Russian literature in a
way that few other questions have in recent years. Admirers of Rasputin insisted on his innocence much in the way that others have de-

fended Solzhenitsyn or Dostoevsky from charges of bias. Others, especially "third wave" émigrés, have tended to associate all of Village
Prose with the worst excesses of anti-Semitism, and their assumption
has been that an objective discussion of *derevenskaia proza* could be in-
terpreted as tacit approval of these extraliterary developments.

In chapter 6, I endeavor to give as objective an analysis as possible
of the relationship between Village Prose and the rise of chauvinism.
While I have no intention of defending any Village Prose writers in
particular, I do defend the right to analyze any literary movement or
writer whose works have aesthetic quality and coherence. Gary Saul
Morson has, I think, already faced this problem, and I endorse his
solution wholeheartedly. He made a detailed analysis of Dostoevsky's
Diary of a Writer, which, as he points out, was very chauvinistic even for
its time, and then suggested that we continue reading and valuing
Dostoevsky. He did not go on to see chauvinism—even potentially—in
everything Dostoevsky wrote, and he did not see this writer as the
cause of anti-Semitism in Russia.[5]

I have devoted considerable thought to the topic of Russian nationalism and chauvinism in the literature of the post-Stalinist period. In
addition, I have spoken about the Village Prose–chauvinism question
with Yurii Afanasiev (a historian and one of the liberal leaders of the
new Soviet parliament), Sergei Kovalev (the most obvious "successor"
to Sakharov), Galina Belaia (a brilliant and liberal literary critic), Sergei Zalygin (a rural writer and editor of the liberal journal *Novyi mir*),
the writer Vladimir Voinovich, and many others. None of my numerous sources saw a direct connection, and all of them felt that to come
to such a conclusion would be a rereading—indeed a misreading—of
both history and literature.

In such a complex situation, it is important to keep in mind the
following facts:

1. Village Prose ended as a literary movement in the late 1970s; the
canonical works that are the subject of this book date almost exclusively from the mid-1950s until 1980. That Village Prose came to an
end is not my judgment only, but the conclusion of the vast majority of
Soviet—and Western—literary critics. The *derevenshchiki* have split up
as a group: some still write about the countryside, some about urban
life, the environment, and a variety of other topics. A few of them,
most notably Astafiev, Belov, and Rasputin, have made certain well-
publicized, xenophobic, and anti-Semitic statements. None of these
sentiments was expressed in their Village Prose works. It is legitimate
to ask what link there might be between the canonical Village Prose
narrative of the decline of one's childhood village and statements
made at a later date by several of the rural writers. It is legitimate to

ask whether the recently ended Village Prose movement could have facilitated the rise of Russian chauvinism a few years later. But there is a difference between asking a difficult question and assuming an easy answer.

2. Anti-Semitism has a long history in Russia. In the early 1700s Peter the Great would not allow foreign Jews to take part in his own perestroika program; at the same time, Russians opposed to Peter assumed that he was a Jewish Antichrist. There are many examples of anti-Semitism through the centuries; in the twentieth century one can point to the pogroms before the Revolution, and to the murder of Yiddish writers and the "Doctors' Plot" in the late Stalinist period. The resurgences of anti-Semitism are independent of a particular writer or group of writers or type of literature. Take away Astafiev, Belov, Rasputin, and all their writings and the results would be the same; it is important to realize that they began to express these sentiments not only after Village Prose had ended but also several years after Pamyat and other like-minded organizations began their activities. This does not lessen their responsibility; it does put their remarks in the proper context of a broad-based, primarily urban movement, whose real leaders and ideologues—people like Stanislav Kuniaev and Igor Shafarevich—are not rural writers. The wave of chauvinism that began to be noticed in the late 1980s is the result of many factors, only one of which is the nostalgia for the rural past that turned into anger at those thought to be the architects of the Revolution and collectivization, which resulted in the virtual destruction of the rural "heart" of Russia.

3. To reread all Village Prose as the breeding ground for chauvinism would make as much sense as rereading all of T. S. Eliot or listening to all of Wagner in order to account for European fascism. What *is* important, as I explain in chapter 6, is to see the ways in which the metaphors of Village Prose were subsequently used by literary critics and demagogues for their own ideological purposes. In the mid-nineteenth century, Goncharov's idyllic novel *Oblomov*, Turgenev's narratives of gentry life, and Ostrovsky's play *The Storm* were enlisted by politicized critics for revolutionary ends. Village Prose has been used in much the same way for reactionary purposes. The fact that a few former Village Prose writers have made extremist statements has stigmatized the whole movement and confused discussions of literary-political ties. Making sense of the literary-critical nexus, that is, the complicated interactions among writers, their works, critics, and ideologues is so crucial for an understanding of modern Russian literature and society that it will be the theme of my next book.

The present book will in no way ignore the relevant political and historical issues, but its main focus is the poetics of Village Prose. It is precisely because Katerina Clark concentrated on an analysis of the Soviet novel—rather than on a discussion of Stalinism—that her book is so valuable.[6] I am attempting to achieve something along similar lines for Village Prose.

While many aspects of the literary process in Russia since the Revolution are unique to that country, there is much in Village Prose itself that has a universal appeal. Any country that has rapidly moved from a predominantly rural life in which subsistence agriculture was the main activity to a more urban, industrialized way of life—with all the losses and changes that implies—has much in common with the Russia depicted in *derevenskaia proza*. The South of Faulkner's novels, the England of Ronald Blythe and Flora Thompson, and the France of John Berger, not to mention the developing world, are closer to rural Russia than the map might suggest. And the radiant nature- and family-centered world of childhood, the very essence of Russian Village Prose, is the most personal—and universal—land of all.

ACKNOWLEDGMENTS

I FIRST BEGAN working on this project in 1984, having moved forward in time from eighteenth-century literature, the subject of my master's thesis, and nineteenth-century linguistic poetics, the subject of my doctoral dissertation and a series of articles. What began as a fascination with the literary style of several Soviet Russian authors of rural background developed into an interest in the aesthetic and ideological characterization of the type of literature commonly known as Village Prose. I have benefited from the work of many scholars and critics, all of whom are acknowledged in the notes. I have also had the pleasure of getting to know—through conferences and correspondence—a number of people whose work in Soviet literature and culture has influenced my own. I would like to mention in particular Deming Brown, Katerina Clark, Geoffrey Hosking, S. Frederick Starr, John Dunlop, Galina Belaia, David Gillespie, Josephine Woll, Cathy Nepomnyashchy, Valerie Nollan, and Gerald Mikkelson, who kindly introduced me to Valentin Rasputin. My most patient and astute manuscript readers have been Caryl Emerson, Gary Saul Morson, and Leonard Babby.

An intensive seminar, "Soviet Literature and Society," sponsored by the Social Science Research Council at Stanford University in July 1986 was invaluable. The Summer Exchange at Moscow University under the auspices of the International Research and Exchanges Board in 1987 included enough extra time for important research and contacts. A summer research grant from the University of Rochester allowed me to attend a conference, "The Topicality of Contemporary Soviet Literature," at the University of Amsterdam in 1988, and an American Council of Learned Societies travel grant in 1990 enabled me to participate in the IV World Congress for Soviet and East European Studies in Harrogate, England. My greatest debt by far is to the Kennan Institute for Advanced Russian Studies in Washington, D.C. where I spent the fall of 1987 as a research scholar. In this most supportive of scholarly environments, with generous colleagues like Robert Belknap and Anders Äslund, the parameters of this book emerged. I would like, finally, to thank the editors at Princeton University Press, especially Robert E. Brown and Lauren Lepow, for their enthusiastic response to *Russian Village Prose*.

A NOTE ON TRANSLITERATION
AND TRANSLATION

FOR DIRECT quotations of Russian words, as well as for end-notes and index, I have used the form of transliteration from Cyrillic—known as Shaw II—that most gracefully fits into a literary text by avoiding diacritical marks. In the text itself, I have used a slightly different version of this system for last names, thus "Tolstoy" and "Yashin," and I have eliminated markings for soft and hard signs in proper names, thus "Astafiev" and "Dal." Unless otherwise noted, translations from Russian texts are my own, including the Aleksei Leonov story "Kondyr" in Appendix I.

RUSSIAN VILLAGE PROSE

ONE

THE PARAMETERS OF VILLAGE PROSE

All villages tell stories.
(John Berger)

Oh my quiet homeland,
I have forgotten nothing.
(Nikolai Rubtsov)[1]

VILLAGE PROSE (*derevenskaia proza*) has most often been
defined as literature with a rural theme, setting, and characters that evolved out of the "Ovechkin-style" essay sometime
in the late 1950s or early 1960s.[2] Included in this definition is the notion that this is an "inside" view of rural life, since the majority of
Village Prose writers (*derevenshchiki*) grew up in villages, in contrast to
the authors of kolkhoz (collective-farm) novels, who were frequently
urban in origin and outlook.[3] The basic characterization of Village
Prose could be expanded from one theme (*tema*) to a collective thematics (*tematika*) that encompassed the rural/urban split, criticism of
government policy in the countryside, the revival of Russian national
and religious sentiment, a search for national values, a concern for the
environment, and a nostalgia generated by the loss of traditional rural
life that was elevated to what Geoffrey Hosking has called "an elegiac
intensity."[4] Within the context of this expanded thematics, the traditional village and its peasants acquired symbolic resonance, and their
decline could be read as having "radical implications" for the Russian
people.[5]

Theme-based definitions of Village Prose are not in themselves
wrong, but they are insufficient; they simply do not capture enough of
the most important qualities of this material, and they give little indication of the crucial ways in which it was a force for aesthetic as well as
ideological renewal in Russian literature. Galina Belaia has repeatedly
complained that superficial themes like "village" and "urban" are not
very useful in the analysis of concrete works of art; she asks for a
newer, deeper "critical code."[6] Along these lines, there is another way
of looking at Village Prose—as not just a theme or set of themes, but
as a thematic orientation that has its own ideological, moral, and aesthetic profile.[7] Liliia Vilchek points us toward an even more compre-

hensive description when she speaks of the "contours" (*kontury*) and "system of coordinates" (*sistema koordinat*) of this literary movement, and, most importantly, of its "code of reading" (*kod prochteniia*)—its semiotic.[8]

In *The Soviet Novel* Katerina Clark provided what amounts to a code of reading for that genre, by carefully reconstructing its "prototypical plot" and definitive characteristics, along with the most important rituals and patterns. While referring extensively to specific works, she gives the reader the clearest possible sense of the invariants, the essence, of the Socialist Realist novel.[9]

This is what I will try to do for Village Prose: construct useful generalizations without violating specific works, or reducing a richly varied literary movement to a single scheme. So much literature on the rural theme has been written since Stalin's death that it can seem at times to be an undifferentiated mass, but, as with the Socialist Realist novel, a canonical work can be identified, and such an identification has an important critical and historical function.

Basically, I envision a *spectrum* of Soviet Russian literature on rural themes, with the Socialist Realist kolkhoz novel at one end, and Russian Village Prose at the other. Literary works about the countryside written after 1953 fit in along the spectrum according to a finite set of constituent properties culled from the reading of a large number of works from this period, and reinforced by an examination of the relevant critical literature. These properties—or parameters—are not meant to exercise a theoretical stranglehold, but to quantify, that is, to make more explicit, the sense among Soviet writers, critics, and readers that a major change took place in Russian rural prose in the 1950s, something with more than simply the politically reformist dimension that we have traditionally used to identify literature of the Thaw.

Not all the parameters carry equal weight in this description: some are core attributes, while others are peripheral. In a given work, of course, there can be a great deal of overlapping—between properties of Village Prose and of War Prose, for example, or even between Village and Urban Prose. As the concept of a spectrum makes clear, a work can exhibit some characteristics of both Village Prose and Socialist Realist Kolkhoz Literature, although one or the other type of literature will generally predominate. The core properties of Village Prose make a contrast at almost every point to those of Kolkhoz Literature, and indeed, contrast is used in both of these types of rural literature as a structural principle: such contrasts as old/new, endings/beginnings, old age/youth, submitting to nature/ruling nature, preservation/destruction, local/national, spiritual/material, continuity/revolution, past/present, and hand/machine. As we scan the spectrum from

Kolkhoz Literature to Village Prose, the positive and negative poles of these contrasting elements are reversed.[10]

The parameters of Village Prose will be sketched out in this introductory chapter, and a number of the core properties—language, cyclical time, childhood memories, loss, the use of the past—will be further elaborated in the chapters that follow. Together they comprise a "code of reading" for Village Prose, which is its most comprehensive description and a necessary heuristic device. To paraphrase Gary Saul Morson, classification is in a large measure interpretation.[11] My translation of Aleksei Leonov's story "Kondyr" and its companion essay show how the code of reading that has evolved in this book can be applied back to specific texts.

The Village

It is axiomatic that "Village Prose"[12]—which is mostly set in the years after the collectivization of agriculture began in the late 1920s—is centered in the village rather than the kolkhoz, even though these may actually occupy the same physical space (kolkhozes generally include a number of villages). The name of the village—Shibanikha in Belov's *The Eve*, Pekashino in Abramov's *The Pryaslins*, Matyora in Rasputin's *Farewell to Matyora*—is more prominent than the name of the kolkhoz, which is used ironically, if at all (kolkhozes were given names like "Victory," "The Path to Socialism," or "Lenin"). The village name gives the residents a distinct identity, a means of differentiating themselves verbally from the residents of the next village, as, for example, *pekashintsy* 'people-from-Pekashino', in a way that the kolkhoz name does not.

The village boundary has traditionally had both a magic and a social power. In Russian folklore, crossing boundaries—of the threshold or the village—made one vulnerable to evil spirits who could harm or even kill you. In a social sense, the people in the adjoining settlements may have had everything in common with each other, but they had different names and often perceived each other as being not only different, but even hostile (*chuzhoi*).

In an interior monologue from Vladimir Lichutin's *The Last Wizard*, an old woman thinks about her son who lives in another village:

> Just think: Kuchema is really close—just fifteen miles down the river— but it isn't at all like here, it's strange. The people there have different blood and different customs. They don't sow barley, and because they haven't worked the land for so long, they're wild and sharp-tongued. In the old days, Pogorelsky women thought of Kuchema as a different

country. Look at my son: he hasn't even lived there fifteen years and already he's changed completely and has taken up all their ways.[13]

To this cast of mind, each village is a separate homeland, a *malaia rodina*. "Every village has its own beliefs—every settlement its own customs."[14]

Moshe Lewin notes that periodic brawls—often planned ahead of time—took place during major religious holidays, usually between the men of neighboring villages. "Atavistic mechanisms, dimly preserved reminiscences of old, protracted, long-solved, and seemingly forgotten land feuds between villages might have kept unextinguished residues of hatred and a desire for vengeance which was ready to flare up on some occasion or other against real or apparent culprits of an almost mythical past."[15]

Allowing for regional variation, the village had a fairly stable set of features: simple houses (wooden in the north and Siberia, wattle-and-daub or stucco in the central and southern regions), and their outbuildings (barns, sheds), vegetable gardens, small orchards, ponds, bathhouses, wells, a church and bell tower (though not in every village), and a cemetery.[16]

Village Prose emphasizes that the village is isolated from the rest of the world. It is linked to the outside by a country road (*proselok*), a turning off from the nearest highroad (*bol'shak*).[17] The isolation served to reinforce differences not only between neighboring rural settlements, but also between rural and urban areas.

Each village constructs "*a living portrait of itself* ... everybody is portrayed and everybody portrays."[18] This is an oral history, built out of the stories of the day and narratives handed down from one generation to another; it is the way that the village defines itself. This ongoing "communal" portrait is not simply gossip: "it is an organic part of the life of the village. Should it cease, the village would disintegrate."[19]

In a discussion of how the Revolution of 1789 was received in rural France, Emmet Kennedy stressed the importance of the village. In Paris, the leading men of letters had initiated a rejection of institutional constraints. "By contrast, authority *was* the village, not something erected over and against it, which helps explain the villages' perpetuation of traditions. The village was the matrix of cultural reproduction and stability." It was ruled by deference, reverence, belief, and habit, "the antithesis of the mocking spirit of Paris."[20] The Russian village had the same enduring stability. Moshe Lewin calls the village "the living cell—of rural society in Russia" about which little has been written. He cautions that "unless we 'crack,' so to speak, the village, something very crucial for the understanding of rural society will be missing. Probably also for the understanding of Russia. It is inside the village that forces were at work—neighborhood networks, family systems, labor processes, social hierarchies and values—that maintained this huge mass of rural humanity and sustained, shaped, sometimes blocked Russia."[21] The peasant commune eventually fell to collectivization, Lewin notes, but the village and the peasantry remained. And their story is told in Village Prose.

Nature

Nature also occupies an important place in Village Prose, though rarely to the exclusion of human beings. Georges Nivat sees a myth— even a cult—of the Russian landscape among writers and artists from the early nineteenth century on, which reemerges in Village Prose; "half-pagan, half-Christian, it measures the immeasurable, the riches/ poverty of the landscape."[22] Tsvetov calls the attitude of the *derevenshchiki* toward nature not that of "feigned rapture" at the beauty of the landscape, but a sense of "kinship."[23] In Village Prose, we see mostly the nature that is part of the villagers' everyday activities—the kitchen garden (*ogorod*), the orchard, ponds and fields, the forest and the river. When the peasant ventures out of the village, it is usually to fish in the river or to gather mushrooms, berries, or firewood in the forest, or—more rarely—to go hunting. The forest is life-sustaining, but also awe-inspiring, and well into the Soviet period it gave rise to a variety of superstitions among rural people, as Vasilii Belov demonstrated in *Harmony* and Iurii Kazakov in "Goblins." The mysterious power of nature still pervaded descriptions of the forest, thunderstorms, and the breakup of river ice in the spring (*ledokhod*). The natural cycles controlled virtually every aspect of the villagers' lives—when they worked, when they rested, when they celebrated.

There is a purer type of nature writing in Soviet Russian literature—as there is a purer form of hunters' narratives—in works by Kazakov, Nagibin, and Astafiev, where the emphasis is on nature to the exclusion of all but one or two observers, usually hunters or fishermen. This type of writing is really a continuation of the Aksakov-Prishvin line in Russian literature and tends to come from writers not of peasant background. Those who actually grew up in a village are less likely to foreground nature and romanticize it.[24] When nature becomes the subject of a work of Village Prose, this focus serves either to emphasize a child's discovery of his surroundings, or to mourn the harm done to nature by poorly planned development or urban hunters and tourists. A whole environmental movement was spawned by rural writers, but its publications are not Village Prose itself, in the same way that Russian chauvinist statements are not Village Prose. The attitude toward nature in Village Prose can be poetic, but it is basically practical; the assumption is that if nature is abused, it will stop providing what people need to live.[25]

Home

The typical Village Prose writer has been called a "bard of the peasant house" (*pevets izby*). Home is important to this literature in its specificity—as the house where the narrator or character grew up—and as emblematic of all rural Russia. Inhabitants' abandoning the peasant house to move to a modern consolidated settlement or to the city is one of the central narratives—along with the return of native sons or daughters—of Village Prose. Most often what we see are very humble dwellings with everyone living in at most two rooms, with some attached structures, and with domestic animals sharing part of the house in the winter. The inventory of the house is simple: the stove and icon-corner are essential, along with a table, some benches, a hanging cradle, a trunk, and a few utensils and tools. In the works that are set in the postwar period, there is greater variety in the furnishings—a clock, a radio, even a television—but the writers are more interested in the older, traditional peasant possessions such as distaffs, embroidered towels, samovars, bast shoes, wooden spoons, and woven baskets.

If the village is the most important rural unit, then the home is the focal point of peasant life on a daily basis.[26] Belov describes it as the "center" from which everything else radiates.[27] In a climate with long, dark winters, and in a type of literature that remains close to memories of childhood, the peasant home with its stove-cum-bed and a grandmother who had an endless supply of fairy tales will have a dominant place. Its destruction will be one of the surest signs of the end of the rural way of life.

Native Realms, Kindred Places

The house is not an impersonal structure—it is *rodnoi* 'one's own, native'. The concept of *rodnoi* is another core attribute of Village Prose. In fact, there is an entire constellation of words with the root *rod-* that play an important role in Village Prose.[28] *Rodina* 'native land' generally refers to Russia, but in canonical Village Prose it is more widely used in the sense of *malaia rodina* 'native region'—rather than the whole country. On an even more intimate level it can refer to the village of one's childhood, which is also called *rodnaia derevnia* (lit. 'native village'). During the 1960s, when the reform essay was yielding to a more lyrical form of rural literature, many works appeared that used words from the *rod-* "family" in the title.

Vladimir Tendriakov's 1964 sketch "Den' na rodine" (A day in the old hometown) is an especially fine example of this kind of transitional work. Here *rodina* is used by the author's father to mean only one thing—the particular village, Makarovskaia, where Tendriakov was born and where he spent the first few months of his life. The strictly local meaning of this "homeland" is further emphasized when Tendriakov mentions that his mother is from the nearby village of Ignashikha, and thus they do not have the same *rodina*.[29]

There is a multitude of little "homelands" in Russian Village Prose, each a microcosm—a miniature, complete universe. While Village Prose may have reflected or even fueled the revival of strong Russian nationalist sentiment, it is most often oriented toward one village or region. Village Prose turns away from gigantism—the large, impersonal, multinational state whose citizens move easily from one territory to another, or, as officials, from kolkhoz to kolkhoz. Rural writers and critics have spoken about the crucial difference between homeland and territory: "a person living on a territory has no sense of home, of a small or large native land."[30] These writers speak of something smaller, more authentically and deeply personal and familiar.

Time

The concepts of *rodnoi* and *rodina* lead to another group of core attributes of Village Prose. THE PAST, MEMORY, NOSTALGIA, and CHILDHOOD are linked by their orientation to TIME. The sense of time in Village Prose is slow, cyclic, focused mostly on everyday life, and often directed toward the past. Even when the setting is the present, it is in the past that narrator and characters look for roots, beauty, traditions, and values; the fear is that in losing the rural past, Russians will also lose their future. The frequent older characters and their recollections provide a natural access to the past, as do the authors' personal memories of a rural childhood. Individual memories blend with a national memory of the rapidly vanishing peasant way of life to create works of great intensity.

Village Prose writers not only foreground memories but also project a sense of nostalgia, that is, the reconstruction or essence of what is basically a "personally experienced past."[31] There is a palpable contrast in Village Prose to the unlived, artificial past of Kolkhoz Literature. Fred Davis, a sociologist of nostalgia, has noted that nostalgia is a "distinctive, aesthetic modality" lacking a "position in objective time."[32] He sees the time perspective as the characteristic that differentiates nostalgia from other forms of consciousness. "Unlike the 'vivid present' of everyday life—that intersection of clock time and our inner time sense—nostalgia leaps backward into the past to rediscover and revere it. Here present clock time loses much of its relevance, and because the rediscovered past is clothed in beauty temporal boundaries are extended in imagination well beyond their actual chronological span."[33]

Nostalgia in literature, when not used superficially, can be a complex emotion, even a spiritual quality. It always involves a sense of sadness at loss, but a sadness that is leavened by a "radiance" or "luminousness," what Russians express with the words *svetlost'* and *svetlyi* (nominal and adjectival forms, respectively). The radiant past (*svetloe proshloe*), radiant memory (*svetlaia pamiat'*), and radiant/luminous sadness (*svetlaia pechal'*) are central to Village Prose—as they are to other memory-oriented literature. The sense of *svetlaia pechal'* is best expressed in these well-known lines from Pushkin: "Darkness covers the Georgian hills; / The Aragva flows noisily before me. / I am sad and yet light-hearted; my sadness is luminous; / My sadness is filled with your presence."[34] Here, a quality of light becomes a quality of memory. The "warm glow from the past" is a universal quality of nostalgia.[35] Consider this extract from the diary of Anaïs Nin.

> But now I see that the extraordinary was in my own vision. . . . I see my life in Paris with the added elements of fiction: lighting, focus, the gold patina which memory adds to it, and they appear to me more vividly, more separated from the quotidian details which dilute it from the unformed, the execrescences, the dust or dullness of familiarity. They are highlighted in this case by poignant memory and a desire to relive it all, now that it is forever lost.[36]

One can find this radiance in certain works of Urban Prose, such as Iurii Trifonov's story "Games at Dusk" and frequently in émigré literature. Vladimir Nabokov's *Speak, Memory* is full of sunlight-dappled memories and "magic lantern" slides of the idyllic childhood he reconstructed.[37] Richard Coe saw in the Childhood genre an attempt to capture a child's sense of time and space, where memories are suffused with a light, a radiance that Coe calls "magical."[38]

There is another side to this nostalgia, the other voice of an "inner dialogue" between a good past and a bad or problematic present.[39] This inner dialogue can break out into the expression of angry, bitter feelings about what seems to have been carelessly and needlessly lost. "This is what we might call, perhaps, 'black' nostalgia: far from being sentimental, it is an outburst of despair or protest against the wanton murder of the countryside, village, and even town, a lament for the deliberate destruction of beauty."[40] Coe assumed that this negative motif is absent from Russian literature after 1917 because "it may be deemed, to say the least, impolitic for a writer to lament over-loudly the way of life that reigned before the Soviets."[41] Actually, Village Prose provides many examples of this angrier, darker nostalgia that borders on an urgent sense of apocalypse. The urgency, the sense of "borrowed time," has to do with the rapid, often poorly planned process of rural transformation, and the destruction of nature in the age of the NTR (scientific-technical revolution) and GES (hydroelectric station). These rural-born writers realize that they are the last to know, by virtue of their own childhoods and the stories told them by older villagers, the ancient patterns of rural life; their memories become an important legacy to the Russian people. The sense that this is a literature of "last things" is strongly expressed in the many metaphors for loss found in Village Prose. As this literary movement waned in the late 1970s and early 1980s, the shadow of the dies irae (day of wrath) began to overwhelm certain works and writers, displacing the formerly predominant "radiant sadness."

A Native Language

Authenticity and sincerity were goals that critics and writers set for the new rural literature in the 1950s, and nowhere is the impact of these goals more noticeable than in the poetics of Village Prose. Dialogue most clearly reflects the contrast to Socialist Realist Kolkhoz Literature—as well as to Youth Prose and Urban Prose—but the narrative language of Village Prose also showed striking improvements over its predecessors in Soviet rural literature, especially in the areas of interior monologue and *skaz* (colloquial) narration. Village Prose writers consciously sought to preserve the traditional local names for fields, woods, and other places important to a given village, as well as local and regional variations on names for common objects, for instance, types of berries and mushrooms. This is what Fedor Abramov called "forest literacy" (*lesnaia gramota*) in his four-volume work *The Pryaslins*. But the energetic, imaginative use of language in much of Village Prose goes far beyond this "forest literacy" and involves the use of linguistic-stylistic devices such as subjectless verbs and indefinite pronouns to indicate the peasant's sense of awe in the face of the elemental forces of nature. The authenticity and intimacy achieved by the language of Village Prose may be what comes across least successfully in translation, but it is no less essential to an understanding of this literature.

These, then, are the "parameters" of Russian Village Prose, contrasting at virtually every point—setting, orientation in time, language—to Socialist Realist Kolkhoz Literature. It will prove more useful in this book to show how works—rather than writers—fit into this scheme; while it is relatively easy to make a strong case for the existence of Village Prose, the writers are more elusive. Not only do they resist being labeled *derevenshchiki*, but a number of them have written other types of literature—Urban Prose, War Prose, ethnographic sketches, studies of icon collecting—as well as much that is publicistic in nature.

There are works that possess all the characteristics of either Village Prose or of Kolkhoz Literature, while others—Abramov's novels, for example—mediate between the two. A small number of works practice a sort of adaptive mimicry: a story takes place on a kolkhoz but is in fact deeply critical of the destruction of rural life, or, conversely, a story seems to be focused on older villagers but really is future-directed, affirming all the values of canonical Socialist Realism. The Soviet literary situation is highly complex, and I hope that the parametric approach employed in this book will shed its own "radiance" on Russian Village Prose—the largest and most coherent body of aesthetically interesting and ideologically significant literature to be published in the Soviet Union during the three decades following Stalin's death.

TWO

THE QUESTION OF GENRE

THE NOVEL was the principal, deliberately monumental genre of Kolkhoz Literature and of Socialist Realism as a whole, the "official repository of state myths."[1] However, beginning with Ovechkin's "District Routine" (1952) there was a conscious rejection of the by-then debased novel in favor of smaller forms. The Ovechkin-style essay (*ocherk*) was stylistically close to Socialist Realism; its innovation lay in criticism of collective-farm administration and admiration for the peasants. It was several years later that writers and critics began looking for inspiration on rural themes to Sergei Aksakov, Gleb Uspensky, Turgenev, Chekhov, Prishvin, and Bunin. A four-volume collection of Aksakov's work had appeared in 1955, and Bunin's work was made available to Soviet readers in an influential three-volume collection a year later. Russian writers—to paraphrase Taine—began to see the countryside through the "intermediation" of these earlier literary figures, and not through the bombast of Panferov, Babaevsky, and Nikolaeva. One can say that the canonical works of Village Prose are both *ante* (referring to prior literary tradition) and *anti* (written against) collective-farm literature.

Shorter forms—*ocherki* and short stories (*rasskazy*)—characterized the first decade of the new rural literature, while longer narratives (*povesti*) dominated the period from the early 1960s until the decline of Village Prose as a movement toward the end of the seventies.[2] Canonical Village Prose included relatively few novels, the most successful being Fedor Abramov's *The Pryaslins* (1958–1978), a four-volume epic about life in the northern village of Pekashino. Historical novels about rural Russia, based more on archival research—or ideological distortions—than on the personal reminiscences of the writer, his family, and fellow villagers, fall largely outside the parameters of Village Prose. In canonical Village Prose, as in the memory-inspired writing of Sergei Aksakov, there is a "displacement of time to the past"; the "remote" time of pastoral prose "is not the objective time of the historical novel, but personal time; the narrated events are remembered events, the personal experience of the narrator also vouches for their validity."[3] This does not mean that Village Prose treats only cyclical and personal time; one of the most salient aspects of this literature is the way that history invades village life. The first segments of Mozhaev's *Peasant Men and Women* and Belov's *The Eve* are for these and other reasons much closer to Village Prose than are the continuations of these chronicles that were published after 1985.

A conventional genre analysis of Russian Village Prose would yield a great deal of conflicting information and few insights. Village Prose—like Russian literature in other periods—tends to resist strict classification by genre. Still, certain generalizations can be made about the forms chosen by the *derevenshchiki*.

The *ocherk* is a genre that has attracted a great deal of attention but which has so far defied the efforts of literary scholars to capture it. While other genres—the short story, story, and novel—can be to some extent described in terms of length or plot development, the boundaries of the *ocherk* are remarkably flexible.[4] Its characteristics are so relative (*uslovnyi*) that one can come up with "a thousand" examples.[5]

Even the *ocherk* that marks the beginning of Village Prose cannot be taken entirely at face value. The author indulges in a bit of "literary mystification," pretending to be merely a reporter witnessing these events when behind this mask he is really giving them shape.[6] Ovechkin imitated a journalistic style and form in order to begin the process of returning rural literature to real life. What is made to look like a problem-oriented, documentary essay is really the beginning of a story, as Ovechkin himself suggests in closing. This essay, he said, had no ending, because it was drawn "almost" from life. "Perhaps it will even turn into a story."[7] In the evolution of Village Prose we see artistic literature being renewed and reshaped from "below" by the use of nonartistic and marginally artistic genres and folklore, while it was also being inspired from "above" by certain nineteenth-century fictional forms. Ovechkin was able to introduce into this early essay material that would have been unacceptable in the traditional novel form of those years, that is, the kolkhoz novel.

Vladimir Soloukhin, in his 1956 poem "Work" ("Rabota") was not very enthusiastic over the prospect of composing even an Ovechkin-style essay. His poetic persona complains at having been ordered to write about a pig farm and the latest statistics on *salo* 'lard'. In order to do this properly he is forced to stifle his lyric impulses, to cover—with writing about agriculture—the sad and luminous features of a beloved face that appears on the page before him.[8]

The assertion of the lyric voice distinguished Russian rural literature of the mid-1950s from that of the previous two decades. Problem-oriented sketches continued to be written, but the new forces in rural literature that had been energized by Ovechkin were not to be limited to that genre. Such works as Dorosh's *Rural Diary* (1956–1970), Nikolai Zhdanov's "A Trip Home" (1956), Soloukhin's *Vladimir Country Roads* (1957), Kazakov's stories "The Woman by the Sea" (1957) and "Old

People" (1958), and Fedor Abramov's *Brothers and Sisters* (1958) soon overshadowed the Ovechkin-type sketch.

As the parameters of Village Prose became more clearly defined in the second half of the 1950s, it was evident that this literary movement would mediate between two modes: the publicistic and the lyric. It would also, for the most part, make its own genre rules. The Kazakov-type story and the rare Village Prose novel had their own physiognomy, but most of the other forms in which Village Prose appeared are—despite the variety of genre designations given them by writers and editors—more or less versions of differing length of what began to look like a genre of its own.[9]

The work of the English rural writer Flora Thompson (1876–1947) has been described in terms that are applicable to much of *derevenskaia proza*; her trilogy *Lark Rise to Candleford* "falls into no obvious category."[10] There are fictional and personal elements, but she writes neither a novel nor an autobiography, and it is too intimate and dwells too much on "humble details" to be social history in the usual sense. "[Her books] are a simple, yet infinitely detailed record of the life of the poor as it was lived in an obscure Oxfordshire hamlet in the eighteen-eighties and nineties, all remembered from a child's experience, all faithfully set down, all true."[11] What Thompson created were the "annals" or "archives" of the poor. She hoped that readers would understand that her intention was to write of "'that more excellent way of life of our forefathers.'"[12]

The new "genre" of Village Prose had as its basis the genuine, long-term rural experiences and memories of the writer. It also drew upon his sense of the depth and beauty of rural traditions and language, as well as his awareness of the difficult history of the collectivized countryside and the seeming impossibility of fair and efficient agricultural management and of industrialization that did not do great harm to nature. The Bakhtinian sense of genre, that it conveys a "vision of the world" through specific examples, surely applies to the case of Village Prose.[13]

A particular sense of experience, never formalized, guides the author's efforts in creating his or her work. Each author who contributes to the genre learns to experience the world in the genre's way, and, if the work is significant and original, to enrich the genre's capacity for future visualization. In short, a genre, understood as a way of seeing, is best described . . . as "form-shaping ideology"—a specific kind of creative activity embodying a specific sense of experience.[14]

The abandon with which writers and editors gave genre designations to rural works shows the essential meaninglessness of these inconsistently applied and often unwieldy labels. How can one justify calling Abramov's "Around and About," Soloukhin's *Vladimir Country Roads*, and Astafiev's *The Final Bow* "stories" (*povesti*), while Rasputin's "Downstream" is called an "essay" (*ocherk*)? And what could be meant by such terms as *povest' v novellakh* (a story in novellas) and *povestvovanie v rasskazakh* (a narration in the form of short stories)? This is only a small sampling of the numerous labels that appeared below the titles of works of Village Prose.[15]

The detective-story genre was borrowed by several rural writers—Boris Mozhaev, Vil Lipatov, and Viktor Astafiev—to polemicize about the ethical and aesthetic questions that had been raised by Village Prose. Folklore genres such as the fairy tale (*skazka*), the humorous anecdotal narrative (*bukhtina*), and the so-called true story (*byl'*) shaped some works of Village Prose; however, the most extensive use of folklore was not for its genre possibilities but as poetic material in epigraphs and inserted texts, and as an influence on narrative style.

A number of *derevenshchiki* devoted their energies to the novel's generic opposite and created collections of very short lyrical essays in the tradition of Turgenev's prose poems. These collections have the most flexible possible boundaries but are meant to reflect broadly unifying themes. Abramov's *Trava-murava* (The thick green grass, 1955–1980) included material that he had not been able to fit into his stories and novels. The title comes from the folk language, where it stands for nature and life as a whole, the grass-covered earth that gives us such pleasure while we are alive and to which we return when we die. Many of the selections are anecdotes that could be seen as narrative segments or embryonic plots for stories. They include overheard conversations, witnessed scenes, and extracts from letters. Along with nature and loss an important—perhaps the most important—theme is the folk language itself. The final section begins with the observation that "the Russian people have an apt expression for everything: for a momentous, joyous occasion, and for a time of great sorrow."[16] Abramov championed the use of folk and regional speech in mainstream literature in light of criticism from some urban quarters. For him, the diversity of the Russian language in the countryside was not an embarrassment, but a national treasure. In his "leaves of grass" he preserved examples that—given his relatively early death—might otherwise have been lost.

"Dom v Verkole" (The house in Verkola), which consists of selections from Abramov's notebooks, contains many more lyrical miniatures and gives evidence that the author saw these as a genre of their own. Abramov's widow and literary executor said that in his later years he was working on a new cycle of these short lyrical stories. The collection would be unified by place (their home, Verkola, the north) and by Abramov's interest in northern *byt* 'the daily cycle'.[17]

Viktor Astafiev's collection of short pieces is called *Zatesi* (Marks/Notches). He said that he had called them short stories at first but found that they were actually "miniatures": "they were outside of genre, not bound by conventional literary forms."[18] Representing twenty-five years of an irregularly kept notebook, these pieces include statements of fact, conversations, everyday truths, and travel notes. Astafiev claims a kinship in *Zatesi* with Turgenev's prose poems and with similar collections by contemporary writers such as Krupin (*Zerna*, Seeds/Kernels), Belov (*Lad*, Harmony), and Souloukhin (*Kameshki na ladoni*, A handful of pebbles). Astafiev's title refers to the ancient custom of marking trees in the taiga so that hunters and others passing by could find their way to the nearest hut, road, or settlement.[19] It was these notches that saved Astafiev as a boy when he became separated from his father on a fishing trip; he sees in them something friendly and even luminous, akin to the light from a distant house that a lonely traveler sees on a cold winter's night.

Zatesi is subtitled "Stories and Essays"; there is a sense that these short works are signposts leading to Russia's rural past, to keep writer and reader alike from getting lost in the modern world. Astafiev's miniatures are more polished than Abramov's, each one a complete, small essay or story about Siberian life. The philosophy behind *Zatesi* is exemplified by the section entitled "Things Ancient and Eternal." As he looks out his window one foggy night, the narrator sees the village horses standing together as they sleep. He is struck by the timelessness of this scene: horses, the forest, flower-carpeted fields, bushes, grasses, and apple trees. He feels sorry for all those who will never know the sleeping village that he sees outside his window.[20]

Alexander Solzhenitsyn's "Prose Poems" to some extent fit under this rubric. They were not published in the Soviet Union, but a number of them were circulated in samizdat copies. In one of them he describes—in a somewhat generalized way—what it is like to travel country roads in central Russia and why the Russian landscape is said to be very "soothing" (*umirotvoriashchii*).

> It is because of the churches. They rise over ridge and hillside, descending towards wide rivers . . . towering above the thatch and wooden huts of everyday life with their slender, carved and fretted belfries. . . .
>
> Wherever you wander, over field and pasture, many miles from any homestead, you are never alone: above the walls of trees, above the hayricks, even above the very curve of the earth itself, the dome of a belfry is always beckoning you, from Gorki Lovetskie, Lyubichi or Gavrilovskoe.[21]

Lest this seem overly idyllic, Solzhenitsyn goes on to say that upon closer inspection, these rural churches turn out to be in a very sorry state.

The Image of the Author

One way to understand what kinds of literature the *derevenshchiki* wrote is to examine the narrative masks they wore. The writers of Kolkhoz Literature saw themselves primarily as rural activists, front-line reporters, and, of course, "engineers of human souls." Village Prose writers saw themselves as witnesses to traditional village life and chroniclers of its rapid decline. They are Old Believers, pilgrims, collectors of antiquities, elegists, mourners, hunters and fishermen, lexicographers, archaeologists, folk storytellers, and the righteous sons of dying mothers. They even identify with the old women—who in the absence of village men are the repositories of the ancient ways—and with migratory birds. The writers are shamans and wizards to whom the secrets of the past have been entrusted and who must pass on their magic lore before they die. They are both the "bearers" and the "recorders" of village life, descendants of Turgenev's peasants who have taken up the pen to tell their own history.[22] Their stories are chronicles, laments, eyewitness accounts, notches on wooden tables and marks on trees that are meant to keep them and their fellow Russians from losing their roots, their memory of the past, and their national distinctiveness.

The "image of the author" in Village Prose has many facets, but there is a unifying theme of the writer's responsibility to record and preserve peasant traditions while lobbying for improvements that might keep rural people from fleeing to urban areas and the government from abandoning what are labeled economically unpromising (*besperspektivnye*) villages, and destroying the environment through hasty development.[23] Long or short, works of Village Prose are based on this self-image and these concerns. In the end it is more useful to try to articulate the author's self-image, to evaluate the balance between publicistic and lyric elements, and to look at the parameters of Village Prose as they apply to a given work, than to insist upon finding a genre pigeonhole in which to place it.

Narrative Patterns in Village Prose

Readers and critics who have looked to Village Prose for plot have found it wanting. The "goal-directed plot is alien to the pastoral world *per se*"; cyclical life, small contained "episodes," and descriptions of place are much more important.[24] A surer path toward an understanding of form in Village Prose is to identify the most frequent and significant narrative patterns.[25] The first pattern that comes to mind is that of RETURN, the attempt of a former villager to return—at least for a short time—to his roots. One of the earliest examples of this is Nikolai Zhdanov's 1956 short story "A Trip Home" ("Poezdka na rodinu"). An urban bureaucrat, Pavel Varygin, travels to his native village of Tyurino after an absence of many years to attend his mother's funeral. The story highlights the familiar concerns of the Ovechkin period: low pay, poor food, constant changes in the size of private plots, and the enormous gaps of understanding and trust between bureaucrats and peasants that led to confused directives and serious crop losses.

On another level, "A Trip Home" is about the hero's journey into his past. When he arrives at the local train station, Varygin recalls the names of all the nearby villages, so familiar to him from childhood. The old wooden church, the funeral service, cemetery crosses against the gray sky, the house with its well-worn table, the old samovar, the cradle hooks—all these evoked "a world he thought had long since ceased to exist."[26] Varygin is interrupted in his reverie by a local woman, who asks whether he thinks that the peasants are being treated justly. Feeling weary and powerless, Varygin rushes back to the city; in his drowsy state on the train, the image of the village comes back to him, but this time it is his deceased mother who asks him about the government's treatment of peasants. As will so often be the case in Village Prose, the return to the village is a poignant and awkward occasion, and the memory of both peasant values and rural problems follows the uprooted village son back to the city.

The narrative of return is both melancholy and luminous. As this narrative developed, it began to involve not simply a personal sense of the passing of one's childhood and the loss of family members, but the acute sense of the end of a way of life, the deracination not just of the hero, but of the Russian people as a whole.

A second narrative line concentrates not on the voluntary uprooting of young villagers but on the forced UPROOTING of old people, either when they become unable to care for themselves and must move in with relatives, or when their entire village is abandoned. In this narrative two threads are intertwined—the death of old peasants and the emptying of peasant homes and villages. In both cases the emphasis is on LOSS, the loss of the knowledge and experience that these old people embody and the emptying of places that for so long had been part of Russian rural life. These narratives begin to appear in Kazakov and others in the late 1950s, but unquestionably the most important early example is Alexander Solzhenitsyn's 1963 story "Matryona's Home." Most narratives of uprooting are quietly told in an elegiac tone, but Solzhenitsyn's dramatic—one might say melodramatic—tale covers the same basic narrative territory. The author wants to show that Russia cannot afford to lose its Matryonas with their old-fashioned ethical and aesthetic values; the spiritual health of the nation literally depends on such people. A Russia without Matryonas will not prosper.

The narratives of RETURN and UPROOTING could be combined in a single story, as they are to some extent in "Matryona's Home." These themes outlasted the decline of Village Prose as a movement. In Boris Ekimov's "Pastush'ia zvezda" (The shepherd's star, 1989), Timofei, a retired shepherd, is talked into selling his house and going to live with his sons near Moscow. But a year spent in what he calls "foreign parts" (*chuzhaia storona*) bores him; he yearns for a place where all the names are familiar and all the land is *iskhozhennoe, svoe* (lit. 'walked over', your own). He makes his way back to his settlement, and eventually to his *malaia rodina* (birthplace), where he takes up his former profession. As in most Village Prose narratives of return, circumstances cause him to leave once more, but the experience has been vital for his spiritual well-being.[27]

The third major pattern is the narrative of a rural CHILDHOOD. At the very heart of canonical Village Prose is childhood in the *malaia rodina*, the place you call home, the place where your *rod* (extended family) has lived for generations and where you first came to know the world. The narrative of childhood may be the archetypal story of loss—compounded by all the changes in rural Russia—but it is a story told with nostalgia, with a luminous touch. This narrative is so central to Village Prose that it will be the subject of the second half of this chapter.

Childhood

Much of Russian Village Prose is based on writers' recollections of the life they knew as children in the countryside. These memories reemerge in full-length memoirs, as reflections on the past in essays, or embedded in fictional works. The form the *derevenshchiki* frequently chose was a mixture of memoir, novel or story, idyll, and social history that Richard Coe has simply called "the Childhood." For Coe, the Childhood has developed into an "independent genre, with its own internal laws, conventions and structures."[28]

The Childhood, of course, existed in Russian literature prior to Village Prose. Some well-known examples are Lev Tolstoy's *Childhood* (1852), Sergei Aksakov's *The Childhood Years of Bagrov's Grandson* (1858), and Maksim Gorky's *Childhood* (publ. 1913).[29] The two distinct branches within this group are the Aksakov-Tolstoy idyllic gentry childhood, and Gorky's horrific lower-class (whether peasant or proletarian) childhood. These two types represent not only differences in class, economic circumstance, and setting, but also in the mode of presentation (a detailed description of the workings of the inner world versus the careful observation of the outer world).

Tolstoy and Sergei Aksakov provided the model for the Russian Childhood; Gorky created its antithesis. Andrew Wachtel calls Gorky's work a parody of the gentry model, an "anti-childhood."[30] Village Prose offers a synthesis of the two types. The Village Prose Childhood is about people who live a very modest, even marginal existence, constantly struggling from one harvest to the next and experiencing the painful realities of collectivization, wartime, and the postwar period. It would seem that Village Prose ought to have a lot more in common with Gorky's somber recollections than with the gentry narrative, but the dominant tone of Russian rural Childhoods of the post-Stalin period is one of calm acceptance, harmony, and beauty. The sour or bitter notes appear in descriptions of the onset of collectivization and the privations of the Second World War and the early postwar years. In general, Village Prose writers present a genuine *skazka* (fairy tale) of their early years, not Gorky's self-proclaimed "bleak fairy-tale" (*surovaia skazka*).[31]

Gorky reminisces about the past, so that he can then overcome it and "rip it out" of his memory. Only then will he be able to focus on the "radiant future."[32] For Village Prose writers, memory is not something to be "ripped out," but something to be restored and cherished; as Rasputin's Darya tells herself: "Truth is in memory. The person without memory is without life."[33] The focus in Village Prose is on the radiance *not* of the future, but of the past, and the past is primarily recovered in the recollection of one's rural childhood.

Vladimir Lichutin confessed that at one point he had lost the "poetry of remembrance," and his early years had seemed bleak to him. But suddenly he began to think about how free and happy he felt then, and he was able to compose (*sochiniat'*) a Childhood and thus recover his former self. During this awakening of his ancestral memory (*rodovaia pamiat'*) he became very interested in the history and culture of the Russian north, but most important of all, he gained LANGUAGE.[34]

The farewell to one's barefoot rural childhood was for a time the leitmotiv of rural prose where it coincided with—and in a sense symbolized—a "final bow" to the traditional village itself.[35] One can even speak of a "chronotope of Childhood" as one of the dominant forms in Village Prose.[36]

Katerina Clark sees Village Prose as a mutation of Stalinist Socialist Realism where events took place "'far away from Moscow.'"[37] In Village Prose the location is not only far from Moscow; it is also far from towns, factories, and trains, and the distance involved is temporal as well as spatial. According to Clark, the chronotope characteristic of Village Prose is "a *place* that also takes one back in *time*."[38] She sees in this chronotope Great Russian chauvinism, a religious vision, nostalgia, and a "proclivity for idealizing retired female collective-farm workers and others of marginal political and economic significance."[39]

The "chronotope of Childhood" seems to capture more of canonical Village Prose than the Clark model. The presence in the narrative of an—albeit at times anachronistic—traditional village in a state of change, the often nostalgic presentation of what must have been a very difficult way of life, the confusion of times, the spiritual depth, the language, and the presence of older women and other so-called marginal types has everything to do with the centrality of the writer's childhood memories to this type of literature. As the last generation to know the traditional village ways and family and village stories from pre-Revolutionary peasant life, the self-imposed task of the *derevenshchiki* was to revive the "forgotten chronotope" of the traditional village.[40]

The village or a favorite place in the surrounding countryside became in this literature the location, the center, of the childhood idyll in the writer's memory. For Mikhail Bakhtin, the most important aspect of an idyll is the relationship between time and space; in the idyll he sees "an organic fastening-down, a grafting of life and its events to a place, to a familiar territory with all its nooks and crannies, its familiar mountains, valleys, fields, rivers and forests, and one's own home. Idyllic life and its events are inseparable from this concrete, spatial corner of the world where fathers and grandfathers lived and where one's children and their grandchildren will live."[41]

This sense of an exact location for childhood is clear in a passage from Vladimir Lichutin's *The Last Wizard*. An old woman named Paraskeva looks out at dusk toward a distant tree-covered hill called "Div'ia gora" (lit. 'Magic Mountain'), where her father had often taken her to gather herbs for tea. She feels that if she could just clamber up to the top of the mountain as she did when she was a little girl, she would be able to "see" her childhood once more.[42] Her son Stepushka feels as if he has returned to childhood when he steps into the small chapel near their house.

Vladimir Soloukhin, in *Kaplia rosy* (A drop of dew, 1960) focuses on just one village, Olepino. "I had no other possibility. It wasn't a matter of choice. For me, there was no other place in the whole world like the village of Olepino; that was where I was born and grew up."[43]

Olepino still exists and Soloukhin describes it in detail in this and other books. But he finds that some part of Olepino has disappeared, what the author calls "the country of my childhood."[44] He tries during return visits to find the stage for his childhood dramas—adventures and games—but he can barely recognize the mountain in the small hill, the steep cliff in the riverbank, and the wild, endless forest in the neighboring Samoilovsky woods. Neither does he recognize himself, "the chief architect of that country. . . . He doesn't exist; he remained there in the warm, golden land of my boyhood years, which also no longer can be found on any map. The names have been preserved: Samoilovsky woods, the Vorshcha River, Zhuravlikha, the village of Olepino, and the Kormilovsky ravine . . . And . . . somehow I still bear the name of the little boy who lived in that special world."[45]

A classic example of the Childhood genre in Village Prose is poet Nikolai Rylenkov's "Skazka moego detstva"(A fairy tale of my childhood). In the introductory section, "Pamiat'" (Memory), Rylenkov uses the term "fairy tale" to emphasize how unreal the story of his early years seems to contemporary children (that is, children of the 1960s). To convince the reader of its authenticity he gives the actual names of his fellow villagers, living and dead. His story is an amalgam of his own memories of events and what his family and other people told him. These memories are intermingled at such a deep level in his soul that he can no longer separate what he has seen himself from what he merely has heard. He narrates his own first impressions of a time (1909–1914) when his family's way of life was about to pass into history, to change so fundamentally that the true story of the old life seems like a legend or fairy tale to young people in the post-Stalin period.

His first memory, typical for the Childhood, is of recovering from an extended illness: he awakens, stretches, hears the voices of his family, and laughs, attracting their attention. The room is filled with a soft, golden light, probably because it is a holiday and the floor has been covered with fresh straw. There is a sense of well-being, and he remembers the joy his parents expressed at the recovery of their only son. "With this, my childhood begins."[46]

Rylenkov describes the expansion of his small world from the big Russian stove, where his grandmother recited *skazki* in a singsong voice, to the whole *izba* and its "inventory," to the village limits.[47] Beyond the village lay ancient forests, inhabited by bears, wolves, elk, and the wood-sprite (*leshii*); it was a special fairy-tale world for the village children, to be conquered when they were a bit older. Nearby was their own little make-believe forest—the fields covered with hemp that could grow higher than the roofs. It was tall and thick enough to hide the children from view for hours on end until the fall harvest. "And now, when I remember my early childhood, more than anything else, there is the wonderfully invigorating smell of the hemp-field."[48] For

Rylenkov, the "grass," to echo Coe's phrase, was not only taller then, but more fragrant as well.

In the frame of the Childhood, Rylenkov describes the established, cyclical ordering of everyday peasant life. Rather than the *odnazhdy* 'one day' and *vdrug* 'suddenly' of fiction, he uses the *kazhdyi den'* 'every day' of Village Prose (or the instrumental of season, e.g., *letom* 'during the summer').

The family in "Skazka" was large and included not only a grandmother, but also a great-grandmother, Katerina. The latter was more than a hundred years old (born ca. 1812) and lived by herself in the ancient *izba* near the main house. Because of her great age, the village children saw her as a sorceress with power over diseases and the elements, and they fully expected to see a thrilling display of *nechistaia sila* 'impure forces, evil spirits' at her death, when the devil would come to claim her soul. Rylenkov re-creates this child's view of the world, achieving at times the atmosphere of a fairy tale: an immeasurably old woman with magic powers, dark lopsided huts, deep forests full of wolves and spirits, an angelic mother bathed in radiant light, and a tall, heroic father. Rylenkov is able, as any successful writer of a memoir of childhood must be, to give us the perceiving child within the remembering adult.

The death of a grandparent is an archetypal ending for a Childhood; this event "marks the conclusion of the childhood, and consequently the completion of the literary form."[49] In Rylenkov's tale, it is the great-grandmother whose fast-approaching demise interrupts the Saturday bathhouse ritual. The little boy sneaks into her hut so that he can watch the devil take her soul, but he is whisked away before she dies. The apple-blossoms that fall into her coffin as it is carried to the cemetery convince the villagers that Katerina was a good witch who had used her special powers to help people, not to harm them.

It seems that this Childhood will end on a note of harmony and peace, until the short but weighty final sentence: "That was in the late spring; in the summer the war began and the fairy tale of my childhood came to an end."[50] It was 1914, and he was five years old. In 1916, his father died, and by 1919 he was a ten-year-old orphan. Perhaps his great-grandmother's death had unleashed evil spirits after all.

Rylenkov wrote a sequel to his "fairy tale" of childhood called "Mne chetyrnadtsat' let" (I am fourteen).[51] The story of this year in his life is framed at the beginning and end by recollections of the death of his parents. His memories are of being on the "threshold of youth," when he was old enough to take on such responsibilities as imparting literacy to village girls but lacked the confidence to respond to their flirting and matchmaking. His favorite occupation was taking the bees out to the fields, where he could read poetry or listen to the old beekeepers talk about the past.

"I Am Fourteen" is a transitional work, balancing the child and the youth, the student and the teacher, village *byt* 'daily routine' (beekeeping, haymaking, the bathhouse, songs, stories, matchmaking, and holidays) and the new world of secondary school, girls, reading literature, and writing. He says that this year was noteworthy because he became more observant, "as though up till then I had been walking along a narrow path, among the tall, thick brush, which hid the horizon from me, and suddenly came out on the edge of it, near the main road, and was overwhelmed by the wide-open spaces that poured into my soul."[52] Leaving childhood is envisioned as moving out of the "tall grass." The "threshold" of this story is not just a personal one; the village (i.e., all rural Russia) is also poised on the brink of change: "And at every step the new existed alongside that which had grown old and obsolete."[53] Rylenkov resisted the tendency toward publicistic comment; when he was advised to write fewer lyric poems and more about how the peasants divided up the land after the Revolution, he replied that this was an appropriate subject for a newspaper article. He recalls his first attempt to write lyric prose—a school essay recalling the day the telegram arrived announcing his father's death.

The canonical Village Prose Childhood resists the publicistic, the exposé. The publicistic voice is that of an anxious, angry, and occasionally self-righteous adult, and when it threatens to dominate a work, there is an awkward sense of mixed genres and moods, as in Vladimir Soloukhin's *Smekh za levym plechom* (*Laughter over the Left Shoulder*), one of the few works of Village Prose that was written in the USSR but first published in the West.[54]

Soloukhin's story is, for much of its length, the transcript of childhood found in many works of Village Prose. There is a large, close, extended family, a two-story peasant house "at the center of the universe,"[55] a garden, village church and bell tower, his mother at prayer before the icons, a meandering river, woods, hills, fields, rural paths and roads, bees, birches, and elaborately celebrated holidays. He has a strong sense of roots and generational life; the adjectives *dedushkin* and *dedovskii* (both mean 'grandfather's') echo throughout the book. The past is radiant in his memory, and he depicts in great detail how the way of life he led as a child has been lost.

Interwoven with all this are elements that make *Laughter* almost an "anti-childhood" (though not a parody), but one that Soloukhin has written more "against" himself, that is, against his own earlier "compromised" works (he cites "A Drop of Dew") than against other writers. He accuses himself of describing certain episodes during the early years of collectivization (when he was a child, thus falling within his childhood experiences) in "gentle, rosy tones," the very term of approbation used by Soviet critics in the fifties to condemn Socialist Realist Kolkhoz Literature.[56]

"A Drop of Dew" (1960) seems an unlikely object for this retrospective self-criticism. It is a canonical description of a barefoot rural boyhood, loosely organized by the narrator's return visit to Olepino. The title comes from a child's delight in the dawn and dusk of early summer, when the sun makes the dewdrops on the grass luminous. What most distressed Soloukhin in later years was what he had omitted from his treatment of collectivization in the earlier work, especially his restrained account of two officials sent into the village to carry out new government policies, officials who were quartered with the Soloukhins because they had the largest house in the village. In "A Drop of Dew" Soloukhin said that since he was only six years old in 1930, he does not remember any of the details of collectivization; he does say with some hint of sarcasm that these two men were the first of an endless chain of officials sent into the countryside. In *Laughter* he describes how the family waited anxiously to hear whether they would be labeled kulaks or not; in the end, one of the officials intervened, and they lost only the use of one floor of their house.

The revised narrative of Soloukhin's childhood is framed by bitter diatribes against twentieth-century ideas of progress, and against virtually everything connected with Soviet life. He focuses on children's exposure to the cult of Lenin in school; his bitterest, most shameful memory is of the Lenin "corner" he set up at home in the presence of parents too frightened to protest. Hence the book's title: the guardian angel behind his right shoulder weeps while the devil laughs "behind his left shoulder."[57]

The sardonic, sour tone of *Laughter* strikes a discordant note, *not* because the criticisms are unjust, but because it is ultimately an expression of extreme self-centeredness, an element foreign to Village Prose, even to the memoir of childhood. Vilchek saw even in Soloukhin's early works, such as "Vladimir Country Roads"(1957) and "A Drop of Dew"(1960), a poorly hidden tendency to turn the search for roots into an exercise in self-praise, along with a certain coldness and sentimentality.[58] This would certainly be an accurate assessment of *Laughter*. What other Village Prose writers describe as typical of village life Soloukhin presents as a personal achievement—*his* birth (recorded, he tells us, in the Soviet encyclopedia and in the English *Who's Who*), *his* soul (including its prebirth journey), *his* consciousness, piety, and superior family and class (the upwardly mobile middle peasant). The frequently expressed sorrow and anger over the fate of hardworking middle peasants (in Belov, for instance) becomes here a simple declaration of the superiority of the middle over the poor peasant and a satisfaction with the relative comfort of his childhood before collectivization. For example, every year during Lent, his father would go into Vladimir to buy the best, tastiest food that still fell within the rules, and it was eaten in abundance. All of this, he said, made Lent go by quickly and pleasantly.

The counterexample of *Laughter over the Left Shoulder* helps us to understand the essence of the canonical Village Prose Childhood, in which writers of rural origin "returned" to their early years through tales infused with lyricism and nostalgia, even if these had been, objectively speaking, hungry and difficult times. The memory of these years was priceless because not only childhood, but the traditional village as well, had vanished forever.[59]

One of the most interesting developments in Russian literature after 1985 was the "surfacing" of works that were written in previous decades but not published. Soloukhin's *Laughter* is one of those works, and Tendriakov's trio of stories about his early years (written 1969–1971; published in the March 1988 *Novyi mir*) is another. Tendriakov has also left us with a "double view" of a childhood that coincided with the onset of collectivization. Born in 1923, he moved around rural Russia as a child because his father was a government official. In "Den' na rodine" (A day in the old hometown), his account of childhood is lyrical and luminous; his memories of his birthplace of Makarovskaia became his personal "fairy tale."[60] The essay ends with his promise to return there—to the "origin of everything"—once again. The Tendriakov childhood memoirs that were published posthumously in 1988, which give a much more harrowing picture of collectivization than Soloukhin's *Laughter*, are ironic, tragic, and grotesque, but the tone is neither bitter nor self-critical.[61]

"Proshchanie s mirom" (Farewell to peace), a similar—and apparently "delayed"—narrative by Vasilii Subbotin (b. 1921) appeared shortly after the Tendriakov stories.[62] Subbotin saw firsthand both a pastoral existence and the violence of the early years of collectivization. As one reviewer noted, this writer is artistically convincing in both his lyrical descriptions of village life and his accounts of the moments when historical forces swept into the village.[63] Subbotin tells of the dekulakization of local families and the sale of their possessions, events that the children could see from their schoolroom. He recalls newspapers in the 1930s that brought word to the village of purge trials and the surprising confessions by the accused. Subbotin tries to recover what he had thought as a nine-year-old when he heard his parents whispering at night about the fate of the kulaks. "I didn't understand very well what was happening, although, perhaps, I did understand something after all; how could I not have understood?"[64] The universal applicability of that question is all too obvious.

How should this kind of "delayed" work be read against the background of several decades of idyllic Village Prose Childhoods? Soloukhin seems to feel that the true story of collectivization cancels out the idyll of childhood, that the idyllic view is false. But, as Coe reminds us, when it comes to memories of childhood, "what *is* accuracy?"[65] Tendriakov and Subbotin deliberately juxtapose the two views of village life, which is probably a more accurate reflection than we find in Soloukhin of the conflicting feelings experienced by children. The pastoral of childhood and the nightmare of collectivization may, after all, be able to coexist in the canon of Village Prose, which respects historical and publicistic material, but not at the expense of the poetry and the "magic" of childhood.[66]

THREE

THE POETICS OF VILLAGE PROSE

What did these writers do for us?
With their help, our language came back to life.
(A. Lanshchikov)[1]

THE LANGUAGE of Village Prose is a feature that immediately distinguishes it from Socialist Realism, and from other post-Stalinist movements such as Youth and Urban Prose. Style is also a characteristic that links Village Prose to folklore and to pre-Revolutionary Russian literature. It is the aspect of Village Prose that has received the least scholarly and critical attention both in the USSR and abroad, and that can be least successfully captured in translation. As the Soviet critic A. Petrik suggested, Village Prose is more than a thematic category; it is artistic, ideological, and in the broadest sense, stylistic. "A scholar who approaches Village Prose as a phenomenon of *style* will make important discoveries."[2] A careful reading of the new rural prose that evolved after Ovechkin's first sketch reveals definite stylistic patterns (*zakonomernosti*) that Petrik felt should be discussed as part of an integrated approach to this literature.

Ovechkin's *ocherk* stimulated criticism that took note of the aesthetic problems of Soviet Russian prose in the early 1950s as well as the need for a more accurate view of life on the collective farm. "District Routine" was seen as the promising beginning of a rural literature that would be both more "sincere" and better written. When we read *back* from Rasputin, the aesthetic improvements over Kolkhoz Literature do not seem impressive, but when one reads *forward* from Babaevsky's *Cavalier of the Golden Star* (1947–1948) and Nikolaeva's *Harvest* (1950), there is much in Ovechkin that is fresh and encouraging.

Pomerantsev in his 1953 essay "On Sincerity in Literature" called most Kolkhoz Literature "a sin against art" and the product of a literary assembly line; writers, he said, had never been ordered to write badly.[3] The following year Fedor Abramov bemoaned the Socialist Realist "pastoral" and came up with the term "curly-headed monotony" (*kudriavoe odnoobrazie*) to characterize one novel in which every living thing, even the bull, had beautiful, curly hair.[4] Ideological and aesthetic complaints were intertwined; poorly written prose was seen as an ineffective instrument for improving kolkhoz productivity. The language of rural characters was seen as too homogenized and too literary, and writers were advised to look deeper into actual rural life and to use literary models from the pre-Revolutionary period.[5]

The first move away from the "poetics" of Kolkhoz Literature came in the form of essays about reforms in collective-farm management and criticism about the current state of affairs. But critics were uncomfortable with the idea of writers simply switching from the "rosy colors" of court bards to the *chernaia kraska* 'dark palette' of investigative reporters. There had to be more attention to style and character, and to language differentiation between characters in place of the linguistic leveling that was typical of Socialist Realism.

Essays on rural themes had their own stylistic problems during the first half of the 1950s; the writers' reformist concerns caused them to include transcripts of Party and kolkhoz meetings, while their growing interest in the peasant led to the inclusion of genuine rural speech wherever possible; the combination of styles was not always successful. Sergei Zalygin had said as early as 1955 that the whole language question in rural literature should be studied very closely.[6] More than thirty years later, shortly after becoming editor of *Novyi mir*, he complained that the criticism of Soviet literature as a whole still concentrated on slogans and ignored the aesthetic qualities of works.

> Take the aesthetics of Soviet prose of the 1960s and 1970s: it is time to sum up this period in the development of our literature. How does it differ aesthetically from the prose of, say, the 1950s and the prewar years? How much we lose when aesthetic criteria are lost! And how much is gained at the same time by the notorious "drab" literature that is created not only by inexperienced writers but also by writers who are, in their own way, quite experienced.[7]

This last point is an important one; it may have been possible for Soviet critics to attack Village Prose on the basis of a "retrograde" ideology and an increasing irrelevance to contemporary problems, but it was a lot harder to ignore or dismiss this literature when genuinely artistic criteria were applied.

Lack of sustained critical attention to the poetics of Village Prose is in almost inverse proportion to the seriousness with which the *derevenshchiki* have regarded the language of their works. Village Prose writers remembered the original mandate of the reformist critics of the 1950s to improve the language of rural literature, and they did not have to go much further than their *malaia rodina* 'native region' to accomplish this. Many went back to the language they had heard and used all through their childhood, renewed and reinforced by frequent visits to their homes or to other rural areas. Valentin Rasputin's experience is typical: "Every year I try to get to a Siberian village, to listen to people's conversations and commit them to memory. The living language interests me, and I'm constantly writing down unusual words. That way, I have a working lexicon of Russian as it is spoken in the contemporary Siberian countryside."[8] Writers from various regions—Siberia, Vologda, Arkhangelsk, Vladimir, Orel—used the language of their native areas to widen the stylistic parameters of Soviet Russian literature.[9]

The increased interest by writers in regional folk language resulted from the village background that most of them shared, and from a sense that it would enable them to record the real life of the still substantial rural population, preserving for posterity a rapidly disappearing linguistic diversity in Russia. Through language the writer could revisit the world of his childhood; Fedor Abramov said that the very sound of "native" (rodnye) words in context returned him to his childhood and thus to the environment from which the writer and all his heroes had emerged.[10] Writer after writer echoed these feelings on the pages of rural literature. In Iurii Kazakov's "Pomorka" (The old woman by the sea, 1957), the first-person narrator visits a northern fishing village. He is intrigued by ninety-year-old Marfa, a canonical Village Prose starukha 'old woman'. At night she prays before an Old Believer icon for all the fishermen at sea, and her prayers awaken in the narrator what Vladimir Lichutin has called rodovaia pamiat' 'ancestral/generational memory': "It's strange—when I hear her prayers it's as if my grandmother is praying, as if I can hear my mother in my sleep, as if all my ancestors, the peasants, the plowmen, plowing the soil from birth to death, bringing forth bread and new lives, buried in forgotten country churchyards, it's as if they are praying—not for themselves, but . . . for Rus—to a mysterious old-fashioned god, to kindly Saint Nikolai."[11]

As a young man in postwar Leningrad, Aleksei Leonov began to acquaint himself for the first time with the works of writers from his native Orel region such as Turgenev, Leskov, Bunin, and Prishvin; he was struck by the similarity between their style and certain aspects of regional folk speech.[12] At the same time, he saw a newspaper article by the linguist Ruben Avanesov which stated that the Orel-Kursk dialects were the foundation of the Russian literary language. "I began to think back to everyday scenes, overheard conversations between the older kids, and the neighbors' swearing, to the deals, games, and disagreements among the boys, and to the proverbs and sayings about work and about lousy weather, failure, and bad luck. It turned out that I had enough linguistic 'luggage' to allow me to describe entire pictures of life in the countryside."[13] Abramov saw the rural speech of the north as an "inexhaustible storehouse" (*neischerpaemaia kladovaia*) for writers.[14] Even though this language was far from being an entirely new source of color and imagery for rural literature, it was a source that had not been used to advantage for decades.

In the Russian village of the writers' youth, oral culture was still very important; it was the people's history as well as their art and entertainment. As with any art, there were skilled practitioners whose talent was much admired. To speak well, explained Vasilii Belov, meant to speak with attention to rhythm and rhyme, and to be both precise and imaginative.[15] The truly talented could improvise, while others just repeated pithy expressions they had heard. In Russian folklore, there were set themes, plots, and character-functions—as Vladimir Propp had explained—but there were also countless ways in which the same basic tale could be varied in the telling. The balance between set themes and opportunities for improvisation was of great interest to a number of Village Prose writers; however, it is a subject they approached not out of theoretical interest, but because they had heard as children, and taken note of as writers, so much living folk speech.

Verbal competition, both planned and spontaneous, among villagers was a frequent occurrence. The *chastushka* (a short, rhymed folk lyric) and other examples of verbal wit (*ostroslovie*) were still living forms. "When peasant men and women get together to relax, you're always amazed by the verbal competition that naturally arises."[16] Abramov saw the north as the last repository of elements of *skomorokh* verbal art.[17] *Chastushki* are seen by Village Prose writers as an important element of folk life, a means of satirical—and often raunchy—commentary on village, local, and even national issues. One verbal "master" familiar to the inhabitants of Belov's village was the half-blind Vasia Cherniaev, who roamed about Russia, periodically returning home, where he recited the "news" in rhymed form, while his hand traced over a scrap of newspaper.[18]

Fedor Abramov said that every hamlet had its male and female champion speakers. In his village there were still a few such old women whom he visited every year, just for the pleasure of listening to their conversation with its remarkable intonation and the rich mixture of lexical elements, which were "affectionate, coarse, businesslike, and sentimental."[19] Writer after writer echoed Abramov's appreciation of rural speech, particularly that of the villages' older inhabitants. The narrator of Solzhenitsyn's *Matryona's Home* is struck by the voice of the first woman he encounters at the early-morning market. "Instead of a normal speaking voice she used an ingratiating sing-song, and her words were the ones I was longing to hear when I left Asia for this place."[20] Matryona's own warm, good-natured words made her sound to the narrator like a grandmother in a fairy tale.

Renewed attention to the language of rural literature—both dialogue and narrative—began in the mid-1950s. Alexander Yashin's 1956 story "Rychagi" (Levers) is structured around the contrast between an unofficial and an official meeting at a kolkhoz, which broadens into a contrast between authentic—in Pomerantsev's terms "sincere"—and inauthentic discourse, and between spontaneous and ritualized behavior. The same group of local leaders who speak so openly and knowledgeably about peasants, agriculture, and the need for frank exchanges of opinion, when they first gather together, fall into their rigidly assigned roles once the Party meeting begins. The overriding theme of this story is the nature of discourse in Soviet literature and life. It is a typical Thaw story, more interesting ideologically than aesthetically, because in the end it is a discussion—rather than an example—of the possibilities of language.[21]

There were a number of aesthetic stimuli in the fifties whose influence cannot be quantified, but which should certainly be noted. New editions of the works of Sergei Aksakov (1955), Nikolai Leskov (1956), and Ivan Bunin (1956) led young writers to look closely at these three figures—and others from the past—as guides for their own work. Bunin was an especially strong influence, both on his own, as a bridge between classical Russian realism and the twentieth century, and through the medium of Kazakov's stories.[22] Even more important was the republication of Vladimir Dal's four-volume *Tolkovyi slovar'* (Explanatory dictionary, 1955).[23] Dal's dictionary and collection of folk sayings helped rural writers to refine and expand the language of their village childhood, which after years in the city—where literary life takes place in twentieth-century Russia—may have been rusty. Part of the Village Prose writers' act of going "backward" in time involved going back linguistically to the pre-Revolutionary period, and Dal was of preeminent importance to their work. Dal's work assumes a symbolic function in Viktor Astafiev's "post–Village Prose" story "A Sad Detective" (1986); urban pseudo-intellectuals have an unused and expensive edition of Dal in their living room, while the hero keeps a worn copy of Dal's folk sayings on his desk, which inspires him at the end of the story to go on with his writing. This could, by extension, be seen to symbolize the difference between a superficial, decorative use of folk language and a deeper, more authentic use, something that was much on the minds of writers and critics.

Both rural and urban writers turned to popular speech in the 1950s to renew the literary language, to rescue it from "stylistic stereotyping, linguistic leveling, a lack of personality and expression, and a skimpy vocabulary"; the appearance of works that were full of jargon, foreign borrowings, technical terms, neologisms, and archaic and dialect forms made a "stunning contrast" to the language of a typical work of Socialist Realism.[24] Aksenov's urban slang had a rural counterpart in the monologues and dialogues of Belov's characters. In both innovative Youth Prose and traditionalist Village Prose, writers were at times given to stylistic excess. Youth Prose, with its celebration of ephemeral and largely borrowed or newly created urban slang, was in general judged more harshly than Village Prose, whose excesses were at least based on a deeply rooted native tradition, that is, on the use of a resource that was unarguably *rodnoi* 'native'.[25] In the way Village Prose was written, and in the way it was received, latent Russian nationalist feelings certainly played some part.

Village Prose writers handled folk speech with varying degrees of skill. Marietta Chudakova took note of those who actually "permitted" their characters to do the speaking, for example, Rasputin and his heroine Anna in *Poslednii srok* (*Borrowed Time*).

> He did not take the position of an interviewing journalist, did not attempt to grasp new material . . . on the run. . . . He listens without interrupting her [Anna], without rushing, without organizing her remarks around what seems to him most central and important, but leaving her in harmony with her own standard of values . . . one cannot shake off the strange feeling that the author was not the "creator" of his heroine's language, but its audience, and that along with us he was following her speech with unflagging attention, straining to hear.[26]

Chudakova contrasts this to Viktor Likhonosov, who in "Brianskie" (Briansk people) and other works comments ecstatically and condescendingly on the folk quality of his characters' speech, rarely letting us simply hear them out. "He loses his way in his own evaluations . . . of their manner of speech before we are allowed to hear it ourselves or *instead* of letting us hear it." And often his exalted praise is not justified by the speech itself.[27]

One of the finest examples of the recording or re-creating of folk speech in Village Prose is the drunken monologue spoken by Ivan Afrikanovich to his horse Parmen, a stylistic tour de force that takes up the first five pages of Belov's *Privychnoe delo* (That's how things are), a section ironically named "Priamym khodom" (Straight ahead).

> – Parme-en? Eto gde u menia Parmenko-to? A vot on, Parmenko. Zamerz? Zamerz, paren', zamerz. Durachok ty, Parmenko. Molchit u menia Parmenko. Vot, nu-ka my domoi poedem. Khosh' domoi-to? Parmen', ty Parmen . . .

Ivan Afrikanovich ele razviazal zamershie vozhzhi.
– Ty vot stoial? Stoial. Zhdal Ivana Afrikanovicha? Zhdal, skazhi. A
Ivan Afrikanovich chego delal? A ia, Parmesha, malen'ko vypil, vypil,
drug moi, ty uzh menia ne osudi.

["Par-men? Now where's he got to, my Parmenko? A-a-ah, there you are,
Parmenko. Cold, are you? Yea, you're cold, lad, cold. You're just a great
fool, Parmenko. And Parmenko doesn't say a word back. Well, we'll go
home now, home. Want to go home? Eh, Parmen, Parmen . . ."
Ivan Afrikanovich's clumsy fingers could hardly unfasten the stiff fro-
zen reins.
"So you've been waiting here? Yea, standing. Waiting for Ivan Afri-
kanovich? Yea, waiting, you say. And what was Ivan Afrikanovich doing?
Just having a l'il drink, pal, a l'il drink and another l'il drink and another
. . . Now don't judge me harshly, don't be hard on me."][28]

The narrator briefly describes the hero's actions but does not comment on this speech; he simply presents it and stands back. After a
while he tells the reader that Ivan Afrikanovich eventually sobered up
and stopped talking. The title of the work is Ivan's own favorite
phrase (although with the order reversed—he says, "Delo privychnoe"), and it expresses his grudging acceptance of whatever life sends
his way. Given this initial monologue, the interior monologues of Ivan
and other characters—including a cow—inserted fairy tales, fishing
stories, folk ditties (chastushki), and local discussions of "Fedor Cas-
trov"[sic] and other world leaders, this is a work of very fresh, if not
entirely pure, language.

The contemporary folk language of the 1960s was not a mertvyi
zapovednik 'a quiet preserve', but a busy lexical marketplace. Abramov
saw in it a juxtaposition of "the deep-rooted ancient speech, dialect
words and expressions, jargon, and the most popular scientific-technical terms, along with the language of contemporary literature, newspapers, radio, and television." The way urban and foreign terms were
incorporated—often incorrectly—into rural speech could be used for
comic effect. Abramov gives the example of the unexpected colloquial
use of the rather formal and abstract word otnoshenie 'attitude, relationship': "Govoriat: 'Tak v kakikh zhe oni otnosheniiakh?'—'Da oni
uzhe za potseluinye otnosheniia pereshli'" ("People say: 'What kind of
relationship do they have?'—'Well, they've already progressed beyond
a kissing relationship.'"[29]

The humor could have a sharp edge to it as in Puti-pereput'e (The
crossroads), the third volume of Abramov's The Pryaslins, in which the
word kotedzh 'cottage' is explained to a peasant who does not trust
the government to deliver on its promises, and where piknik is defined

for a man who has never had much leisure time. "'A picnic,' Egorsha began to explain, 'is like a fishing trip out in the open air, only with women and lots to drink. You see, during the summertime, the bosses always like to spend their day off in the countryside.'"[30] The bureaucrats have time for summer *pikniki*, unlike the peasants whose lives they so thoroughly control. Urban words are frequently foregrounded to reveal the gaps between urban and rural life and the shallowness of those rural people who have been transformed by their exposure to the city.

In Shukshin's "Raskas" (A storey [*sic*]), the hero has come to hate the word *repetitsiia* 'rehearsal', sensing that his wife's involvement in a local theater group will increase her desire to leave the village. Shukshin's "Raskas" is an example of the various ways that an author could use the resources of the folk language. This sad-comic tale of a truck driver who returns to his village to find that his wife has left him contains monologues, dialogues, a quotation from a letter, and an entire inserted text, all reflecting rural speech. Most significant is Shukshin's use of *skaz*. *Skaz* is "narrative related in *erlebte Rede* or 'quoted speech,' i.e., language marked as not the author's own" and as "deviating from the literary norm."[31] Shukshin helped to revive the skaz technique in the post-Stalinist period, as did such writers as Solzhenitsyn and Aksenov.

The first-person narrator of "A Storey" begins in a very breezy, conversational tone: "Ot Ivana Petina ushla zhena. Da kak ushla! . . . Priamo kak v starykh dobrykh romanakh—bezhala s ofitserom" ("Ivan Petin's wife had left him. And the way she did it! Just like in one of those good old novels—she ran off with an officer.").[32] An even more striking example of skaz is the husband's first-person written account of his troubles that he wants to publish in the local newspaper.

> Znachit bylo tak: ia priezhaiu—nastole zapiska. Ia ee ne budu piriskazyvat': ona tam obzyvat'sia nachala. Glavnoe ia zhe znaiu, pochemu ona sdelela takoi fint ushami. Ei vse govorili, chto ona pokhozhaia na kakuiu-to artistku. Ia zabyl na kakuiu. No ona durochka ne ponimaet: nu i chto? Malo li na kogo ia pokhozhii, ia i davai teper' skakat' kak blokha na zerkale.

> [It was this way: I came home and theres this note on the table. I aint going into it exept to say she just gives me hell in it. Mainly I know why she pulled a trick like that. Everyone kept telling her she looked like some actriss. I forget which one. But shes a fool and didnt understand. What's the big deal in that? I look like a lot of people but I dont go jumping around like I got ants in my pants.][33]

THE POETICS OF VILLAGE PROSE 37

Even the title of the story as a whole, the misspelled—but phonetically correct word *raskas*—is an example of skaz.

Another bravura performance of the skaz technique is Vasilii Belov's "Bukhtiny vologodskie" (Vologda whimsies, 1969), which is presented as a genuine transcript of the "tall tales" of retired stove-maker Kuzma Ivanovich Barakhvostov. The "author's" role has been reduced to providing the title, a few parenthetical remarks and explanatory notes, and a division by theme. Kuzma begins by explaining how he did not want to be born in 1916 because of the war and short-ages, but when he "heard" that peasants were receiving land after the Revolution, he had to hurry up and be born so that he would not miss out on this opportunity.

> Den' rozhdeniia proshel blagopoluchno. . . . Starushki soslepu pup na moem brukhe zaviazali ne plotno. Ia chikhnul, zaviazka lopnula. Vse starushki rukami vsplesnuli: "Ai, kakoi fuligan!" Khoteli vdrugoriad' zaviazat', a nitok netu. Pobezhali, truperdy, za l'nom, davai kudel'iu katat'. Chtoby nitok napriast'. Tut uzh ia etikh starukh i pravda chut' ne obmatiugal.[34]

> [My birth went okay. . . . But the half-blind old women didn't tie up my belly button tight enough. I sneezed and it came undone. All the old ladies clapped their hands and said: "What a stinker!" They wanted to tie it up again, but there wasn't any thread. So the old fools ran off to get flax and make some thread. At this point I was ready to curse them out.]

In general, though, the *derevenshchiki* made relatively little use of the skaz technique, which is surprising, considering the resources at the disposal of rural-born writers (with a little help from Dal).[35] The most logical reason for this is that skaz has been used more often than not for comic effect, and these writers wanted to change the view of rural characters as country bumpkins, to show them as dignified and interesting human beings as Turgenev, Tolstoy, and others had done before them. While there is humor in Village Prose, it is not directed at the rural characters but instead rises naturally among them.

Marietta Chudakova, one of the few scholars to take a serious look at the poetics of Russian prose in the 1960s, felt that the simple act of recording folk speech—however accurately done—would not be enough to renew the literary language. And "stylizations in the manner of 'the folk tongue' only frightened away the reader."[36] She was not satisfied with skaz narration that, though expressive, drowns out the author's own voice and alienates the author from the hero; she dismissed it as a "half-Philistine language that seems genuinely folk because we are not used to it."[37] In this kind of narrative, concludes

Chudakova, the folk language is still raw material and not a finished product, and the result is not *bol'shaia literatura* (lit. 'big literature', i.e., first-rate, artistically significant literature).

Abramov felt strongly that writers should not make up words—this was not, after all, a *zaum*-creating avant-garde but a "rear guard" in search of a disappearing past.[38] Village Prose writers ought to listen closely to the language of the people; for Abramov, creativity lay in the selections made from this treasure chest and the way the material is made an integral part of a given work of literature. If the writer penetrated the inner world of his characters, then their speech would affect his own narrative language. "I really like the kind of text where the author's speech and the hero's are merged at a very deep level."[39]

The merging of the language of author and hero could take the form of interior monologue, a stylistic device that had virtually been banned from Soviet literature in the 1930s, but which returned to both rural and urban prose in the Thaw years.[40] Most Village Prose writers concentrated on writing accurate rural dialogue, supplemented by narrative commentary. Some, though, chose in addition to incorporate rural language into "direct interior monologue" (*vnutrenii monolog*)—which has the form of direct speech—and "indirect interior monologue"—which has features of both direct and indirect speech. Interior monologue can be found, for instance, in the novellas of Valentin Rasputin; he was even criticized for getting too close to his characters in this way.[41] Vladimir Lichutin's energetic and original style is also marked by the use of interior monologue. In his epic work *The Last Wizard* several characters take part in the narrative in this way, including old Parania, whose son has just arrived from the city.

> Nebos' khorosho-to ne pozhivesh' v gorode, tam prismotret' nekomu. A kurit' tak i ne brosil, ne uspel nogi za porog zanesti, uzh zuby papirosoi zatknul, a znachit, ves' vecher promolchit, da i spat' molchkom liazhet.
>
> Gor'kaia eta mysl' chut'-chut' zamutila Paraskevinu radost'. Molchun syn, sama vinovata. . . .
>
> Paraskeva zatashchila na stol samovar, chai po chashkam razlila, pridvinula k synu i maslo, i rybu, i moloka . . . esh', synok, esh'.[42]

> [You could hardly live well in the city with no one to take care of you. And he hadn't stopped smoking. No sooner was he in the house than he had stuck a cigarette in his mouth, which meant that he would sit in silence the whole evening and go to bed without saying a thing.
>
> This bitter thought disturbed Paraskeva's happiness a little. Her son was a silent fellow and it was her fault. . . .
>
> Paraskeva dragged the samovar onto the table, poured the tea into the cups, and moved the butter, fish, and milk toward him: eat, son, eat.]

Attaining the correct balance between the languages of author and character was a difficult process; as Belov said, one of the two is forever putting words into the other's mouth, and the result is stylistic incompatibility. Belov was looking for a subtle, elusive, and fluid line of contact between these two linguistic components, desiring neither a concrete divison between them, nor their full merging.[43] The point of contact he sought was in fact found, and not just by Belov.

When Chudakova wrote her article in 1972, she saw the beginnings of change in the use of unassimilated colloquial language by both rural and urban writers. Belov and Rasputin, for example, seemed to be moving toward a more confident use of folk speech in their works, bridging the gap between the freshness of the quoted remarks and the relative staleness of the narrative language framing them.[44] The most finely crafted examples of the new narrative language moved literary style beyond what Chudakova saw as the bookishness and chilliness of the Bunin-Kazakov tradition. In *Privychnoe delo*, for instance, Belov had found the linguistic-stylistic means to express "an entire cast of thought, an entire concept of the world."[45]

In canonical Village Prose there are many instances in which the continuing influence of folk beliefs is revealed not only on the surface of life in reference to superstitions and traditions, but also within the narrative language. This occurs not through direct quotation or by means of interior monologue, but through the influence of the folk worldview and folk language on the author's narrative style. The sense of an impersonal—and yet animate—Nature is reinforced by the frequent impersonal constructions and other "masking devices."[46] These constructions help the reader to feel, along with the characters, that so much of what happens in their lives, whether the result of nature or history, is beyond their control. There are invisible, unknown, but palpably animate forces at work in these stories, though there is very little that could be called mysticism. In Ronald Blythe's *Akenfield*, a chronicle of rural England in the 1960s, the village minister tries to explain this type of rural belief: "Fatalism is the real controlling force, this and the nature gods, the spirits of trees and water and sky and plants. These beliefs seem to have no language, but they rule."[47]

Sometimes, the residual belief in folk spirits is stated directly, as in Abramov's story "Alka." The influence of folk language shows up in superficial ways, such as repetition: "Krutila-vertela, prygala-bezhala—po vereteikam, po kholmikam, po belym" (lit. 'It twisted-turned, jumped-ran—along the fields, along the hills, along the white ones').[48] Alka's aunt, coming upon beautiful, amber-colored berries in the woods, crosses herself and bows to the right and left in a traditional gesture, while her more worldly niece is busy covering herself with mosquito repellent. The two women get lost and are unable to "read" the trees for signs, not knowing the language of the forest. "Vdrug, kak v skazke, zachikhalo, zafyrkalo gde-to sleva v storone, tetka pomertvela: nechistaia sila, nu, a Al'ka s rasprostertymi rukami kinulas' navstrechu etoi nechistoi sile"(Suddenly, just like in a fairy tale, there was a sneezing and snorting from somewhere over to the left of them. The aunt froze: it was an evil spirit, and Alka was heading straight toward it with arms outstretched).[49] The "evil spirit," whose activities could be referred to in this indirect way is actually a tractor—the device is "laid bare" in an ironic bit of folk stylization. When Alka enters her dead mother's house she is still open to the idea of *nechistaia sila* 'evil spirits', and the sound she hears is referred to simply by the verb *miauknulo* 'there-was-a-mewing' even though she knows that what she hears is the tomcat Busik.[50]

In Rasputin's "Vasily and Vasilisa" the feminine personal pronoun *ona* 'she/it' is used—without a direct referent—in a conversation between two old women to mean the work, the daily burdens that a person drags along through life; this use of the pronoun gives it a mysterious animacy. Avdotia complains that when she comes for a visit, Vasilisa has no time to sit down for a chat. Vasilisa responds that what with one thing and another she is on her feet all day long.

> – Ee i za tyshchu let ne pererabotat'! – krichit babka Avdot'ia. – Popomni, Vasilisa, ona vse ravno posle nas ostanetsia. Khosh' konem vozi, a ostanetsia.
> – Ostanetsia, ostanetsia, – kivaet Vasilisa. – Ee iz odnogo dnia v drugoi peretashchish', a uzh nado dal'she tashchit'. Tak i kochuesh', kak tsygan s torboi.
> – I nikuda ne denesh'sia!
> – A kuda denesh'sia?
> – Net, net.
> Oni dolgo i soglasno kivaiut drug drugu golovami.

> ["You'll never finish it all in a thousand years," cries Granny Avdotya. "Think of it, Vasilisa, it'll still be there when we're gone, try as you may."
> "So it will, so it will," nods Vasilisa. "You drag it from one day to the next, you've still got more to do. So you journey on like a gipsy with his sack."
> "And you never get anywhere!"
> "Where'd you get to?"
> "No, no."
> They nod to one another in agreement for a long time.][51]

The *ona* is a sort of personified *byt* 'daily routine', but *ona* is feminine, while the word *byt* is masculine; this personification through masking relates *ona* to something more powerful than mere everyday routine, something like *sud'ba* 'fate' (a feminine noun).

Pronominal masks are relatively rare in Soviet Russian Village Prose because they reflect a belief in spirits that is no longer very common and would have attracted the negative attention of critics; this was certainly the case with Rasputin's mysterious Master of the island in *Farewell to Matyora*. Neuter verbal forms—which impersonal constructions take in the absence of a subject—are a less direct way of inferring the presence of unknown and usually dangerous forces. They transcend any superficial folk influence and are fully integrated into the narrative language.

In "Vniz i vverkh po techeniiu" ("Downstream," 1972) Rasputin describes the all-important first thunderstorm of spring as both terrifying and wonderful to the six-year-old boy who has gone out in the middle of the night to see it.

> Gde-to daleko v taige *zarokotalo, nabralo* silu i *pokatilos', pokatilos'* priamo na derevniu, grozia razdavit' i smiat' ee, i, tol'ko chut'-chut' ne dokativshis', *razdavilos'*.

> [Somewhere far off in the taiga *there began a rumbling which gathered* strength and *rolled, rolled* straight up to the village, threatening to crush and overrun it; having almost reached the village, it *subsided*.][52]

Having established the sense of a powerful, impersonal natural force, the narrator then announces simply: "Nadvigalas' groza" (A storm was approaching). This "force" moves toward the Angara, where it speeds up the process of *ledokhod*, the annual breaking-up of the ice in the river, the real focus of the boy's attention.

> V zhutkom i neozhidanno-radostnom predchuvstvii on vskinul golovu i uvidel, kak, lomaia led, *vynosit* seredinu reki. Ee tol'ko-tol'ko *sorvalo*, ee polosa byla sovsem neshirokoi.

> [With frightening and unexpectedly joyous foreboding he threw his head back and saw the ice breaking and *exposing* the water in the middle of the river. The river had only just *begun to break* loose; the strip of exposed water was still quite narrow.][53]

No English translation can do justice to the rich meaning conveyed by the impersonal verbs *vynosit* 'is carried away' and *sorvalo* 'broke away'. Rasputin describes an event wherein one can observe the activities of unseen forces but cannot control or explain these forces with the name of an agent.

Viktor Astafiev uses the same stylistic device to convey the drama of this annual event, so important in the rural world. In "Predchuvstvie ledokhoda" (Signs of spring), the lengthy, step-by-step description of *ledokhod* includes numerous impersonal constructions.

Sdavilo led, *zapolnilo* pustoty i protaliny.... Beloi priazhei, grubym shvom *proshilo* reku naiskvos'.... *plastanulo* reku nadvoe....

A na reke uzhe vo vsiu shir' *lomalo, korezhilo* led i *provalilo* v tartararu.[54]

[The ice *was being squeezed* and *was filling up* the empty expanses, the thawed patches of earth.... It was as if a white seam *had been crudely stitched* across the river.... the river *had been cut* in two....

And along the whole width of the river, the ice *was going down* into the netherworld.]

Astafiev's grandmother took an icon of the Savior and headed for the river with other villagers to make peace with the elements.

These impersonals are strongly supported by evidences of the cultural phenomenon of dual faith.[55] In this same chapter from Astafiev there is a scene from the year 1934 in which terrified local officials, returning from an interrogation and mysterious imprisonment at a regional center, make frantic efforts to get across the dangerous ice floes. They cross themselves and pray quietly so as not to anger the river. This scene reinforces the sense in Village Prose that both Nature and the State are impersonal, potentially dangerous forces whose activities cannot be controlled. In 1934, Nature was the less frightening of the two.

The sense of the power behind a river's movement, along with the flow of history and the cycle of life, is taken up again by Rasputin in *Farewell to Matyora* (1976). The news that the island will be flooded by the waters of the artifically expanded river has frightened the older residents. When Bogodul shouts something unintelligible about grave robbing, Darya does not immediately dismiss this as a real possibility.

Takoe teper' vremia, chto i nel'zia poverit', da prikhoditsia; skazhi kto, budto ostrov *sorvalo* i *poneslo* kak shchepku,—nado vybegat' i smotret', ne *poneslo* li vzapravdu.

[These were times when you couldn't believe things, but had to: if someone said that the island *took off* and *was being swept downstream* like a twig, you had to run out and look to see if it really *wasn't floating downstream*.][56]

Everything that had formerly seemed eternal was now being swept away.

The old women feel this way not just about the island but about people in general. In "Vasilii i Vasilisa" they dragged (*tashchit'*) the unidentified *ona* (she/it; referring to the daily cycle of tasks that are never completed) around with them as their fate. In *Farewell to*

Matyora, the same verb is used impersonally to show how people themselves are "dragged" through life.

> – My uzhe teper' i tak i etak ne svoim khodom zhivem. *Tashchit* . . . Kudy *zatashchit*, tam i ladno.
> – Chto *tashchit* . . . pravda, chto *tashchit* , – soglasilas' Dar'ia.

> ["We're not living on our own power now anyway. We're *being dragged* and wherever they *drag* us is fine with me."
> "You're right about *being dragged* . . ." Darya agreed.][57]

Watching the figure of her son hunched over in a small boat as if "fleeing some outside force," Darya understands that he is not his own boss.

> I ne Sonia im rukovodit, etogo on ne pozvolit,—prosto *podkhvatilo* vsekh ikh i *neset, neset* kuda-to, ne davaia oglianut'sia . . . svoim shagom malo kto khodit.

> [. . . And Sonya wasn't his boss, either—he wouldn't allow that—they *were* all *swept up* and *carried off* somewhere, without a chance to look back. There weren't many who set their own pace.][58]

Even the majestic larch, which has already faced the impersonal storm "during which lightening *cut off* the top of the tsar larch and *threw it down* on the ground" ("v kotoruiu *srezalo* molniei 'tsarskomu listveniu' verkhushku i *kinulo* ee na zemliu"), must now face the impersonal forces of progress that take the form of fire and flood and chain saws.[59]

Village Names

While such events as the spring thaw, thunderstorms, fire, disease, or war—which seem to come mysteriously from outside the "magic" boundary of the village—are often attributed to nameless agents, within the village a very detailed system of "naming" is at work. People, places, and objects have local designations that might not be entirely clear to an outsider. Richard Coe speaks of attention to the detailed "inventories of a small world" as an essential characteristic of the genre he calls the "Childhood."[60] It is not surprising, then, that Village Prose, which is to a large extent based on memories of a rural childhood, should be so attentive to specific names. With not only childhood, but the traditional objects of rural life and the villages themselves disappearing, it was all the more important to the *derevenshchiki* that their works be a repository for lost names.

Lukashin, the ill-fated kolkhoz chairman in Abramov's novel *At the Crossroads*, came to Pekashino only five years before, and it has taken him all this time to learn what everyone else had begun to acquire as a child: the hundreds of local names for fields, lakes, rivers, pastures, and all the other important places on "the very complicated and confusing Pekashino map." He felt that he had to attain what he calls "forest literacy" in order to be an effective leader.[61] For Emmet Kennedy, there was something quite similar at work in rural France: "Culture meant knowing by heart every nook and cranny, every major rock, every gully, every copse and rivulet of a score of square kilometers."[62]

The specific, colorful names of villages do more than differentiate one location from another. They are a link to the pre-kolkhoz past, providing a sense of continuity and a national or regional identity. Rylenkov explained in "The Fairy Tale of My Childhood" that before the Revolution, every village had not one but three names. The first was the official name used by government authorities, the second was what early inhabitants had called it, and the third was a sort of nickname that was used derisively by people from neighboring villages with which, as Moshe Lewin explained, there was by definition an age-old rivalry. Rylenkov's native village was called Alekseevka, Novaia Lomnia (from *lomat'* 'to break [one's back]'), and Korchevka (which refers to the process of clearing the land of tree stumps). Local legends explained the origin of the unofficial name, for instance, in the case of Korchevka and Novaia Lomnia, serfs sent to settle in the area first had to break their backs pulling out tree stumps.

The hero of Boris Ekimov's "The Shepherd's Star" revisits his native region; when he looks into the distance he sees the pastures, lakes, small villages, riverbanks, and orchards where he spent his life as a shepherd. As he remembers these places name by name, he recalls the special events connected with each one, the specific ways in which everything he saw was *svoe* 'his own'.[63]

In Rasputin's "Downstream," the writer-narrator suddenly remembered that the islands near his village no longer existed; the floodwaters from the hydroelectric project had covered such places as Khlebnik (*khleb* 'bread, grain') and Beryozovik (*bereza* 'birch tree', *berezovik* 'brown mushroom'), where as a boy he had picked currants, wild onions, and garlic; where he had grazed horses, plowed fields, and cut hay. The rising waters washed the soil of the islands away, and they disappeared beneath the waves. "There are no more islands, and their names, forlorn and empty since they've lost their true meaning, are heard less and less and are receding into the distance from whence they are not fated to return."[64] The loss of the very names of these islands and villages—names that were not randomly chosen but linked to the life of the region in very direct and poetic ways—was painful for the narrator to recall.

In Soloukhin's *Laughter over the Left Shoulder* the pain is transformed into anger as the author recalls how after 1931 the centuries-old names of villages near his Olepino—such as Prokoshikha, Brod, Ostanikha, Kurianikha, Venki, Pugovitsino, Vishenki, Lutino, Krivets, Rozhdestveno, Ratmirovo, Spasskoe, Snegirevo, Ratislova—were eclipsed in documents, speeches, and newspapers by the names of the kolkhozes that were established in each village or, more often, uniting several settlements.[65] The village names, which had evolved over the centuries, were linked to nature, culture—including Russian Orthodoxy—and local events; the kolkhoz names had an international, political significance and were the work of an instant, the stroke of a pen. These new names, like other aspects of the collectivized countryside, showed an orientation not toward the past, but toward the "radiant future": "The Red Communist Avant-garde," "The Path to Socialism," "The Warrior," "The Red Banner," "The First of May," and "Forward." Soloukhin's own village of Olepino was lucky at first, as part of an innocuous "Cultural Activist" kolkhoz, but its name was later changed to "The Fortieth Anniversary of October," then to "Khrushchev," and then to "Lenin."[66]

Vladimir Krupin connects the names of villages that have disappeared with the maiming of the naturally beautiful landscape. On an *ocherk*-writing trip to a kolkhoz near his parents' village, recounted in "Sorokovoi den'" (The fortieth day) he asks his guide to stop at a place that he remembers as having an impressive view of the surrounding countryside, but to his surprise "a sad landscape opened up before me." "'This is where Bryzgalovo village used to be, and that was Vinnyi Kliuch, and over there Chernyi Voron, Prutki, and Krasnyi Iar'. . . the official explained, pointing to a landscape dotted with telephone poles, disfigured fields, broken thickets, and the iron skeletons of machinery."[67] Village Prose tells of a thousand such vistas throughout Russia that have lost their colorful specificity to an anonymous technical progress.

In Alexander Solzhenitsyn's story "Matryona's Home," there is a partial deromanticization of this topos of Village Prose. The narrator, eager to get to the heart of Russia after years of exile in central Asia, eagerly accepts a teaching assignment in the village of Vysokoe pole (High field). It "did not belie its name" with its gentle hills, deep forest, and a dammed-up pool. He would gladly stay there forever—but there is no food to buy. His next assignment, to Torfprodukt (Peat product) evokes from the narrator a sigh and thoughts of Russia's past: "Torfprodukt? Turgenev never knew that you can put words like that together in Russian."[68] Fortunately, Torfprodukt is surrounded by villages with more appetizing names: Talnovo, Chaslitsy, Ovinsty, Spudni, Shevertni, and Shestimirovo, stretching into a region of lakes and forests. "The names were like a soothing breeze to me. They had a promise of backwoods Russia."[69] He settles in Talnovo and reaches the heart of the country when he moves into Matryona's home.

The first names and nicknames of rural inhabitants, especially the older ones, are another colorful and distinctive feature of Village Prose. Matryona, Bogodul, Ivan Afrikanovich, Pelagaia, and Evsei would be rare in Youth or Urban Prose, but these and numerous other names used almost exclusively by peasants in the past are common in Village Prose, as are diminutives, patronymics as a replacement for a first or last name, and the use of an adjective indicating place of origin or a nickname instead of a last name. Astafiev wrote of the death of old Aunt Agafia, or, as the locals called her, "Agafia from Sergeevsk."[70] In the context of a hamlet and a few surrounding settlements, a last name was not necessary; "Sergeevskaia" would be enough to distinguish her from any other Agafias. The narrator also remembers how ever since his mother died when he was ten, the women from his part of the village have called him by the affectionate diminutive "Vitenka" as if he were their own son. Sixty years later the remaining old women still address him that way. It is an intimate linguistic detail that gives an accurate sense of traditional village life.

Village Prose writers used these names to achieve a realistic feeling for the rural life they knew so well, and which was so rapidly changing in the postwar period. Vladimir Krupin presents the reader of "The Fortieth Day" with a long list of his forebears. It may seem an odd, even an unnecessary or self-indulgent act—after all, none of these people will figure in the story, but, as with many of the stylistic gestures of Village Prose writers, this one has cultural significance. It is the fortieth day of Krupin's trip to the countryside; Russian Orthodox believers remember their dead on the fortieth day. Because the upheavals and changes of the twentieth century have sent his relatives to the far corners of Russia, he cannot visit their graves in the village cemetery; the only remembrance of them possible at this point is the simple recital of their names.

When Astafiev's Aunt Agafia died, he found photos of her deceased in-laws Lukasha and Akulina in her house, and he wondered who would commemorate them in the future. The responsibility of remembering the names of the deceased is taken seriously in Village Prose, in a way that is reminiscent of Anna Akhmatova's moving epilogue to the poem "Requiem" in which she expresses—but does not fulfill—her desire to name all the women who stood with her outside the prison walls. In Russian Village Prose, the act of remembering people and places that would otherwise be forgotten has a spiritual, cultural, and ultimately political resonance. One of the manifestations of the decline of village life is the loss of its distinctive language, a language that can conjure up a whole way of life in the radiant past, and one of the most important accomplishments of Village Prose was to preserve the living voices of the countryside—the voices of a rural childhood—in Russian literature.

FOUR

TIME, BACKWARD!

> How quiet and sleepy everything is in the three or four
> villages which compose this little plot of land!
> (Ivan Goncharov, *Oblomov*)

> This feeling resembled a memory, but a memory of
> what? It was almost as if you could remember
> something that had never been.
> (L. N. Tolstoy, *Childhood*)

THE TREATMENT of time is one of the core attributes of Russian Village Prose and one of the surest means of distinguishing it from Socialist Realism. The latter's goal of depicting "reality in its revolutionary development" is forcefully expressed in Valentin Kataev's 1932 novel *Time, Forward!* (*Vremia, vpered!*) where the industrialization effort—specifically the attempt to set records for pouring concrete—is seen in terms of the speeding up of time. "Time was concentrated. It flew. It interfered. He must tear himself out of it, free himself. He must outdistance it. Smetana was almost running."[1]

Vladimir Mayakovsky, in suggesting this title to Kataev, declared that "Time, Forward!" was "the very essence of our life today."[2] It is a phrase characteristic of the literary treatment of time that grew out of the Russian avant-garde movement and which was retained by official Socialist Realist theory in 1934, not just for literature on urban and industrial themes but for kolkhoz novels as well. Stories about the countryside were meant to show a relentless struggle to transform the slow cycles of rural *byt*, which clearly stood in the way of a mechanized and collectivized future.[3] The necessity of speeding away from the past is clearly stated in Ilyenkov's novel *Driving Axle*: "This deeply rooted atavistic lure of the village was a drag upon the people; even on the threshold of a new life it tugged at them, making their long march into the future harder."[4]

After several decades of novelists forcibly accelerating time, the Village Prose writers put the brakes on the speeding rural literary machine. As Geoffrey Hosking observed, "At a stroke the Promethean Soviet drive towards the future had been inverted, had become the worship of a lost Golden Age."[5] "Time, Backward!"—the mirror image of Kataev's title—successfully captures the contrast between

fast-paced, future-oriented Socialist Realist works, and slow, past-ori-
ented Village Prose. The literary practices of the *derevenshchiki*
evolved into a philosophical—ultimately ideological—position that
pitted what John Berger has aptly termed the "culture of survival"
against the "culture of progress." In the former it is the past that
looms large and brings all events into focus; in the latter it is the future
toward which all attention is directed. The significance of an experience in one culture is the "mirror opposite" of a similar experience in
the other culture.[6] The Village Prose writer Vladimir Lichutin sees a
contrast between biological and spiritual time. "The natural and biological moves forward in time, but the spiritual moves in a long procession backward, from one ancestor to another, into the depths of the
centuries. . . . it was only the fantasy of an unstable soul that created
the . . . legend of speeded-up time."[7]

To fully understand canonical Socialist Realist works one has to see
their orientation toward the future, to speed, and to a wholesale rejection of the traditional in favor of creating a new world. An appreciation of Village Prose involves looking at the writers' interest in the
past, in a faithfully observed structure of rural activities, and in memory. The image of the "long road" (*doroga dlinnaia*) is a useful one for
Village Prose, referring not only to slow journeys through the Russian
countryside, but also to the "long road" back to the writers' village
childhood and to the past of rural Russia.[8]

The treatment of time—the way it is slowed down and pushed backward—not only distinguishes Village Prose from Socialist Realism but
also marks a point of contrast with much contemporary urban literature.[9] The Village Prose writers generally pay more attention to a rich,
multilayered sense of time than to innovative plots or original characters. As a heuristic device, I have identified some of the more important kinds of "time" that operate in Village Prose: historical, literary,
cyclical, generational, childhood, and "borrowed" or apocalyptic time.
They are of course intermingled in a given work, but each has its own
resonance, its own specific power.

Historical Time

If one were to describe a typical approach to time in Village Prose, it
would combine elements of the cyclical, the historical, and the personal, with an emphasis on the past over the present or the future.
Because this literature is written for the most part by people who have
firsthand experience with rural life, one would expect the cyclical to
dominate, but not to the exclusion of historical events and developments. "Those who have a unilinear view of time cannot come to terms

with the idea of cyclic time: it creates a moral vertigo since all their morality is based on cause and effect. Those who have a cyclic view of time are easily able to accept the convention of historic time, which is simply a trace of the turning wheel."[10]

Although Village Prose had its immediate origins in Ovechkin's essays critical of the present situation on the kolkhoz (i.e., in the early 1950s), it evolved into a literature primarily concerned with the past. In the late 1970s, when some writers returned to descriptions of contemporary rural life, critics saw these new works as part of "a different literary galaxy."[11] But, even once it is established that Village Prose has dealt primarily with the past, there is still the question of *where* in the past Village Prose locates itself, and whose past it tells. The frequent ambiguity about exactly when a given work is taking place led Geoffrey Hosking to remark that the *derevenshchiki* prefer to depict the village "not as it was *at the time of writing*, but as it used to be somewhat earlier."[12] They break away from a publicistic attachment to the present moment that is typical of Soviet literature, finding instead a breathing space in a more relaxed—and elusive—notion of time. The temporal vagueness of Village Prose has to do with the distillation and collapsing of events in one's memory; it also happens to serve very well the needs of an incipient ideology. The misreading of this deliberately vague temporal scheme has led to a questioning of the factual accuracy of the picture of rural Russia presented by Village Prose, when what was really being offered was *pravda*—a moral and personal truth—and not fact.

When it attends to history, Village Prose retells a story of peasant life in the Soviet period that had been simplified, falsified, and generally glossed over in collective-farm novels. Its rural chronicle gives a fuller account of the Soviet past, one that is based on memories from the *malaia rodina*—the writers' own villages and families. The complexities of collectivization, the wartime rural home front, and the postwar period come alive because we learn how the writers' parents, grandparents, brothers, and sisters were affected. The *derevenshchiki* emphasize not just major historical forces and events, but also the traditional patterns of village life that were irrevocably altered in the twentieth century. It is the local repercussions that we see, not the events themselves. The writers' favorite characters were usually old men and women, the bearers of tradition, rather than Kolkhoz Literature's youthful carriers of change.

With the exception of collectivization, the Village Prose writers portray historical and natural forces in elemental, impersonal terms. Nature sets the river ice in motion each spring, and the government sends floodwaters down the Angara—and the peasants do not make distinctions. Characters are not so much passive as they are driven creatures, surviving at the pleasure of forces stronger than any human being. Some of the most powerful passages in Village Prose, Aleksei Leonov and Abramov on the war years, and Rasputin on the flooding of villages and whole islands for hydroelectric projects, express the feeling of acceptance of the inevitable. Darya, in Rasputin's *Farewell to Matyora*, repeatedly remarks that everyone is pulled and swept along through life and it is a rare person who sets his own pace. Tatiana Averkina in Leonov's story "Along Summer and Winter Roads" shows the truth of this observation as she makes her way one cold winter evening during the war after having traded her most precious possession—a shawl—for enough food to keep her children alive. "The wind swept the snow from the lane, it spun her around and no matter which way she turned it struck her in the face, blinded her, and blew under her skirt. And, bending her back to the wind and holding onto the hem of her skirt, Tatiana set off like a homeless dog who's suddenly found a bone."[13] Tatiana is quite a different figure from the all-powerful masters of history and nature that Socialist Realism envisioned. Backs to the wind, these peasant characters try not to transform, but to survive, to make it not all the way to the "radiant future" but just to the next harvest.

Even when a very specific historical period like the Second World War establishes a time frame, Village Prose writers do not concentrate on major battles, campaigns, or historical figures. They are interested not so much in individual heroics as in the survival of the village and, by extension, of all Russia. They foreground daily life, with the emphasis on how much harder it is to survive during wartime when most of the men are away and the remaining villagers—women, old people, and children—must fuel the war effort. Village Prose writers brought these simple peasants into official history from which they had for the most part been excluded. In a nation of hero-cities, there are no "hero-villages" except in these works. In addition, most of these writers were children or young boys during the early forties, and a rural child's view of the world colors their depiction of the war.

Until the Gorbachev era, the excesses of collectivization were hinted at—rather than discussed frankly—in rural literature. By the time the constraints of censorship had for the most part been lifted, Village Prose had ceased to operate as a coherent movement, and the fuller portrayals of this tragic period appeared in works that were more documentary than lyric. Belov, Mozhaev, and others have begun to shift from the almost exclusive use of the memories of their own childhoods and the stories from their *malaia rodina* to the use of newly accessible archival materials. Regrettably, some of them have wound up exchanging one myth of collectivization—the Soviet story of a smooth, successful, justifiable process—for another—the Jew as the enemy of the Russian peasant and virtually the sole agent of change.

Cyclical Time

Village Prose is dominated by cyclical time, primarily the natural cycle of the seasons, and it shows the way that cycle is intertwined with work patterns, folk customs, and the church calendar. The remarkable calming effect of much Village Prose, even amid scenes of historical upheaval and personal tragedy for peasants, is due largely to the sense of a predictable cycle of such events as spring thunder and flooding, plowing, sowing, early summer haymaking, fishing, long summer days, the last swim and the first apples in August, mushroom gathering, the harvest, followed by flax spinning and the repair of fishing nets indoors during the long winter evenings, and the wait for the cow to calve and once again give milk. Then the cycle is repeated, always with the same contours, but with no day or year exactly like the previous one. Each season has its structure of activities, holidays, games, clothing, food, songs, sayings, and superstitions, and its own rhythm.

Leonov's Tatiana Averkina knows this cycle well; it is the way she keeps track of her family history. In labor in a root cellar a few months after the beginning of the war, with the enemy nearby, she remembers when her other children were born, not as numbers on a calendar, but according to where these births fit into the natural cycle.

> When Ivan was born the fruit trees were in bloom and bees and flies were buzzing. . . . And Fedor was born when the apples were ripe. That was a really good year for apples. . . . Masha appeared on Christmas Eve. It was very snowy . . . and there was a whistling in the stovepipe. . . . When Verka arrived they were gathering mushrooms in the woods. . . . Mishka was born with the first snow on a pale-blue evening. The cow had calved the very same day. . . . In March noisy Aliosha showed up. The starlings were flying above the treetops, fighting over bird houses. . . . And just before haymaking, when the meadow was dandelion yellow and a hazy heat poured over the growing grain and furrows were hidden by the tops of potato plants, Petia entered the world.[14]

In Viktor Perepelka's "The Old Almanac"("Starinnyi kalendar'") the narrator spends a day in his old village, a place "lost in the roadless backwoods" where nothing ever happened except that once a crop duster landed by mistake, giving people a marker by which to tell time, for example: "'It was the year after the plane landed in the field.'"[15] In the ruins of his family home the narrator finds a few pages from his great-grandfather's almanac. A monument to *dvoeverie* 'dual faith', that amalgam of Russian Orthodoxy and folk beliefs which is so characteristic of rural Russia, the pages of the calendar connect cycles in nature and the spirit world to the months and the saints' days. "'On St. Nikita's day, the water-sprite wakes up and invites the mermaids to a feast.'"[16] Fishermen must make an offering to the spirits on this day so that their homes and family members will be safe. The almanac tells you when to expect the migration of birds, how to know what the fall and winter will be like, and at what times to exercise special care, for example, on St. Ilya's (Elijah's) day (July 20, O.S.). "'On St. Ilya's day before dinner—it is summer, after dinner—it is fall. On St. Ilya's day don't drive the cattle out to pasture: wild beasts and vermin roam the fields.'"[17] St. Ilya, a marked contrast to the generally helpful St. Nicholas, seems to have taken on some characteristics of the old Slavic thunder god Perun, and although he might provide much-needed rain, he could also send dangerous lightning and hail. Not only were the cattle not sent out on his day, but peasants themselves stayed away from the fields, fasting and setting out offerings to placate him.[18]

Kondyr, the eponymous hero of Aleksei Leonov's story, looks up at the moon and instinctively makes the sign of the cross.[19] A residual dual faith is evident as well in Viktor Astafiev's "Predchuvstvie ledokhoda"(Signs of spring).[20] His description of the annual breakup of the ice in the Yenisei connects this all-important moment in the natural cycle with the Easter season. His grandmother experienced this violent event as *svetoprestavlenie* 'the end of world, doomsday, chaos', and, taking an icon of the Savior, would head a procession of women to the river's edge. There she led the others in prayers and deep reverential bows that were as much to the river as to the Mother of God.[21]

Valentin Rasputin's story "Vasilii i Vasilisa"(Vasilii and Vasilisa, 1967) is attuned to the patterns of the day and season. The present tense of much of the story reinforces this sense of repetition, as does the use of the instrumental of seasons, e.g., *letom* 'during the summer', and *zimoi* 'during the winter'. The daily and seasonal tasks that structure life, but are never finished, acquire in this story an almost personified form as *ona* 'it (fem.), she'—a figure that will outlive us. Before we learn anything else, we hear about Vasilisa's morning routine, and how she tells time: "Her day was divided not by hours but by samovars: first samovar, second, third."[22] It is only after we have heard about Vasilii's morning routine that we are told about their highly unusual domestic arrangements: for thirty years—after a drunken assault that caused Vasilisa to suffer a miscarriage—the husband has lived in "exile" in the barn. But everything in this story is incorporated into *byt*: the separate dwelling places, Vasilii's return from the war (in autumn at potato-lifting time), his temporary addition of a second "wife" in the barn, and the daily glass of tea that he receives across a "demilitarized zone" in the middle of the kitchen table. When Vasilii is ill, he expresses a wish not to die at night. "'I want to die in the daytime. People talking, hens flapping their wings, dogs barking.'"[23] *Byt*, the daily routine, can even dull the fear of death; one is reminded of the peasant Gerasim in Tolstoy's story "The Death of Ivan Ilych," who takes care of his dying employer with the same briskly cheerful competence that he would bring to any other task.

The last chapter of Belov's novel *Privychnoe delo* (That's how things are) finds Ivan Afrikanovich sitting on the shore of the village lake in the late autumn. Though it is the fortieth day after his wife Katerina's death, he focuses not on the end of life, but on its endless cycles. The winter will come in stages and will be very long, but one day the warmth will return and the fish will begin to stir again, the ice will break up, and the frogs and grouse will make themselves heard. "And this cycle has no end."[24] It is his detailed contemplation of seasonal change that brings an unexpected peace to Ivan Afrikanovich's troubled soul. He goes to his wife's grave for the first time, bringing her rowanberries—a gift from the world of the living. He will go on, submitting not only to the harsh reality of her death, but also to the cycle of life. The end of this work first shows Ivan stretched out on his wife's grave; then the narrative view rises above that to an impersonal scene from nature. "A noisy flock of starlings flew over the church. There was an acrid, ancient smell of smoke. The sky was blue. From somewhere on the other side of the brightly-colored trees, the first breath of winter blew into the villages."[25]

The cyclical structuring of life in Village Prose seems to lift the village out of history and put it down in a protected place in the primordial forest, and yet troubles are never far away: Leonov's Kondyr walks in the ancient Dubrava woods on the eve of his forced move from the village, but the walk, however pleasant, changes nothing. Spring arrives at the beginning of Rasputin's *Farewell to Matyora*, "one more in the never-ending cycle," but it is the last spring for the island.[26] Vasily Belov calls these two aspects of Village Prose *lad* 'harmony' and *razlad* 'disharmony, discord'.[27] The distilled vision of *lad* and *byt* 'daily routine' is presented most fully in Belov's book of essays on folk aesthetics called *Harmony* (*Lad*), which provides a remarkable description of daily life in northern Russian villages near Vologda. Time was experienced differently in the countryside than in urban areas, Belov tells us, without clocks and without speed, but rather with an eye to the sun's position and a steady, stubborn effort.

Belov describes how village life was structured first by the season and agricultural activities and then by subdivisions such as ordinary days and holidays, fasting and nonfasting time, days of the week, and times of the day. He takes one crop—flax—and details how the transformation from flaxseed to such products as linen and linseed oil structures a year's activities for the village women: planting, pulling, threshing, spreading out, the pressing of oil, flax breaking, separating fibers by beating them, combing, spinning, weaving, bleaching the fabric, and finally sewing. Failure to complete an activity at the proper time risked economic and social failure.

Food, children's games, ritual celebrations, courtship, and marriage were all part of various cycles. Belov emphasizes that in all these cycles—in all of village life—there was both the following of an inherited pattern and the uniqueness of a given performance. Each house, icon, lament, fairy tale, or embroidered towel could be recognizably "correct" and yet unlike any other. All villages celebrated the major feasts, but each village chose its own summer and winter "beer holiday" (*pivnoi prazdnik*).[28] In all of this, the individual's life is seen as a particular performance of the pattern, and not more than that. This is not a way of life or a type of literature that foregrounds either the "novel" or the individual. Continuity was all-important; change was feared and resisted. John Berger has captured this sense of life in *Pig Earth*. "The peasant sees life as an interlude because of the dual contrary movement through time of his thoughts and feelings. . . . His determination is to hand on the means of survival . . . to his children. His ideals are located in the past; his obligations are to the future, which he himself will not live to see. After his death he will not be transported into the future—his notion of immortality is different: he will return to the past."[29]

It is this emphasis on cycles and the detailed representation of *byt*—along with the reliance on childhood memories—that allows the *derevenshchiki* not only to move time backward but also to slow it down. Kataev's *Time, Forward!* intentionally matches the tempo of a speeding train; Belov's slow horse and its besotted driver at the beginning of *That's How Things Are* proceed at a very different pace. For Village Prose writers there is a value in the time-honored daily round itself, in learning, living, and passing on the tradition, not in speeding away from it. In Lichutin's story "Grandmothers and Uncles," an old woman answers complaints about the senselessness of the daily struggle with the statement that "we live to continue the family (*rod*). That is the reason for our endless work."[30]

Literary Time

The cyclical time of Village Prose, with its folk calendar, not only reflects rural life as the writers knew it—or as they had heard about it from older peasants—but also continues a literary tradition that dates back to Karamzin's "Poor Liza." The *derevenshchiki* have been influenced by this literary tradition and its use of time at many points along the way by, among others, Aksakov, Goncharov, Turgenev, Tolstoy, the Populists, the peasant writers of the 1920s, and Prishvin; they have literary grandparents among turn-of-the-century writers such as Bunin and Gippius. In *Oblomov* (1859), Goncharov says that during the hero's childhood, the rural gentry and their serfs kept track of time by the holy days, the seasons, and family events. "They never referred to dates or months."[31] In the 1895 Gippius story "Outside of Time: An Old Etude," the young gentry narrator goes to spend the summer with relatives at a remote estate. Here he soon finds himself unable to maintain an exact sense of time. "I don't know how much time had passed since I had come to Osokino. The days came and went; I had lost track and didn't even want to count them. I only knew that the hay had been mowed long ago, and that the rye had already turned yellow and bent to the ground, and that frequent winds had started to ripple the water of the large lake."[32] When he tells his cousin that he knows neither the date nor even the month, she replies that it is sufficient to know the days of the week—by such signs as the ringing of church bells on Sunday—and the seasons. Of course, this level of nonchalance was a luxury that peasants could not afford, but the temporal atmosphere of Village Prose is still closer to that of a story set on a nineteenth-century gentry estate than to later, more "proletarian" works.[33] In Bunin's story "Antonov Apples" (1900) time comes to a standstill at dusk in early autumn when the poignant, bittersweet fragrance of ripe apples fills the air, and the horses slowly pull the threshing machine in never-ending circles, often falling asleep in the process.[34] These seemingly endless, slow circles are emblematic of the temporal structure of Village Prose.

The sense of time in Village Prose is not only *anti–* but also *ante–* Socialist Realism; it effectively bypasses Socialist Realism and goes back to both traditional peasant life and to the depiction of that life in pre-Revolutionary Russian literature. What Ilyenkov feared, these writers celebrate. They countered fast tractors with slow horses.

Generational Time, Ancestral Memory

There is a sense of time in Village Prose that involves one's *rodina* 'native land, homeland' and its people. This homeland can be Russia or the entire Slavic world, but it can also—on a smaller scale—comprise a region (central Russia, the north, Siberia), or a single village and villagers related to you past, present, and future. Vladimir Lichutin called the awareness of *rod* (i.e., relatedness in time, place, and person) *rodovaia pamiat'* (lit. 'generational or ancestral memory'). This memory might "appear" to you suddenly as a tiny candle lighting up the dark recesses of the soul. You realize that "you arose much earlier than the moment of your birth," that you are not an alienated person, but one whose connections stretch back through the centuries.[35]

Lichutin confesses that at first he saw nothing poetic in a childhood spent in a cramped, unattractive home that did not even have a Russian stove, but then he came to recall carefree moments spent outdoors, and by the time he reached his thirties, a happy childhood began to shape itself in his memory. "And it's only now, in my thirties, that looking at the vaguely oscillating image of my past self, I've suddenly become convinced that although I was a fatherless, hungry kid, I wasn't at all unhappy. It means that as a child you might be hungry or full, shoeless, poorly clothed, dirty or well-cared-for, homeless or spoiled, but you cannot be unhappy or joyless—that is childhood's inscrutable secret. Childhood is childhood."[36] At some point a fog lifted and ancestral memory began to stir in his soul. Visits to his mother's village were a necessary link in the process of "reunifying" his memory, providing himself with a *rodovaia pamiat'*. The experience of shared patterns of everyday life (*byt*) over the generations is the foundation of this feeling of connectedness (*rod*) and a means of protection against a destructive cultural and personal vacuum.

Lichutin links ancestral memory to "spiritual" memory (*dukhovnaia pamiat'*) and contrasts both to reason (*razum*).[37] After his epiphany, he found that he could strengthen his ancestral memory by traveling through the Russian north, by studying the rich folklore of that area, and by recalling stories told him by older relatives, especially his grandfather, through whom he was able to extend his spiritual life back to the previous century and his great-grandfather.

Ancestral memory has more than a personal significance. Lichutin tells of his own experiences in the hope that this will inspire others. *Rodovaia pamiat'* is a force that could strengthen the nation, one person at a time. "Ancestral memory is the knowledge of life that has been swept away and lost in its primordial state. It's so easy to lose it, but you can only reconstruct it bit by bit: sometimes you find that you discover once again something you knew as a child and had already forgotten."[38] In Lichutin's essays from the late 1970s and early 1980s—when Village Prose as a school had already declined—we can see the lyrical-philosophical elements of Village Prose acquiring the mythic trappings of ideology.

Vladimir Krupin works hard at maintaining his "ancestral memory" in "The Fortieth Day." While visiting his parents, he senses the unity of his family members, living and dead, as they visit him in his dreams and gaze at him from photographs. Despite his family's frequent moves around the country and the lack of a village to call his own, he still tries to remember the names of all the families he can count as "kinfolk" (*rodnia*) and the locations of all the widely scattered family graves. He estimates that by the year 2000, no one would have the energy to visit them all.[39]

In Abramov's posthumously published "Poezdka v proshloe" (A Journey into the past, wr. 1963–1974, publ. 1989), we see a more painful search for ancestral memory. The hero, Miksha (Nikifor Ivanovich Kobylin), has many years before changed his last name to distance himself from his old-fashioned father and to impress his two uncles—both Bolshevik activists. When a mysterious stranger forces him to act as a guide to an abandoned, overgrown former settlement for exiled kulaks, Miksha must confront the painful fact of dekulakization that the region experienced and that his uncles had supervised. "He had seen a lot in his lifetime. He had spent time in both the war and the camps. In '45, he took Berlin with Zhukov—but he had never seen anything like this. He had never walked down the main street of a settlement and had to push the overgrown bushes away with his arms, as if he were deep in the forest."[40] The stranger turns out to be the person who killed one of his uncles when this "hero" raped the boy's sister. Once his pride in his uncles—the reason for separating himself from his roots—disappears, Miksha sets out to learn his father's story, and in that way to reconnect himself to the *rod*. He discovers genuine local heroes, his father and the village teacher among others. On his way home through the icy autumn night, he stops by the village chapel—a place where the uprooted kulaks took shelter and where many of them died—and it seems to him that the place is brightly lit. He hears people singing, the way they did in 1930, in voices that reduced his father and other villagers to tears.

> I'm coming father!
> He had never visited his father's grave, never shed a tear in the cemetery next to the church, and why? Was he not his father's son?
> The bells were ringing . . . The song rose and fell with longing and pain . . .
> He strode toward his father.[41]

The candle that lights up the soul—ancestral memory—enables Miksha to find his authentic past. The fact that he dies in the process is of little consequence to the author; Abramov refers ironically to a local newspaper article that attributes the death to drunkenness. Miksha dies on his father's grave, having returned to his *rod* and to his past. In this "epitaph" to the Village Prose movement, Abramov has offered a "symbolic working out of repentance," a theme that has dominated post-1985 discourse in the USSR.[42]

The theme of a common Russian identity found in some Village Prose led to writing that was not always as artistically refined as it was ideologically stimulating. The feeling for local roots and generational unity, one of the distinctive features of Village Prose, has been much more effectively expressed because it is personally known and felt and is not a politicized abstraction. A constellation of words related to *rodnoi* and *rodnoe* links land, language, home, renewal, and a bond among the dead, the living, and those not yet born. This sense of the common life of various generations is particularly strong in the "Grandmother's Birthday" chapter of Viktor Astafiev's *The Final Bow*.

> Soon after St. Ilya's day, when the mowing was over, all our numerous relatives would show up at our house for a visit or, to be more precise, to celebrate granny's birthday. It happened only once in every two or three years. More often than that would have cost too much. No one ever arranged for granny's sons, daughters, grandchildren, and other relations to make their visit in any particular year, at any particular time. But by some kind of intuition they themselves knew when to come.[43]

Fortunately, Astafiev's grandparents shared this intuition and prepared well in advance for these epic feasts.

Village Prose tells of more than the bonds between blood relations. Fedor Abramov, at the beginning of his epic *The Pryaslins* (1958–1978) sees the true chronicle of the village of Pekashino written on a wooden table in a haymaking hut where the men and boys of the village had carved their names and made their marks over the years. Aleksei Leonov's hero Kondyr contemplates the family table with marks made over the decades by his grandfather and father as they cut their home-grown tobacco. The ties between generations of people performing similar tasks are there for all to see. Although the local women have left no analogous "chronicle," their links and their story are no less compelling for these authors.

Sometimes the bond takes the form of an emotional expression of remembrance, as when Nastasia in Viktor Perepelka's "The Last Day in the Old House" "talks" to her dead husband in the village cemetery before moving in with her daughter; Belov's *That's How Things Are* ends with Ivan Afrikanovich at his wife's grave, trying to tell her of both his grief and his decision to go on. At other times there is a sense of real communication with those who have gone ahead into the other world, for instance, in Leonov's "Kondyr," Boris Ekimov's "The Last Peasant House," and most importantly in Rasputin's *Farewell to*

Matyora. In the latter work, old Darya, after holding a vigil in the island's devastated graveyard, finally receives the guidance that she has been seeking as to how best to bid farewell to the family home before it is burned down to make way for floodwaters from the new dam. Darya thinks about the living and the dead as well as about the different generations alive at one time.[44] Sitting with her son Pavel and grandson Andrei, she silently contemplates her own death, envisioning it in terms of the most commonplace of objects. "There it is, one thread with knots. It seemed that there were so many years between knots . . . where are they? My knot is going to be stretched out and smoothed over, they'll let the smooth end go so that it'll be invisible . . . so that they can tie a new one on the other end. Where will the string be pulled now? What will happen?"[45]

A mysterious catlike creature called the Master (*khoziain*, a euphemism for the *domovoi* or house-spirit), a kind of island spirit, watches over his domain at night. "Only at night, casting off from the solid land, the living and the dead meet—the dead come to them in body and word and ask for the truth, in order to pass it on even further, to those whom they remembered."[46] A chain of memory—which is equated with truth—leads backward in time. At the beginning of *Farewell (Proshchanie)*, the Soviet film based on this book, director Elem Klimov shows five hooded figures in monklike translucent white robes—which on closer inspection turn out to be raincoats—crossing the mist-shrouded Angara River in a small boat. As they land, the four men "become" government workers from the mainland who are to clear the island of all structures; the fifth, a female figure, disappears from view. This scene serves as a tribute to Klimov's wife, the filmmaker Larisa Shepitko, and four of her crew, who were killed in an accident at the onset of what was to have been her film. Though this scene was obviously not in Rasputin's text, it fits beautifully and eerily the book's elegiacal sensibilities.[47] Having the same figures simultaneously play the living and the dead is an astonishingly effective, unforgettable filmic gesture. At least for a moment, there is a real sense of access to the "other world," the kind of access Village Prose characters sometimes experience when they think about the *rod* to which they belong, and whom they must honor and serve.

The *predki* 'ancestors' were always important in Russian folklore and Russian Orthodoxy, and Village Prose reflects these still-active beliefs. In general, death in the countryside, as it has usually been represented in Russian literature, was accepted as part of the natural cycle, which makes a striking contrast to death in the world of the educated and the city-dweller, a contrast noted by Tolstoy in such works as *War and Peace* and "The Death of Ivan Ilyich."[48] The old peasants die while thinking of those who came before them, with whom they will soon be reunited.[49]

Childhood Time

Memories of childhood can be seen as a "subset" of the deeper ancestral memory. In Village Prose, the child's memories shape the sense of time as well as linking the individual to previous generations, to the whole *rod*. The form the writers choose—what Coe calls the Childhood—is a mixture of autobiography, novel, idyll, and social history. (It is discussed in chapter 2 as the "chronotope of Childhood," my adaptation of Bakhtin's term.) Viktor Astafiev evokes the spirit of this idyll when he says, "Oh my memory, work another miracle. . . . resurrect the little boy in me, let me calm and purify myself by his side."[50] To move time "backward" is to be purified and comforted.

The memories that go into this latter-day Russian idyll must be from a specific place familiar to the narrator and inexpressibly dear to him. Lichutin says that "it is not the earth in general that calls to you, but those places connected to your father and mother." He feels that the idea of a "homeland" is too vague for us; we have to make it more concrete, to narrow it down to a place about which we remember everything.[51] Vladimir Nabokov in *Speak, Memory* insisted that his nostalgia was not for lost wealth, but for lost childhood, and not for all of Russia, but for "*one* locality in Russia," the estate where he grew up; this view is echoed by rural writers.[52] While Socialist Realist Kolkhoz Literature used generic rural locations (what Katerina Clark calls "far away from Moscow"), in the Village Prose memoir of childhood there is one village, one name, that evokes the past; the Village Prose Childhood is in many ways a universal narrative, but one that relies heavily on the specific. One analysis of Evgenii Nosov's stories emphasizes that he counteracted a literature which had no language, landscape, or character of its own with a literature of specific villages and their inhabitants, and an identifiable regional variant of Russian.[53] The place may be concrete; the time is not. Perhaps what the writers of the post-Stalinist period express is more the *memory* of an idyll than the idyll itself.[54] They had seen the impoverished tail end of traditional village life, and much of what they knew came from the stories told them by older relatives and villagers.

In *The Final Bow*, Viktor Astafiev lays bare the transformation that childhood memories naturally undergo, the way that one could remember—as Tolstoy said in *Childhood*—things that never took place, or took place in quite a different way. Astafiev's narrator analyzes his grandmother's favorite story about his mother, who bowed and cried every time she passed the former house of her in-laws, sent away as kulaks during collectivization.

> After my mother's death, grandmother Katerina Petrovna often told me this story, and every time she told it she added something, not just tears, but details about my mother's personality, her habits, and her actions. As the years passed, my mother's image became more and more radiant in grandmother's memory. For that reason it is sacred to me, although I understand that this image of my mother is one that was reborn and re-created by my grandmother's guilt over a daughter who died young and by my longing for my mother. This image can hardly be reconciled with the reality of the simple, hardworking peasant woman that she was. Mama was and will now forever remain the finest, purest person, not even a person, but a deified figure.[55]

Lichutin writes of a mother who has almost disappeared from his memory, "leaving only a vague and oscillating image of 'mother.'"[56]

Vladimir Tendriakov, in "A Day in the Old Hometown," recalls a month-long visit he made as a five-year-old with his father to the village in which Tendriakov was born. It was a damp, gray summer morning when they arrived, but the father was excited by the sight of the simple houses.

> "Look!"—He touched my shoulder. "Look—it's your hometown!"
> I was forever hearing that there was a place on earth called My Hometown. I couldn't remember it—I was taken away from there in swaddling clothes. They told me about it at bedtime along with fairy tales, and in the end the village of Makarovskaia itself became like something in a fairy tale—indistinct and wonderful.[57]

The fairy tale became real on that visit, and the events of the summer—such as catching his first big fish—were engraved in his memory for a lifetime, to be summoned up from the depths in his years away from the village. Several times he uses the prose refrain: "Then I was five years old, now I'm forty." The "day" in the title is the one-day visit he makes as a forty-year-old man. One of the most frequent narrative patterns in Village Prose is that of RETURN, generally the return to the village of an uprooted native son or daughter who recalls the past in lyric tones, is distressed by present conditions, and then leaves. The lyric, even luminous, feeling is strongest when the work is told in the first person.

In Valentin Rasputin's story "Downstream," the hero travels down the Angara to his native village, recalling as he goes various points along the current of his past. The most vivid moment of a youth spent on the river was when the annual breakup of the river-ice coincided with his sixth birthday. The little boy went down to the river in the middle of the night to observe this dramatic event and was caught in a terrifying thunderstorm, the first that spring, which helped the river break loose from winter's icy grip. There are calmer moments to recall as well—summer mushroom and berry picking with his family, and spearfishing on autumn nights with his grandfather. "Memories linked to the river lived within him distinct from other memories; they lived like a warm, heartfelt sorrow beside which he would often rest and warm himself before moving on. He understood: childhood had preserved them—everything relating to first impressions is preserved for a long time, perhaps forever, but the crux of the matter was that out of many other things childhood had set precisely these apart."[58]

Village Prose expresses a sense of the primordial—the misty beginnings of time in forest and field—as well as each individual's beginning in childhood. Of equal importance is its focus on the end of time in the deaths of older peasants, the abandoning of whole villages, and in the perceived threat to the distinctive rural character of Russia itself. If the past of Village Prose is full, radiant, and complex, the present is experienced as a time of loss, and the future is seen as a cultural and moral vacuum.[59] The elegiacal tone of Village Prose—at times bordering on the apocalyptic—is so important to an understanding of this literature that it will be the subject of the following chapter.

FIVE

BORROWED TIME: METAPHORS FOR LOSS

IN VILLAGE PROSE

> This is the peasant Atlantis, which has already
> sunk to the bottom of the ocean.
> *(Igor Zolotussky)*

> We measure time not only by what we
> acquire, but also by what we lose.
> *(Vladimir Lichutin)*[1]

VILLAGE PROSE is simultaneously a literature of first and last things. The first things are the primordial setting, the ties to pre-Revolutionary life and literature, and the memories of childhood. The last things are the ways in which traditional rural life and the very existence of the small village are coming to an end. The importance of endings, the past, and progressive loss is reflected in such titles as *Poslednii srok* (*Borrowed Time*; Rasputin), *Poslednii poklon* (The final bow; Astafiev), *Poslednii koldun* (The last wizard; Lichutin), "Posledniaia okhota" and "Poslednii starik derevni"(The final hunt, and The last old man in the village; Abramov), "Posledniaia khata"(The last peasant house; Ekimov), and Viktor Perepelka's "Poslednii den' v svoem dome"(The last day in the old house) and "Krai medlennogo vremeni"(The land where time slowed down).[2] There are titles in a similar vein using the words for "old" and "farewell." Vladimir Soloukhin has also noticed the way titles followed certain patterns and added to this list Belov's *Kanuny* (The eve) and Vladimir Krupin's "Sorokovoi den'"(The fortieth day), which in Russian Orthodoxy is the day that the soul of the deceased person finally leaves the earth and when a large wake is usually held to commemorate the loved one.[3] The orientation toward things that are coming to an end also shows up in the emphasis on the village (versus the kolkhoz), in the mainly older characters, and in the houses, artifacts, and customs of traditional rural *byt* that function as important images and symbols in these works.[4] The changes that have taken place in the countryside are perceived by the *derevenshchiki* as a process of loss, both personal and national. For them, the old rural life and with it the very roots of the Russian character are slipping away quickly and forever. When old people die and young people leave, there is no hope for the village.

The narrative of the decline of rural life is not new to Russian literature. From the 1850s to the Revolution, the gentry estate was the most important rural setting in literature and its gradual decline was used to symbolize a general malaise. The death of the estate and the life it represented is announced first tentatively in works like Goncharov's *Oblomov* and Turgenev's *Fathers and Sons* and then decisively by Chekhov. At the end of the first act of *The Cherry Orchard* (1903), the shepherd playing his reed pipe in the distance is a teasing reminder of the pastoral that is no more, an "idyllic scene, set up only to be destroyed."[5] The haunting sounds of a breaking string and of an ax striking the cherry trees punctuate the tension felt at the loss of the house to a former peasant who will tear it down to make room for summer cottages. The final scene of the old servant Firs left to die in the closed-up mansion foreshadows the end of estate life for peasants as well as for gentry.[6]

There was no return to the gentry estate in Russian literature after this work, except for those nostalgic, backward glances that reinforced a sense of irrevocable decline; for example, in the stories of Ivan Bunin. Bunin uses the estate and nearby village in "Antonov Apples" (1900), "Dry Valley" (1911), and "The Last Day" (1913) as a setting to illustrate "the transition from the realized ideal to its incipient destruction."[7] The first part of Vasilii Belov's novel *The Eve* (*Kanuny*, 1977, 1987), set in the late 1920s, returns briefly to a mansion house to show that the dwelling and its still-living former master are attractive but now peripheral and vulnerable to the violent forces of change. Belov's work reminds the reader that what has been lost is not only the estate as a rural chronotope, but also the voice of the gentry, both as character and writer. The Soviet publication in the glasnost years of Vladimir Nabokov's autobiographical *Drugie berega* (lit. 'Other shores', trans. into English as *Speak, Memory*) underscored the fact that the Russian estate of the author's childhood had become a "foreign shore" to émigré and Soviet reader alike—as it was to Nabokov himself. In post-Stalinist Village Prose, simple peasant homes in small villages were shown to be as vulnerable to the forces of change as the gentry mansions before them.

Although the peasant himself and the communal village are important to Tolstoy, Dostoevsky, and the Populists, their focus is on peasant-centered—though not peasant-formulated—programs rather than on a sense of loss.[8] Other works of the pre-Revolutionary period, such as Chekhov's "Peasants" (1897) and Bunin's "The Epitaph"

(1900) and "The Village" (1910) depict the hopelessness and desperate poverty of the countryside as the old structures of rural life broke down. Bunin accepted the fact that life would not stand still but saw that both the by-now largely impoverished gentry and the peasants would say farewell to the old ways with great sadness.

The avant-garde artistic and political movements of the early twentieth century concentrated on the city, and the rural theme was pushed into the background of literary life, with the exception of the works of Mikhail Prishvin and poet Sergei Esenin. Esenin was part of Nikolai Kliuev's loosely organized group of peasant writers and poets who used materials from folk culture to present a generally utopian picture of a mythic village recoiling from the industrial future.[9] Esenin's lyrical hero proclaimed himself the "last poet of the village," who heard the "moon's wooden clock wheezing out my final hour."[10]

The countryside once again became an important literary setting after the beginning of collectivization in 1928 and the institutionalization of Socialist Realism in 1934. Kolkhoz Literature, a subgenre of Socialist Realism, was charged with proclaiming and promoting the program of rapid, uncompromising rural transformation. Kolkhoz Literature emphasizes beginnings, the future, and progressive gains. We can see this in the young Party and kolkhoz officials and agronomists who populate these works, in images and symbols such as tractors, combines, trucks, and rural power stations, new buildings, lightbulbs, and radios, and especially in the titles: *Combines* (Zhuravlev), "The Story of the Director of the MTS [Machine Tractor Station] and the Chief Agronomist" (Nikolaeva), *Virgin Soil Upturned* (Sholokhov), *A Light over the Earth* and *Cavalier of the Golden Star* (Babaevsky), *Happiness* (Pavlenko), "Spring at the 'Victory' Kolkhoz" (Gribachev), *Movement* (Kataev), *The Creation of the World* (Zakrutkin), "Time to Build" (Galkin), *Wholeheartedly* (Maltsev), and "A Flag over the Village Soviet" (Nedogonov).[11]

Kolkhoz Literature told the story of the countryside as it was being pushed into the future, as Vasily Ilyenkov forcefully proclaimed in the novel *Driving Axle*: "He thought of that other tomorrow. Thousands of workers would abandon their machines and scatter along muddy roads and medieval trails, so as to destroy ancient field boundaries, uproot the stubborn habit of individual farming and rouse the peasants to a new order of life . . . class energy would push the creaking wheels of the rural cart out of its rut."[12]

The ancient, natural living and working structure of the village must yield to the new rational organization of the agricultural work force along industrial principles. The primary setting in Kolkhoz Literature is neither estate nor village but the collective-farm office or regional Party headquarters, places where important decisions were being made. Traditional peasants and their dwellings are seen as being out of step with the modern age. Semyon Babaevsky lays bare the urban animus behind rural change in his novel *Privol'e* (Wide open spaces, 1979) when the narrator notes that the attractive new cottages in a steppe settlement make a sharp contrast to the modest older houses that surround them "in the same way that an urban member of the intelligentsia stands out when placed next to a peasant."

The new rural writing that began with Ovechkin's essays in 1952—and which evolved into the Village Prose movement—took a more critical look at the collectivized countryside. Ovechkin, Dorosh, Soloukhin, Yashin, Kazakov, and many others began to question the dissolution of the village, the deracination of the peasant, and the devaluation of traditional rural ways. The writers found much to value in the old life, and they often expressed a deep sadness over how much had been lost.

A number of these writers—those actually of rural origin—moved from a focus on the impoverished present *backward* to show the countryside of their childhood years. They portray a village largely isolated from linear time, but with history poised to invade and destroy that timeless state. In their works the chronotope of the village is in the process of being destroyed. The reasons given by the *derevenshchiki* for rural decline are many: the Revolution and Civil War, collectivization, World War II, twentieth-century modernization and industrialization of rural areas, government neglect and mismanagement, mass migration to towns and cities, and environmental damage. The peasant home and village were so self-contained and central to rural culture that the abandonment and destruction of these native places is a poignant event. Village Prose shows how home by home, village by village, rural Russia is losing its distinctive way of life; writers worry about the long-term consequences of such a loss. Theirs is a nostalgia tinged with anxiety and anger.

Village Prose writers re-create what Katerina Clark has called the "iconic version of the traditional Russian village" including old peasant houses, a church, cemetery, lake or river, forest, bathhouse, mushrooms, berries, and birch trees.[13] The writers do this not to paint a naively idyllic picture, but to make a strong contrast to Kolkhoz Literature and to show that the village, along with its oldest inhabitants, is dying. And since the traditional villages are being abandoned, modernized, or absorbed into larger units, everything within them, from old peasants to bast shoes, is an image of loss. The younger generation has not inherited the skills, tastes, or forbearance that would keep the chain of village life from being broken. The canonical work of Village

Prose is infused with the atmosphere of diminution, of the penultimate moment, when the extent of loss is already known or guessed.

There is a tension in Village Prose between the vivid and almost atemporal depictions of traditional village life and contemporary realities. Igor Zolotussky noted that Feodor Abramov's prose "was filled with voices, laughter, wailing, the rush of northern rivers, filled with the smell of pine forests and with the swaying of grass taller than a man." As the reader wanders through Abramov's landscape, "it might seem that all was not lost," but this, the critic reminds us, is a poetic illusion.[14]

The most important narrative in Village Prose is that of the temporary RETURN of an uprooted peasant who tries to reconstitute the chronotope of Childhood or "ancestral memory." Gelasii Chudinov in Lichutin's "Grandmothers and Uncles" journeys from the city to the rural suburb where he grew up; he fears that soon he will have no home or family to come back to: "Everything around him was unavoidably aging. Grandfather Spira and his grandmothers Mania and Natalia were all dead, and one day he would go up to the familiar door of his house and see a rusty lock . . . and the three narrow windows covered with dark boards."[15] Gelia goes further back into his past by journeying to his mother's native village, which, though obviously dying, is lit up by the rays of the setting sun. The large family home is almost empty—"orphaned"—but the radiant presence of his Uncle Kronia, a truly Tolstoyan figure, heals Gelia's soul, as work in his mother's garden had helped to heal his body.

The return trips in Village Prose are most often like the one described in "Grandmothers and Uncles." The loss is noted in some detail, but it does not dominate the work to the exclusion of a feeling of radiant sadness. One remembers with fondness and even reverence that which was lost, and the very act of remembering brings back something of the past.

Another common narrative line is a variation on the idea of UPROOTING: an older villager is pressured into moving from the ancestral home and dies in the process, and that person's special knowledge of the old life is gone forever. Unlike Tolstoy, the *derevenshchiki* are not interested in "dying" as a theme in itself, but in the deaths of old villagers as symbolic of the end of a way of life. Belov, Astafiev, Abramov, Rasputin, and other writers reenacted a traditional farewell to their homes and native regions, but in their works this ritual acquired, in the words of Georgii Tsvetov, a "sharply contemporary meaning." The ritual-centered period of the 1960s and 1970s in rural literature saw the rise of the *rasskaz-epitaf* (story-epitaph) in the manner of Bunin's "Antonov Apples" with its luminous sadness (*svetlaia pechal'*).[16]

Solzhenitsyn's story "Matryona's Home" is one of the first examples of the narrative of uprooting: Matryona's house was literally broken in two by greedy in-laws, who could not wait for her to die. In the process of hauling half the dwelling to a new site, Matryona is crushed by a train, itself a common symbol of progress and object of fear for peasants. For Sergei Esenin, the train heralded the new world of iron and steel that would destroy the Russian village.[17]

In Evgenii Nosov's "Domoi za mater'iu"(Going home to get mother) the hero Vasiukov, who lives in the north with his wife, is traveling to his native Orel region to fetch his mother from the village and bring her back with him so that she can take care of the grandchildren. On the train he meets an old woman who is "fragile, ancient, barely alive."[18] This woman was also forced by her children to sell her small house and possessions and go all over the country to help them both to care for the grandchildren and to qualify for larger apartments.[19] She feels the break with her village very keenly—"her roots were completely destroyed"—and now that she is older and less useful, the children treat her as a burden, so she is returning to the *rodina* to die. She may not have a home there, but she can no longer spend all her time in transit—having nothing in common with the hero of Aksenov's "Halfway to the Moon," who happily crisscrosses the country in airplanes until his money and his vacation time are used up. She is confident that someone will give her shelter until the not-too-distant day when she is carried to the village cemetery. Vasiukov leaves her sitting perfectly still in the Orel station, in stark contrast to the hectic life she was forced to lead after leaving the village. In this anonymous old woman Nosov has successfully created a character with elements of both the typical and the poignantly specific.[20]

Grandmother Polia in Boris Ekimov's story "The Last Peasant House" faces two threats. The first is from a fellow villager who wants her large garden; the second, more serious threat is from her son-in-law, who intends to tear down the wattle-and-daub hut she built by herself after the war, and to replace it with a modern house. The tree that marks her son's grave will have to go, and the grave itself will be obscured. Unable to convince her family that the humble dwelling's significance lies in the labor that went into it, for it represents survival with dignity, she retreats to it to say farewell, to pray once more, and then to remove "the now unnecessary icon."[21] On the eve of its destruction, Polia dies in the old place, dreaming of her mother and her dead son, and of the simple peasant house in the next world in which she will see them both again.

In Aleksei Leonov's "Kondyr," a ninety-year-old man must move with his children to a new settlement because their village is being abandoned. On his last day in the old village he reminisces about his long life:

> ... the day had come for him to see his roots torn away from Mother Earth. Their possessions would be loaded in the car and taken away, and the walls of the house would be broken up into bricks and dragged off to build a poultry-yard or pig-barn for the sovkhoz. He had often felt pain for other people's houses, and at the thoughtlessness of people who moved to other villages or even to far-off places. Now it was his turn to experience this intense pain, which was so much like death.[22]

All around the village Kondyr sees lifeless, abandoned houses; his own house, though doomed, still has the warmth of human habitation. The wooden table, soon to be discarded, bears the marks of use by his grandfather and father, and the stove is worn from all those who sat on it through the long winters; the new house will not have a Russian stove. After the move, Kondyr leaves the housewarming in the new, consolidated village and sets off for his old home, determined to save it. While he is resting from his journey, his dreams of the past merge with the present moment and he dies, sharing the fate of his village.

Viktor Perepelka in "The Last Day in the Old House" depicts Nastasia, an old woman no longer able to fully care for herself, as she takes leave of her village before setting off to join her daughter's family in another settlement. Visiting her husband's grave, she recalls how they built their house without any help. Nastasia had hoped that one of her daughters would come back to live in it, "but they never said a word about it—it's clear that the umbilical cord is cut forever. But what is it they like so much about the city?"[23] Nastasia dies on the way to her daughter's house.

Vladimir Lichutin's "last wizard," Gelasii Sozontovich, takes a final look around his old house, which must be destroyed to make way for a new school. Every object—net, rake, pitchfork, scythe, sled—holds a memory for him. The house itself is like an old peasant, creaking with age and pleading to be left alone in its final years. During the last weeks of his life, when he is an unwelcome boarder with his grandson, the old man constantly dreams of his home and deeply regrets that he neglected to invite the house-spirit (*domovoi*) to move with him.[24] Elsewhere in the same story, the kolkhoz chairman Radiushin visits his native village and sees many uninhabited dwellings. "The boarded-up houses are sad, but even more unbearable is the sight of houses that were simply abandoned. The windows seem to look at you and the doors have been left invitingly open, but if you step across the threshold, it's like looking into a grave."[25]

Vladimir Soloukhin's mother spent her old age moving between their village of Olepino, Moscow, and Minsk, where she died. The account of her burial in "Pokhorony Stepanidy Ivanovny" ("Stepanida Ivanovna's Funeral," wr. 1967, publ. 1987) is a scathing, almost inappropriately hilarious account of life and death in the Soviet Union. The theme of loss is emphasized in the reactions of villagers to the traditional religious funeral that Soloukhin managed to arrange for his mother despite the fact that such an event was officially forbidden. When the priest arrived at the family home, volunteers came forward who still remembered the ritual songs. Villagers wept openly during the service. "Not, I think, for Stepanida Ivanovna (her time had come, it was inevitable, and we're all headed there), but for something they had remembered, something they had recognized, something they had lost that had been taken away from them and almost forgotten but had been returned to them at least for this one day."[26]

The death of a ninety-year-old woman, Auntie Agafia, in her own home in Astafiev's *The Final Bow* moves the author to comment: "What a rare bit of luck these days—to live all ninety years in your own country, in your native village, in your own place, in the rural world that has been inexpressibly near and dear to you since childhood."[27] To leave the world from the same home into which one entered it and to repose in the same cemetery as one's relations has become a great rarity, as Krupin lamented in "The Fortieth Day." In an age of rural transformation the stable family nest has become the exception, and in Astafiev's story it dies with Auntie Agafia.

In Village Prose, the traditional home stands for all rural Russia: the village, its everyday life and culture, the family, work, and beauty. The house is a frequent and important symbol, and abandoning it is a painful event, often connected with death. Abramov called the emptied houses "wooden mausoleums" and hoped that they were at least the resting places of the souls of dead soldiers. Astafiev, in "The Blind Fisherman," calls a remote house where a peasant died alone, with no one to bury him, a "sepulchre."[28] The last volume of Abramov's Pekashino tetralogy is simply called *Dom* (The house/home). This melancholy-luminous chronicle of rural life in the 1970s ends with Liza Priaslina mortally injuring herself while restoring a carved wooden horse to the roof of her renovated ancestral home. Because of her "sacrificial" death, this house, ironically, will once again become home to an extended family, as her estranged brother Mikhail takes on the task of raising her youngest children.[29]

In the narrative of uprooting, Village Prose writers show an attachment to the traditional dwelling, and disdain for the modern housing that replaces it and for the policy of consolidated villages. In addition, by connecting uprooting and death, the writers show the still-strong influence of Russian folklore, which—along with literature about the gentry estate—is an important source of inspiration for Village Prose.

In Russian folk belief, changes in the dwelling-place—people's building or moving; a bride or a soldier's leaving home—are closely linked to the activities of place-spirits. Because the act of crossing boundaries, whether the threshold or the village limits, might offend the *domovoi* 'house-spirit', there are fairly elaborate rituals to insure that everything goes well.[30] Special precautions were taken for building and moving since it was believed that someone in the family might die in the process.[31] Not only was the *domovoi* invited to leave the old house and enter the new one, but a sacrifice, either real—an animal's head—or symbolic was placed underneath the corner opposite where the stove would stand. This corner of the room, once a place for ancestral images, later became the repository for icons and other ritual objects such as embroidered towels and decorated eggs; it was a place that anyone crossing the threshold would turn to first if he was not an evil spirit in human guise.

The belief in place-spirits and the sense that boundary crossing, building, and moving made one vulnerable to the spirit world shows up in Russian Village Prose as the narrative of "dangerous uprooting."[32] This motif is especially strong in the works of Valentin Rasputin. In "Vek zhivi—vek liubi" ("You Live and Love"), the construction of a hydroelectric station led to a rerouting of an important railway line and the abandonment of a number of villages. Day-trippers in search of berries still got off the train at the old stops: "The people disappearing into the dark wasteland, past the dead houses, as if past so many coffins, seemed as if they were heading in search of their own eternal resting-place bearing in their strange containers the sum of their lives. . . . Sanya had a clear and overwhelming sensation that he was seeing from the inside an ancient burial ground and, above the houses, as if over graves, stood headstones, as was right and proper."[33]

In "Downstream," Viktor, a writer, travels down the Angara River by steamship to see his family. His previous trip, five years earlier, had been made just before the village was flooded to form a reservoir for a hydroelectric project; several villages were moved inland and consolidated. Villagers then referred to the impending move sorrowfully as "the end of the world" (*svetoprestavlenie*).[34] To Viktor the former site of his family home looked like a grave. Five years later the old village is an indistinguishable part of a large new settlement, and Viktor does not even recognize the old house in its new location. The kolkhoz part of the village has been moved far out into the steppe and their old neighbor Lukeya has gone with it. Viktor's grandmother recalls this when Viktor arrives:

"There was Lukeya who left and she didn't last a year. How did that happen? And what if they had let her be? . . . She died, Lukeya did, may the heavenly kingdom be hers, she died. She couldn't even last a year in the new place. People say she kept longing for the old place, kept begging to go back. Here at least, the fir trees look like home, but over there everything to the last drop is foreign. And so she couldn't bear it. They say she wept bitterly before she died."[35]

Viktor also has problems adjusting to the new setting, and he soon leaves. He will go back to the city, try to accept the realities of his displaced home and waning youth, and then return as a "different" person to see the place as if for the first time. The story is really a paradigm for Village Prose: the rural-born writer tries to confront transformation but comes into painful conflict with the main source of his creativity, his childhood memories. This literature is the meeting-place of *razlad* and *lad*, that is, of discord and harmony.

As Viktor traveled downstream, the sides of the steamship scraped against trees from islands that were flooded by the same project. He suddenly realized that these colorfully named islands no longer existed. The imminent disappearance beneath the waves of one such island is the subject of *Farewell to Matyora* (1976), Rasputin's most dramatic vision of the impact of change. In this work, the centuries-old village is shown on the eve of its destruction by fire to clear the land and then by flood.[36] The kolkhoz has been disbanded, and most of the residents have moved off the island to a new consolidated settlement attached to a *sovkhoz* 'state farm'.[37] Only a handful of old people who want to put off moving as long as possible are left to tend their gardens till the end of the summer.

Although the peasants accept the flooding and the move as just one more impersonal force that they cannot hope to control or turn back, they do object to the way that the move is carried out, especially to the "arsonists" who are sent by the state to destroy the village cemetery, the forests, and the houses. These men care for nothing but the present and the promise of a comfortable future, while the villagers revere the memories and values of the past. For Darya, "truth is in memory. The person without memory is without life."[38] She agonizes over the proper way to bid farewell to her home until she senses that her parents have sent word from the other world for her to prepare the house for its end.

If in Ekimov's story there are quiet prayers in the old house, in *Farewell to Matyora* there is a full-scale wake. During the days before it is to be burned down, Darya with great difficulty whitewashes the house, scrubs the floor and windows, and spreads grass and fir branches around in their proper ritual places. Although it changes nothing, to Darya this procedure is of great importance.

> You don't put a person in his coffin without washing him and dressing him in his best—that was the custom. So how could she send off her own house, out of which her father and mother, grandfather and grand-mother, were carried and in which she had spent her entire life, except for what was left, and deny it the same dressing up? No, the others could do what they wanted, but she understood things. She would see the house off properly. It stood and stood, poor thing, for some one hundred fifty years, and now it was over, now it would be gone.[39]

She spends her last night in the old house in prayer, and in the morning takes her trunk with her burial outfit in it, makes a sign of the cross in the direction of the icon corner, and leaves. With a true feeling for ritual and for sacred space, she forbids the arsonists to set foot in the house before burning it. Vladimir Soloukhin described Darya's action as neither social, economic, nor even practical, but rather as "purely spiritual."[40]

We are told in some detail about the new settlement where Darya and the others are to live after leaving their island homes. There are two-family houses with all the conveniences that Matyora lacked, but the drawbacks seem to outweigh any advantages: the houses are too close together, the vegetable gardens are tiny, there is no room for a cow and no way to feed it, the soil is poor, and the cellars are continually flooded. The settlement itself is inexplicably set five miles away from the new shoreline. The older inhabitants of Matyora cannot easily imagine themselves in these new surroundings. One old couple moves to a new city, but there the man refuses to leave his apartment and soon dies—symbolically estranged from both nature and the community. The few villagers who are left on the island would rather die than move.

The end of *Farewell to Matyora* is deliberately ambiguous. The old people are huddled together in the last structure left on the island. Darya's son and several other men set out in a boat to take the remaining people off Matyora but get hopelessly lost in the fog. The final sounds of the novel are of the lost boat moving further and further away from its destination, and of the Master, a place-spirit for the whole island, howling for the last time.[41] Rasputin uses an expanded notion of reality to stage his apocalyptic finale, but that does not weaken his observations about the excesses and mistakes of rural transformation. Mixing social and political commentary with the fantastic is a Russian literary tradition that goes back at least as far as Pushkin and can be found in the works of such writers as Gogol, Dostoevsky, Bely, Zamyatin, Bulgakov, and Sinyavsky.

In Vladimir Lichutin's "Grandmothers and Uncles" (1976), the hero looks down the river from the city in the direction of his rural home and sees—in an optical illusion—the island villages partially submerged beneath the water. This story, published in the same year as *Farewell to Matyora*, suggests—as did Rasputin's novel and his earlier story "Downstream"—that rural Russia was being drowned by the forces of progress.[42]

Rasputin saw *Farewell to Matyora* as bringing to an end his own writing about the traditional village. He compared it to the act of sons visiting their dying mother, and declared it a turning point in his work. He would follow the islanders to a new settlement and see what would happen to them there.[43] By allowing himself to be swept along by currents both literal and figurative, Rasputin opens up the possibility of exploring the negative impact of rural transformation not only on traditional villages but also on the new settlements that replace them, something that he does in the 1985 story "The Fire." Rasputin has shown that this theme can be simultaneously addressed in abstract and concrete ways as apocalypse and as the loss of material objects.

In *Lad* (Harmony), Belov tries to stop time through both verbal and (in the illustrated book version) visual still lifes. Customs and objects are deliberately suspended in time and space for the duration of the book. Rasputin allows time to do its work in order to see what changes and what remains. Critics like Igor Dedkov worry about how much can really be saved.

> The sad thing is that behind the image of Matyora, there is an entire old peasant world, and you can't preserve and display that in a museum like a plow or a distaff; it is man's breadth and depth, his experience, his culture, and no matter how conscientious our memory, will it be able to preserve all the best things, will it remember and transmit them further, not like relics, but as living customs, as ways of living and working?[44]

The underlying assumption in Village Prose that the thousand-year-old rural chain of life is being—or has already been—broken is directly tied to concrete images in the works. That "the former life has been ruptured" in Rasputin's "You Live and Love" is illustrated by the sight of abandoned houses.[45] In Astafiev's "The Sad Detective," the sight of a family heirloom, an old trunk, elicits from the hero Soshnin the comment: "Why should we talk nonsense about the bonds of time! They've been broken, truly broken, the expression is no longer a metaphor, but has an ominous ring to it."[46]

Astafiev's trunk is a very powerful image of loss, of a break in the chain of memories. The work in which it appears—an example of "post–Village Prose"—is about people with rural roots who are living in a provincial city. At the end of the story, Soshnin, an ex-detective turned writer, is reunited with his estranged family. Waking up in the middle of the night, he goes to check on his sleeping daughter.

> Having kicked off the blanket and let the pillow fall, with arms and legs dangling, the girl trustingly embraced Granny Lina's old trunk, made by skilled craftsmen from Viatsk and warmed by the little girl's body since her earliest childhood. Before that, this trunk had been warmed by distant relatives of Sveta and used to store their wedding dresses, their simple country dowry of yarn, scarves, coins and candies tied up in small bundles, floor-coverings, tablecloths, and lace. She had never and would never see or know these relations, and would never find out anything about them.[47]

The ties of memories are broken; Sveta will inherit the object but lose the context in which the object "lived" and was valued. The trunk plays a prominent role in the numerous Village Prose memoirs of childhood, the archetypal story of loss. Its contents, the few heirlooms and ritual items that peasants possessed, such as wedding and funeral clothes, are themselves subject to loss, as we see in Aleksei Leonov's story "Along Summer and Winter Roads." During wartime evacuation, Tatiana Averkina must raid the family trunk in order to feed her family. Keeping out of her daughters' sight, she takes a cashmere shawl, which had been handed down by the women of her family since the eighteenth century, and brings it to a war profiteer. As Tatiana tries on the shawl to demonstrate its beauty to the prospective buyer, its significance to the family is painfully clear to her:

> From the shawl came the trunk's smell of olden times—and in her mind there appeared in rapid succession great-grandmothers and grandmothers, handing the precious object from one person to the next. And here she was knocking down the price for this wretched, cursed profiteer. . . . Neither her grandchildren nor her great-grandchildren would get to see this shawl and they would not remember their grandmother, because there wouldn't be anything to remember her by.[48]

Like Astafiev's trunk, the shawl in Leonov's story is an object torn out of its context—its *rod*—and out of its time. Because peasants had so few objects to be remembered by and almost no letters or photographs, each object takes on a special commemorative meaning.

In "Konchina" (The demise), Astafiev mentions photographs that he saw at a village wake. The older mourners remembered that the subjects of the photographs were Lukasha and Akulina, but Astafiev cannot recall exactly how they were related to the late Agafia. "Aunt Agafia prayed for them and honored their memory with candles on holy days. But who would remember them now?"[49] Not only would there be no one left to honor the dead—a responsibility not to be taken lightly in either Russian folk belief or Russian Orthodoxy—but in a few short years, no one would even be able to identify the photos. The faded rural photograph, hanging on the edge of oblivion, is a power-ful—and universal—symbol of irreparable breaks in the chain of memory. As Lichutin has said, "We go from one person's memory to another" ("Pamiat' idet po pamiati").[50] One break in the chain ends this process forever.

The theme of collecting provides Village Prose writers with another way of discussing the loss of the context of rural culture. They are skeptical about the gathering of rural objects as a way to heal the break in time. Vasilii Belov in *Harmony* writes disparagingly of published lists of proverbs where there is no indication of when to use them.[51] In "The Sad Detective" Astafiev wickedly satirizes the provincial intelli-gentsia's habit of juxtaposing genuine folk objects, folksy souvenirs, and reproductions of European art in their apartments. It is a passage that brings to mind Sologub's savaging of the Populist president of the district rural council in *The Petty Demon* (1907): "Everything in this house spoke of the desire to live simply and well and to work for the common good. The eye was struck by many objects that were reminis-cent of country life and simplicity: an armchair with a shaftbow for the back and axe-handles for arm rests; an inkstand in the form of a horseshoe; a bast shoe for an ashtray."[52]

Hordes of souvenir-hungry Muscovites pillaging the countryside figure among the subjects of Astafiev's story cycle called "Mesto de-istviia" (The place of action) in the May 1986 issue of *Nash sovremennik*. In Evgenii Nosov's story "I uplyvaiut parakhody, i ostaiutsia berega" (And the boats sail away, and the shores remain, 1970) there is, as the title suggests, a strongly expressed contrast between the ephemeral and worldly—in the form of tourists coming across Lake Onega to briefly visit the nearly depopulated islands—and the timeless spiri-tuality of the islands themselves with their marvelous churches "not made by human hands."[53] As the main character Savonia watches one such boat sail away, the narrator widens the distance between these two "worlds": "Behind him, shrouded in mist, the island churches faintly glimmered. They seemed to soar over the tarnished silver of Onega's waters, like a ghostly illusion or something in a dream."[54] The churches, we are told at the beginning of the story, silently and thoughtfully gaze into the distance, taking no notice of the visiting ships.

The narrator of Abramov's story "Wooden Horses" goes to the countryside to steep himself in folk traditions and collect peasant tools. In the quiet village of Pizhma, there are no radios or cars, and the seven remaining houses and the handmade objects in them are for him an entire peasant museum. However, a visiting peasant woman, Milentevna, so impresses him with her living folk qualities that he decides to return to the city to try to actively emulate her and his late peasant mother. He has learned to value the effort that went into making and wearing smooth the spindle and plow-handle even more than the objects themselves. This story is a somewhat rare example in canonical Village Prose of the sense of loss being in some way ameliorated by a plan for spiritual development.[55] In Vladimir Krupin's *The Water of Life* this fear of relic collecting's replacing living custom and memory is stated directly: "And who remembers anymore the sickle, the scythe, a horse with a plow and a woodsman's ax? Soon you'll be able to see people plowing and cutting wood the way they've done it for a thousand years only in the movies, and it's easy to imagine how little Masha [the hero's daughter] will look at them—as if they're lunatics. And in another hundred years—who will even explain it?"[56]

Folk songs, another collector's item, have strong symbolic value as indicators of the state of oral culture as a whole. In Yashin's "Vologda Wedding," the village girls have only the sketchiest knowledge of the ritual wedding songs, and funeral laments are known only by the older women in Rasputin's *Borrowed Time*.[57] In Belov's *Carpenters' Tales*, the narrator, a former villager back on vacation, finds two eternally warring old men naturally united in song, a song that excludes him: "Then he and Aviner, bowing their heads, quietly and harmoniously took up the ancient song. I couldn't join in—I didn't know any of the words."[58]

Objects have no context, tools are discarded because no one knows how to use them, and folk songs are only half-remembered. Sometimes people stay in the village but lose the old ways; sometimes they migrate to urban areas and forget their rural roots, like the hero of Shukshin's story "Snowball Berry Red" who "forgets" what to do in the bathhouse and how to use a plow. In Aleksei Leonov's short story "The Widowed Well" the whole village disappears, and all that is left is one well, for "in dead villages the wells die last."[59]

Anna, in Rasputin's *Borrowed Time*, has just a little while left to teach her daughter Varvara the traditional laments so that there will be a proper funeral. In the same author's "Oh, You Old Woman," the last shaman dies before she can disclose her secrets to her granddaughter.

The fact that there is no one to whom she can pass on her knowledge is a source of great torment.

> For hundreds and thousands of years her fathers and grandfathers and their fathers all had a mysterious power, which she also possessed, and which was highly valued. And now all of this had come to an end. A person who is the last in his family is unfortunate. But a person who has stolen from his people an ancient skill and carried it with him to the grave, not having communicated it to anyone—what can you call this person, who stole his people's greatest riches?[60]

Sometimes we see time literally running out and a tradition dies before our eyes. Gelasii Sozontovich, Lichutin's "last wizard," has forgotten almost everything, although "there was a time when I knew angry words to separate lovers or to take away sorrow." In his final days, Gelasii is pursued by people who want him to display his magic power for personal or ethnographic purposes—or even to heal himself—but he can no longer help anyone; all he can remember is some old recruiting songs. His death is a long and bizarre process; prophetic dreams disturb his rest and drive him up to the roof of the house, where he perches like an alien bird or a tormented demon. Gelasii dies after a raging thunderstorm, as befits a wizard.[61]

Despite the emphasis on the decline of Russian rural life, many works that focus on loss end not on a note of gloom or self-indulgent mourning, but with a mixture of sadness at loss and the pleasure of remembering something beautiful and *rodnoi* 'native, one's own'. Even after the many bitter passages of "The Sad Detective," at the very end Soshnin goes to his desk, looks at a well-worn copy of Dal's Russian proverbs, and begins once more to write. The need to compensate through writing for the wound in time has led him to embark on a new work, which, we are led to believe, will be more authentic than his "sad detective story." In Village Prose and "post–Village Prose," the act of remembering and recording can be creative and life-affirming and can mitigate to a certain extent the loss.

An elegiacal tone is a core attribute of canonical Village Prose works; the less frequent apocalyptic strain is one that—while never dominant—outlived the movement itself and can be seen in many of the essays and stories of the "post–Village Prose" years, and in the ideological pronouncements of such erstwhile Village Prose writers as Belov, Rasputin, and Astafiev.[62]

Apocalypse is the furthest possible extension of the idea of loss: one is no longer speaking of the loss of one's youth, one's childhood home, or even one's village. What is at stake is nature, Russia and its people, and the whole world.

There is a sense of apocalypse in the posthumously published Abramov story "A Journey into the Past." As he makes his way home, the hero Miksha thinks that he hears church bells and sees the local church filled with light as it was in 1930 when exiled kulaks took refuge in it, emerging in the evening to sing. In the drafts that were published along with the story, Miksha sees the living and dead gathered together, candles in hand.[63] In a cacophonous finale, the wind howls, the bells ring, the exiles sing church songs, his uncles sing "The Internationale," and the old women weep.[64] This scene's power is intensified by the fact that the Old Believers—of whom Abramov was so fond—in the early years of the Schism often barricaded themselves in churches which they then set on fire. The Abramov story could hardly have been influential since it was largely unknown and definitely unpublished during the height of Village Prose, but it demonstrates one direction a leading rural writer was taking, if only in works "for the drawer."

There are other explorations of the "end" in canonical Village Prose: the deaths of old people, the abandoning of villages, the loss of the traditional rural way of life, and the harm done to nature. After 1985, in the literature that followed the decline of Village Prose as a coherent movement, the apocalyptic theme takes on a more ideological and more abstract form, and is no longer so closely tied to specifically rural metaphors for loss; no longer part of a radiant memory of the past, it is an anxious and angry projection into the future.

SIX

THE VILLAGE PROSE WRITERS AND

THEIR CRITICS

"See what your nihilists are doing!
They're setting Petersburg on fire!"
(An acquaintance of Turgenev)[1]

WITHIN the canon of Village Prose, it is difficult to draw precise borders between fiction and nonfiction. This is partly for generic reasons: the *derevenshchiki* have included publicistic (and autobiographical) material in their artistic works, as well as contributing many essays, speeches, and interviews on the "burning questions" of the day (*zlobodnevnye voprosy*), especially after the decline of the movement in the late 1970s. Non–Village Prose writers have satirized their rural colleagues, parodied certain of the conventions of Village Prose, and even mimicked the style of Village Prose to benefit from its popularity. Of greatest importance is the interaction between literature and criticism, with critics taking the ideas and images they found in Village Prose and attempting to translate them into ideological concepts. Village Prose and what was written about it came to occupy what might be called a "paraliterary space": "the space of debate, quotation, partisanship, betrayal, reconciliation . . . not the space of unity, coherence, or resolution that we think of as constituting a work of literature."[2] In this politicized—at times highly charged—literary context, Village Prose has been not so much an object of literary-critical study as "an occasion for argument about the most important contemporary problems."[3]

The discourse that was stimulated by Village Prose and which at times engulfed the movement has led to both interesting commentary and major rereadings of some of the primary Village Prose texts and of the movement as a whole.[4] It may even have pushed some of the writers toward a more publicistic type of fiction in the "post–Village Prose" period. One need look no further than Alexander Ostrovsky's play *The Storm* (1859) and Nikolai Dobroliubov's essay "A Ray of Light in the Realm of Darkness" (1860) to understand the nature of the relationship between Village Prose and some of the criticism it engendered, and to realize that this relationship is not new to Russian literature.[5]

The close ties between *derevenskaia proza* and criticism began with the first installment of Valentin Ovechkin's "Raionnye budni" (District routine) in *Novyi mir* in 1952 and the publication of Pomerantsev's article "On Sincerity in Literature" in the same journal the following year. Pomerantsev wittily attacked such postwar kolkhoz novels as Babaevsky's *Cavalier of the Golden Star* (1947–1948) and Nikolaeva's *Harvest* (1950) and then went on to speak approvingly of "District Routine" from both an ideological and aesthetic point of view. The mini-flood of critical works that followed effectively swept Kolkhoz Literature away, leaving a vacuum that was filled by Village Prose. Twenty-five years later, Babaevsky was still trying to recoup his losses when he wrote *Privol'e* (The wide-open spaces), a Socialist Realist kolkhoz novel that mimicked certain aspects of Village Prose.[6] Rural writers themselves were involved in the critical discourse from the very beginning: Fedor Abramov, Sergei Zalygin, Vladimir Tendriakov, Efim Dorosh, and Ovechkin, for example, all contributed essays in the mid-1950s on the theme of "the kolkhoz and literature."[7]

Official encouragement of a new, more critical rural *ocherk* in the style of Ovechkin stemmed from the Party's desire to improve the perpetually sorry state of agriculture, especially at the level of local leadership. The critics, however, also focused on the literary "landscape," promoting the new rural literature by attacking postwar Kolkhoz Literature for such qualities as *lakirovka* (varnishing of reality), *shablony* (clichés), *shtampy* (stock phrases), insincerity, tedium, lack of conflict, and a superficial knowledge of rural life, all of which led to unbelievable situations, characters, language, and resolutions of problems. They called Kolkhoz Literature a pastoral or idyll—in the negative sense—a charge that was later made against Village Prose itself at the height of its popularity. These early essays questioned the unthinking praise that postwar kolkhoz novels had received from most critics, and the negative examples that were quoted from Kolkhoz Literature were both funny and effective. The attack on Kolkhoz Literature was often placed in the context of the Party's program for the countryside; it was charged that because of serious artistic weaknesses, Kolkhoz Literature had not been a very useful weapon for publicizing agricultural policy.

Critics wanted the new rural literature to display the qualities they had missed in Kolkhoz Literature: unvarnished reality, sincerity, conflict, attention to language and style, deeper psychological portraits of characters, and a genuine knowledge of the countryside. They encouraged the cultivation of a number of genres, particularly the artistic essay (*ocherk*) and the story (both *rasskaz* and *povest'*), expecting that it would take some time before the new rural novel would replace the devalued kolkhoz novel. The artistic development of these writers was to be guided—according to the critics—by the closer study of the nineteenth-century canon: Turgenev, Tolstoy, Shchedrin, Gleb Uspensky, Korolenko, Chekhov, and Bunin were among the most frequently mentioned names. Soviet literature was not offered as a model but implicitly or explicitly shown to be an *anti-model* (despite the obligatory praise of Sholokhov and favorable mention of Leonid Leonov's novels). The critical literature devoted to the Ovechkin-style *ocherk* was an important step in the process of undermining Socialist Realism aesthetically while seeming to uphold it ideologically.

As rural literature evolved further away from Kolkhoz Literature with the appearance of such works as Dorosh's *Derevenskii dnevnik* (Village diary, 1956–1970), and Soloukhin's *Vladimirskie proselki* (Vladimir country roads, 1957), criticism changed along with it.[8] The writers had gone beyond the confines of the kolkhoz office to look more closely at the daily lives of simple country people in their cultural and natural surroundings. As the focus switched from the Soviet collective farm to the Russian village, critics searched for a new label for this expanding literary movement; by the mid-1960s the interim, genre-bound term *derevenskii ocherk* 'village/rural essay' had been replaced by the more flexible *derevenskaia proza* 'village prose'.

"Village Prose" has always been a problematic term in Soviet literary-critical discourse; *derevenshchik* 'Village-Prose-writer' is even less popular among those to whom it is applied, who feel that it marginalizes them.[9] Soviet articles on rural literature often began with an attempt at defining *derevenskaia proza* and most often put it in quotation marks, preceded by the phrase *tak nazyvaemaia* 'so-called', shifting the ultimate responsibility for the term to some anonymous persons, *kotorye tak nazyvaiut* 'who use this name'.

Objections to the term *derevenskaia proza* were made both on ideological and aesthetic levels. A "Village Prose" implied an "Urban Prose" (*gorodskaia proza*), reinforcing differences when the basic divisions in both life and literature were supposed to have been eliminated. While Kolkhoz Literature showed the growing *smychka* 'union, linking' of country and city as the village became part of an agricultural production line, Village Prose hinted broadly at the failure and basic undesirability of this process. In an important sense then, Village Prose restores and emphasizes *difference* where unity and homogeneity had been the goal; and, to the extent that Village Prose is perceived as nationalistic, it is seen as stressing a Russian over a Soviet identity.

On the aesthetic plane, there were objections to the dividing up of the literature into so many kinds of prose: village, urban, war, Moscow, confessional, intellectual, production, adventure, documentary, *byt*, and the prose of the "forty-year-olds."[10] It seemed to some critics that this process could lead to an arbitrary and almost unlimited number of subdivisions—by theme or location, or even by the age of the writer—and a real narrowing of the critical view; it also allowed subtle moves by both writer and critic away from the confines of Socialist Realism. For other critics the concern was the difficulty of clearly defining and characterizing a literary school that was made to include such a diverse group of writers, styles, subjects, and approaches. To address this problem, there were suggestions for even finer divisions of the material: e.g., Orel, Siberian, and Vologda schools, ecological prose, and *literatura proshchaniia* 'the literature of farewell'.[11] Still others were troubled not by the grouping but merely by the specific words *derevenskaia proza*, and they suggested substitutes that emphasized other qualities. Alternative labels for this prose were *sel'skaia* 'rural', *liricheskaia* 'lyric', *nostal'gicheskaia* 'nostalgia', *derevne-opisatel'skaia* 'descriptive-of-the-countryside', *pamiatlivaia* 'memory-oriented, commemorative', and the unwieldy "theme of the peasantry and the countryside in Soviet prose of the second half of the 1960s and in the 1970s."[12] Vilchek says that after "chronic" discussions of the term and its implications, the furor died down and the name was accepted with the caveat "so-called" making it an impersonal "act of nature" for which no one need take the blame. Tsvetov is less sanguine, stating that "the phenomenon remains, develops, evolves, is in the center of critical attention; it is argued about and studied, but it has no name."[13] What is most important is that astute critics like Petrik, Tsvetov, and Vilchek, who have carefully studied rural literature in the post-Stalinist period, as well as Valentin Rasputin—its greatest talent—identified a unified literary movement whose unity might have been lost from view without the use of the term "Village Prose."

The critics did more than just argue about what to call this popular literary movement, although that discussion itself involved much more than metacritical wrangling. Judgments of "Ovechkin-school" essays could be based on the improvement they marked over the kolkhoz novel in setting forth the problems of agriculture; but the type of rural literature that began to appear around 1956 forced a discussion centered on what might be termed a major change of chronotopes, i.e., from the Soviet collective farm and the present to the Russian village and the past. A steady stream of works with such high-water marks as Solzhenitsyn's "Matryona's Home" and Abramov's "Round and About" (both from 1963) made an indelible impression on the reading public and critics alike and led to one of the liveliest (especially in 1967–1969 and 1979–1980) and most protracted discourses on a single topic in Soviet Russian literary history.[14] Looking at old peasants instead of young kolkhoz officials led to descriptions of the values, roots, and vestiges of traditional rural culture. Listening to the grandfathers and grandmothers meant presenting to readers a rural idiom that had been all but banished from Socialist Realism. And focusing on the village where the writer had grown up involved reducing the Soviet "fatherland" not just to the Russian republic but to the *malaia rodina* (small homeland), that is, one small village and the surrounding region.

A number of critics were quick to praise Village Prose because it was a tremendous improvement in the artistic quality of Soviet Russian literature. For them, Village Prose was realistic, poetic, sincere, and genuine—a worthy successor to the great nineteenth-century canon that had ended with Bunin. The attention that Village Prose paid to hard work was helpful in obscuring the fact that villagers preferred to use traditional methods and lavished much of their effort on their private plots. The close-up view of life in the "hero-village" during World War II marked these as demonstrably patriotic works that overlapped with the increasingly important genre of War Prose. The rural idiom, when used in moderation, was seen as enriching the Russian literary language. When all else failed, the critics would say that Village Prose was the transcript of the writer's rural childhood, where it would be natural and acceptable to find luminous memories and expressions of sorrow at how much of the old village had been lost.

Negative criticism saw in Village Prose a literature that was patriarchal (i.e., that frankly admired pre-Revolutionary life in the countryside), sentimental, and cloyingly folksy—in short, a false and potentially harmful idyll; as a literary movement, it clearly had little to do with the goals and coordinates of Socialist Realism. While those who favored Village Prose pointed to the obvious laudable qualities of the village characters—hard work, loyalty, unselfishness, devotion to the land, powers of endurance—their opponents had little trouble showing that Solzhenitsyn's Matryona and Belov's Ivan Afrikanovich were not what Socialist Realist theory had in mind under the rubric "positive hero." They could find few officials or young people who were presented in a favorable light in these works; generally in Village Prose such characters are at the very least shallow and misinformed. Village Prose foregrounded the old, the unambitious, and the eccentric, who could be defended more on artistic than on ideological grounds.

Lev Anninsky complained (in 1971) that there *had* been a viable rural literature in the Gleb Uspensky–Ovechkin tradition but that although it continued to be written and published, it had been rejected by readers and talented writers. The real literary "action" was in a parallel line of lyrical stories and philosophical essays by writers like Belov, Shukshin, and Soloukhin. "In place of the sober manager there was the village dreamer, the muzhik, the joker, the oddball, the wise man, the ancient village grandfather who kept the old ways. . . . it's like Gleb Uspensky being replaced by Nikolai Leskov."[15] Readers who are familiar with both Uspensky and Leskov may question the seriousness of Anninsky's objection. Worse than all the village grandfathers—in the eyes of some critics—were the old women, the Annas, Matryonas, and Daryas who are easily the most memorable characters of Russian Village Prose. Critics were heard to speculate on just how many more *driakhlye starukhi* 'decrepit old ladies' one would have to endure before this trend ran its course. What was there for the reader to emulate in these women, whose primary function seemed to be to mourn the quickly receding past? Fedor Abramov countered this attack by describing the heroic exploits of the Russian *baba* during and after the war when she almost single-handedly kept the army and the cities fed and clothed while bearing the loss of husband and sons. "Is it such a surprise, then, that the old peasant woman . . . has temporarily pushed other characters into the background? No, this is no idealization of the patriarchal way of life, no oft-mentioned nostalgia for the disappearing land of peasant houses, as several critics and writers have thoughtlessly and arrogantly suggested. It is a son's belated gratitude."[16]

When Village Prose overlapped with war literature, the treatment of the positive hero became a much more sensitive topic. Many of the *derevenshchiki* had experienced the wartime and early postwar village firsthand; a few had been old enough to serve in the military. They wrote movingly of struggle and suffering caused mostly by the enemy, but exacerbated by mismanagement and human failings on the Soviet side (e.g., in Abramov's *Brothers and Sisters*). This view was accepted up to a certain point, but characters like Andrei and Nastena in Rasputin's *Live and Remember* stretched the limits of official tolerance. An artistically less persuasive writer might have stumbled badly with such a pair. There was apprehension in the mid-1970s about the *degeroizatsiia* 'deheroicization' of war literature, a tendency that was said by Iurii Prodan to have sinister origins: "Deheroicization did not arise by chance. Its sources can be found abroad, in the camp of our ideological adversaries."[17]

One of Prodan's examples of "deheroicization" is a scene from a rural novella by Aleksei Leonov called "I ostalis' zhit'" (And they came through it alive) in which the kolkhoz chairman comes out to the fields to read Stalin's speech about the German invasion (one is reminded of Vladimir Voinovich's comical treatment of this moment). In Leonov's story, the women sigh, the hero Konstantin Nikitich thinks about his grown sons who are sure to be drafted, and one clearly negative character, the bookkeeper Khanin, fondles a young woman amid giggling and whispering. The critic asks: "Could it possibly have happened that way? . . . It is very hard to believe Leonov."[18] Prodan insists that rural literature paint the home front in sober tones, free from comic elements, with every character's total attention on the war effort, but *without* saying that the work at home was exhausting, unrewarded, or dangerous. Socialist Realist literature on the war may have made life seem too easy, wrote Prodan, but it was no more acceptable to make it seem too difficult.[19]

Along with extensive ideological criticism of Village Prose, by the mid-1970s it was said that Village Prose, which began in part as an *answer* to the *shtampy* and *shablony* of Socialist Realist Kolkhoz Literature, was itself seriously clichéd, an endless repetition of the prosaic that no longer offered anything new. The "magic circle" of the village, the seasons, and the agricultural year became in the eyes of some critics a literary liability. The very fabric of village life was repetition—of tasks, rituals, sayings, and folktales. The narrative patterns of Village Prose were few—childhood, wartime suffering, return, uprooting, the death of an old peasant, the end of the village—and most of these revolved around MEMORY and LOSS. The range of characters was mostly limited to old people and children, the settings to the peasant house, the field and forest, and the village cemetery.

As early as 1973, there were complaints about the number of writers who were sending their heroes back to the "land of childhood."[20] Once in the village, these characters drank, reminisced, wept drunken tears at the graves of their ancestors, and then—refreshed—returned to the city. The heroes noticed the smallest details of village life—but little beyond that. A typical bit of dialogue in one of these stories is: "Do you remember?" "Yes. I do remember." Viktor Kochetkov sought to rescue the village from the grip of childhood memories and return it to the "working territory" of the modern world, because "a blind love for one's roots can do more harm than one's indifference."[21] Vladimir Gusev complained of rural writers herding readers "first out into the open air that everyone's sick and tired of (*na lono vsem nadoevshei prirody*), then into a comfortless log house, and finally into a church; you would think that there was nothing else to be concerned with in the twentieth century."[22] By 1981, Igor Shaitanov could write with obvious impatience: "Everything that could be remembered has been remembered. Only the names of villages and family members change."[23] Even Viktor Astafiev eventually complained about the tidal wave of imitative, mediocre manuscripts about "the same old village" that were sent to him for a reading. "It's just one continuous idyll, written in an urban apartment by a person who is too lazy to go to the countryside. He yearns for the birch tree under his window, the poplar, and his grandfather, who spends all his time sitting on a dirt embankment. Some of these grandfathers must be 150 years old by now."[24]

Fedor Abramov vigorously defended Village Prose, especially at the Sixth Congress of Soviet Writers (1976) in a speech entitled "Daily Bread and Spiritual Sustenance." While he admitted that, like any literary group, not all the Village Prose writers were equally gifted, the movement as a whole had earned its place at the forefront of contemporary Soviet literature. He reviewed the charges made against Village Prose—of shallowness, backwardness, and avoidance of the demands of the present—and rejected them. Rather than being a retreat from the writer's avant-garde role, said Abramov, Village Prose is an indication of the maturity of Soviet literature. The disappearance of the thousand-year-old village way of life is not a fashionable theme but a topic of the utmost importance to the life of the nation. This period of great change is the best time to look at what is disappearing: the ethics, aesthetics, folklore, and language, that is, the *culture* of the village. For Abramov, one cannot possibly understand the Russian national character without understanding the village; the theme of Russia can never go out of style. The values, the spiritual culture of a thousand years' duration is just as important to study and preserve as the environment and monuments of material culture. This is what Dmitrii Likhachev calls *ekologiia kul'tury* 'the ecology of culture'.[25]

Criticism of Village Prose found its way into fiction and even poetry. Andrei Voznesensky mocked the rustic values of Village Prose in his 1975 poem "Dialog obyvatelia i poeta o NTR" (A dialogue between a Philistine and a poet about the NTR) in which the poetic persona declares his support for the much-maligned scientific-technical revolution (NTR). "With all due respect to water-carriers' yokes / I want the most remote place to have running water and the free movement of thought."[26]

In other cases it is the Village Prose writers themselves who are criticized as much as what they wrote. Daniil Granin's "Obratnyi bilet" (Return ticket, 1976) has the first-person narrator's reverie about his childhood interrupted by a friend who declares that the story of a trip to one's native region is no longer a fresh idea, but a theme fit only for those who have nothing else to say.

"They long for the countryside now that they've gotten themselves fashionable apartments in the city and have to use an elevator and wash in a bathtub. The poor dears go to their native places to get a rest from all this!" Disturbing his own philosophical calm, he cursed these literary cheats and hypocrites. "They go to the sauna but sing hymns to the old-fashioned bathhouse ... they sing of the old women, symbols of hard work and morality, but they themselves don't show up at harvesttime. And you want to get involved with them?"[27]

The narrator's only answer to this diatribe is that, independent of the rural writers, he likes to visit places familiar from his childhood. Boris Pankin called Granin's story "a peculiar reaction, whether intentional or unintentional, to the wave of reminiscences." It is an attempt to "conceptualize" and then "rise above" this current.[28] While George Gibian felt that Granin succeeded in going beyond Village Prose and had written a much more complex work using similar material, Pankin thought that it had become fashionable by the mid-seventies to complain about the use of reminiscences in Village Prose, and that Granin rushed out "Return Ticket" to take advantage of that fashion. As a result of the author's mixed intentions in writing the work, concludes Pankin, "Return Ticket" is clichéd, contrived, and shallow.[29]

The overly positive image of the decaying *izba* (wooden peasant house) and the common motif of uprooting in Village Prose caught the attention of Vsvelod Kochetov, an orthodox Stalinist literary figure. He pointedly refers to such works as "Matryona's Home" in his novel *Chego zhe ty khochesh'?* (Just what is it you want? 1969). The character Sveshnikov is confronted by Bogoroditsky, the rural author of a long poem called "Na bogomol'e" (A pilgrimage). While reeling from the stench of the writer's garlic folk-cure for colds, Sveshnikov recalls that the hero of the poem left the city for his native northern village of only fifteen households. "Everything in the village is dilapidated, half the houses have been boarded up, the young people have gone to the cities, and only old men and women are left to live out their days sitting in front of their homes. To the hero ... they seem like saints or gods taken from the icons of the neighboring village's church. . . . the icons of these saints and gods no longer exist. But to make up for it there are these living saints, on which the whole world depends."[30]

A young Soviet author named Vladimir Sorokin has written one of the best parodies of Village Prose.[31] In "Proshchanie" (Farewell), the hero, Konstantin, makes a return trip to his native region where he chain-smokes while standing on the edge of a precipice, thinking about his early years in the village. This sketch contains most of the images and phrases that had become clichéd by 1980: the barefoot childhood, the folk musical instruments, birch trees, memories of one's first fish and first kiss, distant roads, and village eccentrics. At the end the hero tries to define the word "homeland" (*rodina*); he finally decides that it is neither land, nor people, nor a government, but rather "a barefoot childhood with a wooden fishing-pole and a jar full of carp." The narrator, clearly fed up with this interior monologue, dismisses his hero with an obscenity.

While there has been praise in émigré journals for the Bunin-like aspects of Village Prose, it has also been strongly criticized, especially by "third wave" writers and critics. Joseph Brodsky wrote dismissively of "'peasant prose,' which, in its Antaeus-like desire to touch the ground, went a bit too far and took root." He called it "largely unpalatable [with a] strong tendency toward nationalistic self-appreciation" and claimed that it marks "a stylistic and aesthetic retreat."[32]

Vladimir Voinovich, who was pressured into emigrating in 1980, satirized Village Prose writers in his play *Tribunal* (The tribunal). The hero, Podoplekov, is himself attending a play called "The Tribunal" when he is put on trial for unnamed crimes. Among the characters who appear on the scene but who refuse to help him is a bearded Village Prose writer carrying a shepherd's staff. What follows is a parody of both the style of Village Prose, especially the use of rural language, and some of the causes espoused by the *derevenshchiki* in their fiction and in public pronouncements. The Writer is willing to fight for taiga mosquitoes and northern rivers and against Trotskyites and other "non-Russians"; he is a Party man who always wears a cross. He feigns ignorance of the needs of city-dwellers like Podoplekov, being just a simple country boy. "I sit myself down in the hayloft and scratch away with my fountain pen. Well, sometimes, you understand, I have to go on business trips to Moscow, Paris, London, and to the Black Sea, but then it's home again to the village and the hayloft."[33] When this characterization is juxtaposed with the play's sardonic portrait of Evtushenko, it becomes clear that *Tribunal* involved not just a parody of Village Prose, but "a settling of scores with his literary adversaries."[34] Voinovich objected to what he saw as the hypocrisy of successful Soviet writers, who would do nothing to jeopardize their success.

In *The Fur Hat* (*Shapka*) Voinovich created the character of Vaska Tryoshkin: "poet, and defender of the Russian national character against chemistry and Jews."[35] Vaska lives in a Moscow apartment building for writers and is disturbed by the number of Jews in the building. When his cat disappears and his Jewish neighbor Yefim Rakhlin receives a new cat-fur hat, Vaska's paranoia reaches its peak; ever the opportunist, Vaska decides that if a Jewish-Masonic conspiracy is really going to take over the world, he might as well join them while he can. This is not a parody of Village Prose, but a satire of the behavior, in the 1980s, of several former rural writers; it seems to be especially directed at Vasilii Belov.

Negative reactions in the émigré literary community follow two basic lines. The first is an expression of aesthetic distaste for the anachronistic folksiness and deliberate provincialism of Village Prose.[36] The second is a political judgment, the assumption that no literature which was both good and truthful got past the censors before Gorbachev. According to this line of thinking, Village Prose writers exploited a residual Russian nationalism of Party and government leaders and the reading public without at the same time telling the whole truth about rural life in the Soviet era. The lament for the Russian village became the "official line," and the *derevenshchiki* were able to establish for themselves a secure and eventually powerful position in the literary establishment that outlasted the decline of the movement as a whole and of their individual talents.[37] Vasilii Aksenov wrote (in 1981) of the powerful protection that Village Prose writers—he called them "KGB favorites"—enjoyed while urban dissidents publishing in samizdat were being arrested in the middle of the night.[38]

In a review of the career of urban playwright Mikhail Shatrov, David Joravsky came up with a term—"licensed critics"—that could be applied to a number of *derevenshchiki*:

> Shatrov has never been one of those rebellious writers, like Sinyavsky or Solzhenitsyn, who knowingly transgress. . . . He has wriggled out of one ban or another . . . exploring the border where Soviet bosses distinguish between constructive criticism and intolerable desecration. He and his kind have been among the few refreshing features of Soviet history, a constantly renewed assortment of almost rebellious writers—or shall we call them licensed critics?—nudging an oppressive system towards reform.[39]

The émigré critic Iurii Maltsev coined the term *promezhutochnaia literatura* 'transitional literature' to refer to those *gosizdat* (passed for publication by Soviet censorship) works—a large percentage of which are Village Prose—that occupy some sort of no-man's-land between Socialist Realism and dissident writing. This "transitional literature," Maltsev claimed, revealed more of Soviet reality than Socialist Realism, but it never went over the line into forbidden territory, and so it never told the whole truth.[40] The fact that franker and more complete appraisals of collectivization—containing their own kinds of lapses and distortions—emerged after 1985 only reinforces this point.

Vladimir Soloukhin lends credence to Maltsev's view in *Laughter over the Left Shoulder*. Engaging in self-criticism, Soloukhin wonders whether his violent childhood reaction to the absurdities and excesses of collectivization was not the most "sincere" moment of his entire life: "And then came the long years of compromise, loyalty, or to express it more profoundly, of collaboration and conformist behavior."[41] In an earlier work, *Kaplia rosy* (A drop of dew, 1960), he had in fact described the process of collectivization in his village, "but that description had, of course, its dose of loyalty and conformity," and everything was padded with *vata* 'cotton wadding' so it could be published. The moment when the Souloukhins were nearly sent away as kulaks is written in "gentle, rosy tones."[42]

This can be seen as a strictly personal confession, but it has, of course, implications for Village Prose as a whole. How much was distorted or suppressed because of self-censorship and the various levels of official censorship? Certainly the Tendriakov stories that appeared posthumously in *Novyi mir* in March 1988 are a much fuller and more shocking eyewitness account of the treatment of suspected kulaks than was published during the author's lifetime; the same can be said of Abramov's "Poezdka v proshloe" (A journey into the past, *Novyi mir*, May 1989). Should an evaluation of Village Prose be based on what was said or what was left unsaid? Did Village Prose evolve from a bold criticism of conditions in the countryside to crass opportunism, or is that simply a latter-day reading of this body of literature? The provocative questions raised by Souloukhin tie in with the charge made by a number of émigrés—and Soviets—that Village Prose writers played it safe and were well rewarded for their restraint. Previously written manuscripts that are surfacing (along with newly written works) on such important topics as collectivization have provided more material—or fuel—for this debate.

One of the thorniest critical debates about the legacy of Russian Village Prose at the end of the 1980s had to do with rural literature and the rise of extreme Russian nationalist groups, especially Pamyat (Memory). Spokesmen for chauvinist organizations have said that they want to stop what they perceive as the "genocide" of the Russian people and thus facilitate a renaissance of Russian national identity. They feel they can achieve this in part by freeing the Russian Republic (RSFSR) from non-Russian influences (e.g., Jewish, Georgian, Western). The Revolution, the destruction of architectural monuments and the environment, collectivization, and sometimes—however illogical and contradictory this may sound—even the conversion of Russia in 988 and Stalin's death in 1953 are seen as the result of anti-Russian conspiracies. Although no one has been able to prove that any Village Prose writer is actually a member of Pamyat, there has been more than enough evidence to show that writers such as Vasilii Belov, Viktor

Astafiev, and Valentin Rasputin are in agreement with some of the group's ideas.[43]

Their public expressions of affinity with some aspects of the chauvinist program, the way some of the former *derevenshchiki* have wielded power in the Russian Republic Writers' Union, and their participation in collective letters have led to a linking both in the USSR and in the West of Village Prose as a whole with Russian chauvinism.[44] Geoffrey Hosking has rightly said that "the failure of a reputable writer like Valentin Rasputin to distance himself from Pamyat' is a political mistake of major proportions."[45] Among the contemporary reevaluations of post-Revolutionary literary history is the rereading of Village Prose as a possible seedbed for Russian chauvinism. In the interest of an accurate assessment of Village Prose I will attempt to untangle this complex situation.

Village Prose was the most promising offshoot of the new rural literature that began with Ovechkin's essays in 1952. After 1956, the dominant voice in rural prose changed its orientation from the badly run kolkhoz of the present to the supposedly better-run village of the past.[46] Working within the limitations imposed by Glavlit censorship, a number of talented writers (and their epigones) evoked the past in elegiac, at times idyllic, tones, basing their stories to a large extent on their own childhood memories, supplemented by stories told them by older villagers. This literature was not merely ethnographic or descriptive of rural *byt*. It also raised such issues as the need to use the peasant's labor more efficiently and to compensate it more justly; the importance of preserving examples of traditional rural architecture and other physical aspects of the old village; respect for the rural contribution to the war effort; the need to strengthen the spiritual aspects of Russian life that had been weakened by atheism, materialism, and urbanization (this is sometimes reflected in positive Old Believer and Orthodox characters); the need to find one's Russian roots and the rapidly fading "memory" of the past; and the importance of protecting the environment.

Criticism picked up on these extraliterary issues—especially in the late sixties and seventies—using them pro or con to evaluate Village Prose as anything from patriarchal and anti-Soviet to deeply patriotic and necessary for the health of the nation.[47] A whole "ideological infrastructure grew up around this rural literature, with critics and journalists supplying the rationale for this new Russophile culture."[48] The Soviet critic A. Petrik sees "a whole pleiad of critics who entered the literary process with articles about 'village prose' and its creators. . . . these works [of criticism] are primarily emotional, subjective, or exclusively publicistic in character."[49] He laments that for the most part the aesthetic achievements of Village Prose were ignored in the heat of these discussions.

In the late 1970s, just before the rise of Pamyat, the already twenty-year-old Village Prose movement was seen as a "moderate element" in the "spectrum of Russian ethnocentricity" which had touched upon problems that had a deep resonance in contemporary Russian society.[50] But mournful evocations of picturesque—yet dying—villages were not entirely neutral; at the very least they had "radical implications" for the Russian people.[51] If one looks at the major Village Prose works of the second half of the 1970s—Rasputin's *Farewell to Matyora* (1976), the first parts of Mozhaev's *Peasant Men and Women* and Belov's *The Eve* (both 1976), Astafiev's *King-Fish* (1976), Abramov's *Home* (1978), Belov's *Harmony* (1978–1981), and Lichutin's *The Last Wizard* (1979)—there is no overt Russian chauvinism, but there is the "potential espousal of the cause of old Russia."[52] In Mozhaev and in Belov's *The Eve* we see increased attention to the fate of the middle peasant during collectivization; the "luminous sadness" (*svetlaia pechal'*) of canonical Village Prose is beginning to give way to a darker anger and resentment.

The years 1980–1985 were relatively quiet ones for the village writers, which reinforced the sense that the lyrical, elegiac, "childhood" period of Village Prose was mostly over. The saga of Matyora was seen to "logically complete the village theme,"[53] and *derevenskaia proza* went through that period of decline and transformation to which all literary movements are subject. The writers' silence was also partly due to accidents of fate: for example, the severe injuries Rasputin suffered in 1980 when he was mugged, and the deaths of Kazakov (1982), Abramov (1983), and Tendriakov (1984).[54] But there was the additional problem of censorship and editorial timidity that kept franker accounts of collectivization from appearing.

In this context, Chingiz Aitmatov's novel *The Day Lasts More Than a Hundred Years* (*I dol'she veka dlitsia den'*, 1980) can be read as both a borrowing of some of the themes and characters of Russian Village Prose for a central Asian (Kazakh) setting, and an attempt to satisfy some of the critics of rural prose by stressing positive aspects of technology. Katerina Clark sees Aitmatov as a "'fellow traveller'" of Village Prose, not only because he is ethnically Kirghiz, but also because his work "conveys both the miniature quality and sense of locale" of *derevenskaia proza*—the *malaia rodina*—along with the larger, multinational, "global" setting that was suggested by critics in the late 1970s.[55] Aitmatov in this, as in other works, has shown himself to be a master of creative adaptation and accommodation.

The works that emerged in the period after 1985 were proof that while lyrical stories and reminiscences were still being written about the Russian village, Village Prose as a whole had fragmented, with writers moving in several directions: to Village Prose themes transposed into more urban settings (Rasputin's *The Fire*, Astafiev's *The Sad Detective*, and Belov's *The Best Is Yet to Come*), to publicistic works on the environment and other issues, and to historical novels about collectivization that make use of archival materials as well as personal experiences (especially the subsequent installments of Mozhaev's and Belov's chronicles).

In some of these "post–Village Prose" works there is evidence of Russian chauvinism that complements what was being stated simultaneously by Pamyat and other groups. *The Sad Detective* contemptuously refers to "Jew-kids" who dared to study German literature alongside the story's Russian hero at a provincial institute.[56] The use of this ethnic slur brought a sharp rebuke from the respected critic Ekaterina Starikova: "[I] find it extremely jarring when the author of *A Sad Detective Story*, who, after all, has even read Nietzsche and a great deal else, allows himself the tone of some kind of Slavic superman. . . . This is home-grown chauvinism in bad taste. . . . Dostoevsky, who was guilty of such remarks, at least had no way of knowing what Auschwitz and Dachau were. . . . But Astaf'ev and we are very well aware of what they were."[57]

Belov's *The Best Is Yet to Come* features a negative Jewish character who breaks up a Russian family, mocks Russian bravery in the war, annoys people with his complaints about anti-Semitism, and plans to emigrate to America with his Russian wife and stepchildren. Vladimir Lakshin notes that Jews are one of the many targets of Belov's "fiery, 'Avvakum-like'" indignation. Some other objects of the author's wrath are Freemasons, lesbians, hypnotists, purebred dogs, computers, White Horse whiskey, and rock music.[58]

The chronicles of collectivization foreground the participation of Jews in the events of 1929–1930 both at the level of activists coming into the village and at the highest level of leadership. There can be no ambiguity about the author's intent at the beginning of *God velikogo pereloma* (The critical year), which continues the story Belov had begun in *The Eve*.

> If one monastery remained that had not been looted, and if in that monastery there had been just one monk-chronicler who had not been repressed, then maybe the following entry would have been recorded in the chronicle: "In the year one thousand nine hundred twenty-nine, during the fast of St. Philip, by the will of our Lord the son of a Grodno pharmacist, Yakov Yakovlev, was set up in the Moscow Kremlin as the commissar over all Christians and tillers of the land."
>
> Such a chronicle did not exist.[59]

Belov sets himself up as a latter-day Russian monk-chronicler to make up for this gap in the historical record. The anger and resentment found in many of these post-1985 works are directed not only toward Jews and their Masonic "co-conspirators," but also toward Georgians (in Astafiev's "Fishing for Gudgeon in Georgia") and other non-Russians, as well as the Western-influenced urban intelligentsia and Western mass culture.

Pamyat arose without the direct help of the *derevenshchiki*, but some rural writers have joined with urban writers such as Iurii Bondarev and Stanislav Kuniaev and other members of the conservative intelligentsia in supporting some of Pamyat's ideas. In his fiction, Rasputin expressed only what might be called "free-floating" anxiety, but he has defended Pamyat in public statements, both in the USSR and abroad.[60] Astafiev's most controversial remarks appeared in an infamous 1986 exchange of letters with the respected literary scholar Natan Eidelman that were widely distributed in the USSR and published abroad.[61]

Of the seventy-four original signatories to the March 1990 "Letter of Russian Writers," at least five (Lichutin, Likhonosov, Krupin, Rasputin, and Proskurin) could be classified as former rural writers (although the mediocre Proskurin could hardly be called a *derevenshchik*).[62] This letter applauds Pamyat, attacks those who are supposedly trying to destroy the Russian people, and even goes so far as to accuse Jews of complicity in pogroms and the Holocaust. While this document has no link whatsoever to canonical Village Prose, and the signatories are primarily urban writers and critics, at least four former Village Prose writers (plus a fifth, Belov, who signed on later) felt comfortable enough with the content of this letter to lend it their names and their not insubstantial credibility with the public. This is not a singular occurrence: Belov and Rasputin have spoken out on similar issues at meetings of the RSFSR Writers' Union.[63] Whether or not interviews with these writers and reports of their public remarks have always been recorded with complete accuracy, the body of evidence is simply too large to ignore.[64] Their past artistic strength has not been matched in the glasnost years by political wisdom or by a generosity of spirit toward those whom they identify as "alien" (*chuzhoi*). They have been unwilling to discuss at any length which aspects of Pamyat's program and methods they do not support, because this would have the effect of further splitting the ranks of the nationalist Right.

The chauvinistic remarks made by several former writers of Village Prose both in post-1985 literary works and in speeches, interviews, and letters have gained a great deal of attention both in the USSR and in the West. Third-wave émigré writers and critics have reacted vigorously to this development, but in their well-founded anxiety about anti-Semitism, they sometimes have focused too narrowly on the *derevenshchiki*, who have been termed collectively "writer-Nazis" by Vasilii Aksenov.[65] More often they are simply called *pochvenniki* (men of the soil).[66] The news of the appointment of Rasputin to Gorbachev's short-lived inner council was received with alarm in the West by those who did not understand that Rasputin is actually more moderate in his beliefs than many other prominent nationalists.[67] Nationalist feeling in Russia is not one kind of emotion or political stance; it ranges from the commendable "cultural ecology" of Dmitrii Likhachev at one end of the spectrum to something close to neo-Nazism (complete with uniforms) at the other end; terms like "conservative" and "right-wing" can also be applied in a number of senses.

Close readings of canonical Village Prose show that it is very nostalgic, and somewhat nationalistic—more at the level of a single village or region (*malaia rodina*) than of Russia as a whole—but only in the use made of it by ideological critics and in the activities of some of its erstwhile writers can it be directly linked to Russian chauvinism.[68]

Were the members of Pamyat nurtured on Village Prose? Perhaps, but they also read Pushkin, Dostoevsky, and other Russian and Soviet classics. The direct Village Prose–Pamyat connection that is assumed by many members of the Moscow intelligentsia, Russian émigrés, and Western scholars is a tenuous one at best, conflating at it does canonical Village Prose texts (1956–1980), criticism inspired by those texts, and comments made by authors both in and out of fiction in the "post–Village Prose" period. This view also ignores the obvious presence of other important factors in the rise of a more extreme Russian nationalism in the 1980s: a backlash against anti-Russian outbursts and movements for independence by other Soviet ethnic groups and republics, the threat posed to Russian domination by the higher birthrate of central Asian peoples, residual Russian xenophobia, the resentment felt against those who not only were allowed to emigrate but then were permitted to visit their former homeland, fear for the environment in the light of the northern river-diversion project (which is expressed as broad-based antiurbanism), the pro-Russian feelings surrounding the celebration of the millennium of Russian Orthodoxy in 1988, the collapse of the economy (always the time to search for a scapegoat), the increased opportunities for self-expression of all kinds afforded by glasnost, and, finally, the legacy of official government anti-Zionist propaganda and of urban right-wing underground movements.

The final factor is one that is least understood—or known—by those who have seen the Village Prose writers as the chief architects of chauvinism. *From under the Rubble* (*Iz-pod glyb*) is probably the most significant collection of samizdat essays from the conservative camp in the seventies. The eleven contributions, by Solzhenitsyn, Shafarevich, Mikhail Agursky, and others, sought to revive the historical debate over Russia's fate, pitting—once again—the national, spiritual, peasant-centered Russia against the Soviet Russia of the Western-oriented urban intelligentsia. In the essay "The Smatterers" ("Obrazovanshchina," 1974), Solzhenitsyn goes so far as to claim that the intelligentsia ceased to exist when it supported—or failed to protest—the destruction of the peasantry that began with collectivization in 1930. "All the outward, international success of our country and the flourishing growth of the thousands of scientific research institutes . . . have been achieved by devastating the Russian village and the traditional Russian way of life."[69] For Solzhenitsyn, the losses are many and include everything from "obedience to elders" and the baking of bread to Russia's folk culture and "historical memory."[70] The samizdat archives of the 1970s include material whose content is very similar to Shafarevich's 1989 essay "Russophobia," to the "Letter of the [seventy-four] Russian Writers," and to similar documents of the glasnost years.[71] In fact, some of the samizdat essays of the early seventies—none by Village Prose writers—are *so* extreme that their authors accuse Solzhenitsyn and Shafarevich of being Russophobic agents of Zionism. There is ample evidence that a conservative and increasingly xenophobic ideology evolved outside of artistic literature in the years before glasnost.

Along with the vital and very positive role that it played in Soviet Russian literature, Village Prose raised many issues of social, economic, and political importance that stimulated extraliterary debate. But while canonical Village Prose engages these ideas mostly at the level of metaphor, character, setting, and dialogue, critics and demagogues—and a few of the rural writers in nonliterary and "post–Village Prose" roles—used these metaphors as ideological stepping-stones. In the process, the chronotope of the traditional village became a "paraliterary space."

SEVEN

TWO DETECTIVES IN SEARCH OF

VILLAGE PROSE

Some pretty weird things have been appearing lately
under the heading of "detective stories."
(Natalia Ilina)[1]

LIKE VILLAGE PROSE, the detective story (*detektiv*) is a synthesis
of theme and genre, with specific characteristics that are relatively easy to identify.[2] The parameters of canonical detective
fiction would seem to differ in most ways from those of *derevenskaia
proza*: a tightly woven plot structure versus apparent plotlessness
(*sobytiia* 'events' as opposed to *byt* 'the daily routine'), a search for the
unknown versus a celebration of the known, the rapid succession of
events in the present versus an orientation toward the past and a slow-
ing down of time, and mostly urban versus rural settings. But the *detektiv* is no more rigid than Village Prose; the borders of each can be
breached, for instance, by digressions of a publicistic or ideological
nature to the extent that they overwhelm the story. These two very
popular types of literature—which share an interest in social order—
could also come together in rural detective stories. In Russian literature of the post-Stalinist period, the rural theme in general, and the
aesthetic and ethical values of Village Prose in particular, influenced—
and were influenced by—a variety of other themes and genres. The
detective story in turn could be set in the countryside and filled with
contemporary rural material. Boris Mozhaev, for example, wrote a
trilogy of *detektivy* that appeared between 1957 and 1974, and which
were subsequently filmed.[3]

In "The Law of the Taiga" ("Vlast' taigi," 1957), the hero is a solidly
built police sergeant named Vasilii Serezhkin; during an investigation
of theft, he discovers that a lumber-camp brigade leader is terrorizing
the people working for him, forcing them to become involved in various criminal activities.[4] Such a message about tyrannical personalities
and their servile followers was transparent in the Thaw year of 1957.

"The Witness Disappears" ("Propazha svidetelia," 1969) introduced
a new detective, police lieutenant Leonid Konkov, who must find out
who murdered a zoologist deep in the taiga. If the 1957 *detektiv* re-

flected the concern in rural literature of the 1950s—the Ovechkin period—over leadership cadres and tyranny, "The Witness Disappears" brings to the detective story an interest in the environment that was becoming increasingly important by the end of the 1960s. This work focuses on poaching, the illegal export of birds, and the destruction of fish-spawning grounds. Both of these Mozhaev stories are tautly written, exciting, and virtually free of commonly accepted characteristics of Socialist Realism.

In the final part of the trilogy, "The Fall of the Forest King" ("Padenie lesnogo korolia," 1974), Mozhaev includes so much material of a digressive and publicistic nature that he loses control over the detective genre. He apparently forgets that Konkov has an assault and a possible murder to solve. Much of the added material would make this story a predecessor of "The Sad Detective" (Astafiev), "The Fire" (Rasputin), and *The Best Is Yet to Come* (Belov), but the ending of "The Fall of the Forest King," where the *detektiv-pravednik* (detective–righteous man) Konkov is saved from punishment—for insubordination—by the Party regional committee, seems to move this work much closer to Socialist Realism.

If Village Prose is not simply a theme or type of material, but a set of parameters that includes a definite orientation in time and space, then works such as Mozhaev's trilogy of rural *detektivy* fall largely outside of Village Prose. There are, however, two other rural detective stories—Lipatov's *A Village Detective* and Astafiev's "A Sad Detective"—that are written with the parameters of Village Prose very much on the writers' mind.

Vil Lipatov's *Derevenskii detektiv* (*A Village Detective*) first appeared in *Znamia* in 1967–1968.[5] The hero of this cycle of stories is sixty-three-year-old Fedor Aniskin, a precinct policeman (*militsioner, uchastkovyi*) who has presided over the same Siberian settlement for more than thirty years. He is tall and stout and so regular in his ways that the village women know when they hear him on his morning rounds that it is time to bake the bread. Even hardened criminals call him "Uncle Aniskin." He deals with crimes ranging from accordion theft to murder, and he always gets his man. Lipatov has said that the character of Aniskin is based on a real-life policeman from the Siberian village in which the author grew up.[6] He also resembles in many respects Vasilii Serezhkin in the first of Mozhaev's Siberian detective stories.

In *A Village Detective*, Lipatov combines two of the most popular literary genres of the sixties: detective fiction and Village Prose. From the *detektiv* there is an eccentric but very effective sleuth, a range of criminal activities to be analyzed and solved, and a certain level of dramatic tension. From canonical Village Prose, Lipatov takes the setting (a village rather than a kolkhoz), a colorful group of rural characters, a sense of the decline of traditional peasant ways, and a distaste for the anonymity and fast pace of urban life.

Soviet critics were not sure how to categorize this work, that is, which "code of reading" to apply to it. They saw it variously as a detective story, a parodic anti–detective story, humorous Village Prose, nonlyrical Village Prose, and a polemic against Village Prose. The journal *Voprosy literatury* offered a parody of Lipatov called "A Rural Sherlock Holmes" in which Aniskin grumbles about "all those Sherlock Holmeses, Agatha Christies, and George Simenons who get up in the morning, drink their coffee, play the violin, and then sit down to write up their cases," while he must combine crime solving with educational work among local hooligans.[7]

From the point of view of the classical Western detective novel, Lipatov's work seems very weak. It conforms more successfully to Soviet norms for the genre. The Russian *detektiv*, seen as part of a larger adventure-suspense-spy genre (the umbrella term is *prikliuchencheskaia literatura* 'adventure literature'), was expected to include a political message along with the action. This is true of detective fiction from the era of "Red Pinkertonism" in the 1920s up to the present.[8] Despite an occasional call by Soviet critics for more entertaining stories and the well-known passion among Soviet readers for translations of the less politicized Western works, the official demand that Soviet *detektivy* be ideologically correct and socially significant prevailed through most of the 1980s.

It was obviously important to keep this popular, mass-market literature from drifting too far away from Socialist Realism.[9] Now that crime in the USSR is covered more thoroughly in the Soviet media and Socialist Realism is not the literary yoke it once was, the *detektiv* may undergo major changes, but in 1967, it was still a very conservative type of literature.[10]

Aniskin is a village elder and an agent of Soviet power; he represents the principle of ORDER in the community. Like a canonical Socialist Realist hero, he is literally larger than everyone else, farseeing, allknowing, and disciplined, drinking only once a year on Victory Day, and then only with a war buddy. The worst crimes in the village are committed by people identified as kulaks and their children; these families are even said to have backed Hitler from afar during the war. All disturbances of order are seen as social crimes; local hooligans are brought before a village meeting for Aniskin's educational speech—inspired by an article from *Pravda*—about the Party, the militia, and offenses against the collective. One character who questions whether he is going to get a fair deal from the justice system is told by a local kolkhoz official: "Who gave you the right to suspect him of being unfair? Do you for one minute imagine he would have an innocent man arrested? This is nineteen sixty-six and your interrogators are Communists."[11]

There is some basis for calling this a detective story when one considers the Soviet profile of the genre.[12] The argument that *A Village Detective* is a parody of *detektivy* is also not entirely without merit.[13] Aniskin is a somewhat ungainly hero with a few genuinely annoying personal habits, like sucking his teeth loudly and repeating "Tak! edak!" (Ho-ho!) as he waddles around the village. One villager, seeing Aniskin in a real quandary, humorously suggests that "it's Sherlock Holmes you want, Sherlock Holmes!"[14] But the edifying side of the book prevails, not unexpectedly, since a small dose of self-parody has been an option for Soviet *detektivy* since the days of Red Pinkertonism.[15]

The critics who read *A Village Detective* as Village Prose had a much more difficult case to prove.[16] Its focus on a Siberian village and the often colorful peasants who live there is more than offset by the enunciation of the very Socialist Realist values that Village Prose stood against. The most convincing critical argument of all is the one that sees Lipatov's work as a *polemic against* Village Prose.[17]

The book is critical of a kulak family, a former priest, and people who worry about man's impact on the environment. The destruction of Russian forests by the lumber industry became an important area of concern for rural writers, especially those from Siberia, in the 1970s and 1980s; even before that, they had expressed a deep concern for nature in general. Aniskin supports the counterargument that cutting down trees only makes the forest healthier. While Village Prose is oriented toward the past, Aniskin apologetically says to the head of the lumber camp: "I suppose I'm no better than Veryutin, thinking only of the past instead of the future. So please forgive me, Comrade Stepanov, for being a fool."[18] Lipatov's style also bears little resemblance to that of canonical Village Prose: it is in places awkward, flawed, and repetitious. We are told that at times Aniskin used the local idiom, but we do not actually "hear" him speak that way. And, in a blizzard scene ("Three Winter Days")—a classic Village Prose occasion for the use of the impersonal constructions that emphasize nature's power—no such forms appear.

Lipatov wrote *A Village Detective* at a time when such works as Solzhenitsyn's "Matryona's Home" (1963) and Belov's *That's How Things Are* (1966) had led to a critical backlash against Village Prose. Article after article in the pages of *Literaturnaia gazeta* and other periodicals debated the extent to which this literary movement was defending the patriarchal past. Lipatov entered the debate clearly on the side of those who found the glorification of the past in Village Prose excessive; he showed that the lyric evocation of traditional village life represented a reactionary stand.[19] Vladimir Bakhtin noted that the work is openly tendentious and publicistic: "Lipatov sees two villages—the one that is living out its last days and which fiercely resists all that is new, and the one that is created by this new life. . . . Vil Lipatov has said things that we need to hear now. He opposes the defense of patriarchal Rus."[20]

Lipatov was able to draw simultaneously on the popularity of two genres, one of which—the *detektiv*—he subjects to gentle parody, and the other—Village Prose—to substantive criticism. He mimics Village Prose to draw the reader in and then tries to undermine some of its most important values, creating what Alexander Kogan called a "plaster cast" that some mistakenly saw as "a model of the world."[21] Village Prose was clearly getting out of hand by the mid-1960s: if Matryona and Ivan Afrikanovich were fiction's newest heroes, what future could there be for orthodox Socialist Realism? *A Village Detective* is an attempt (one that parallels what was going on in criticism) to reroute Village Prose into more acceptable channels. Aniskin tries to keep law and order not just in his Siberian village but in the literary "village" as well.

Twenty years later, Viktor Astafiev's *Pechal'nyi detektiv* (A sad detective) again drew on these two seemingly disparate literary forms in one of the most original and powerful works of the early glasnost period.[22] Even though the detective, Soshnin, has retired because of job-related injuries, and the setting is on the outskirts of a provincial city, this short novel still encompasses the thematics of the *detektiv* —crime and criminals—and many of the characteristics and values of Village Prose.

Astafiev, like Lipatov, chose the detective-story format to interest the mass readership of traditional *detektivy*. The narrator comments on the popularity of this theme: "How many books, films, and plays have there been about criminals, the battles with crime, men and women on crime sprees, dens of iniquity, prisons, hard labor, daring acts, and clever murders."[23] Even Soshnin hums the tune from a popular detective show just before he is assaulted by three thugs outside his own home. Astafiev wants *detektiv* fans and other readers to realize that crime is not a subject for entertainment, but the manifestation of an evil that is corroding the soul of the Russian people. His use of this genre is obviously not without precedent in Russian literature.

> It is the fate of the detective story in Rus to help first-rate literature, to lure some readers and to deceive others.
>
> Viktor Astafiev, however, doesn't intend to lure, to charm, or to entertain. . . .
>
> An essential quality of the detective story is that the hero triumphs and peace and order prevail. This is, so to speak, an optimistic, cheerful detective story. But what we have here is somber and sad.[24]

The hero, now a full-time writer, has as his model Dostoevsky, who, he feels, reached almost to the center of man where the "self-devouring beast" lurks.[25] Soshnin's first book was a collection of stories about police work; however, like Dostoevsky, he wants to go beyond the topicality of the crime question to something much deeper. He tells his editor, the grotesquely drawn Oktiabrina Perfilevna, that his theme is *chelovecheskaia* 'all mankind'. Here Astafiev clearly inscribes himself in the text, speaking to those readers and critics who might see this work as only topical and not concerning the "cursed" questions that have perennially engaged Russian writers.

Soshnin wants to understand the Russian soul, not just the part of it that does evil, but the part that all too easily forgives the evildoer. Historian Moshe Lewin explored this question in *The Making of the Soviet System*. His evidence revealed that in the patriarchal Russian village, thieves might be killed on the spot, while murderers would be handed over to the proper authorities. A thief could even try to save his life by claiming to be a murderer. Lewin's explanation is that "peasants sometimes made a distinction between 'crime' and 'sin.' And they were not in the business of punishing sinful actions."[26] His years in the police force have drained all such sympathy from Soshnin—all he feels now is a weary agitation.

Although he is a second-generation townsman, through his own and his wife Lerka's family Soshnin has maintained strong ties with the nearby countryside. During visits to Lerka's parents in the village we see scenes of rural decline familiar from Village Prose: houses and whole villages abandoned, the young men gone, and women living out a lonely old age. Astafiev lovingly describes genuine peasants—Aunt Lina, Markel Tikhonovich, and Uncle Pasha—juxtaposing them with peasants-turned-bureaucrats (and peasants-turned-criminals). He also contrasts real folk culture with the decorative arrangements of folk objects found in the apartments of urban pseudo-intellectuals. Soshnin has lived all his life on the very edge of the city in an old wooden house—left standing by mistake—that like an *izba* represents for him "the memory of childhood and a place of refuge."[27]

The "village soul" of *A Sad Detective* is further emphasized by two episodes toward the end of the story. The first is the funeral of Granny Tutyshikha, the old woman who lived on the first floor of Soshnin's house. Scenes of the death and burial of old women are used throughout Village Prose to amplify the pervasive sense of loss: when these women die, they take with them not only knowledge of the old ways, but also a strength of character that seems strangely lacking in young people. Survivors are judged in these works by how they behave toward the dying and whether they honor the memory of the dead. The narrator tells of garbage being burned on cemetery ground, mourners getting so drunk that they forget to bury their deceased relative, and of investigator Pesterov, who, instead of attending his mother's funeral in a nearby village, just sends money. By way of contrast, Soshnin willingly goes to the funeral of his elderly neighbor.

While Granny Tutyshikha was hardly an exemplary character, the occasion of her funeral allows Soshnin to visit the local cemetery, which is covered in snow. There he thinks about his own dead, the earth that gave them life and received them when they died, and the cycle of the generations. At the graves of his mother and Aunt Lina, he takes off his hat and bows low to the earth, feeling physical pain but spiritual relief. As he leaves the cemetery he encounters his estranged wife and his daughter, who on the pretext of attending the *pominki* 'wake' follow him home. Reverence for the dead has saved his family.

That night Soshnin has a troubling dream, in which it is springtime and his daughter Svetka is playing on the river ice as it begins to break up. He attempts a rescue, but just when he reaches her, the sheet of ice she is standing on turns into a sheet of paper that shoots upward into the starry sky. At this point, Soshnin awakens. Critic Iurii Kariakin was also troubled by this dream, but for aesthetic reasons. He sees it as a made-to-order illustration for the author's moral agenda. "It is suspiciously well-formed and literary, that is, too much governed by reason."[28] For Kariakin, this is another example of how writers of publicistic works were being forgiven grievous artistic sins.

The literary or ideological dream actually has a lengthy pedigree in Russian literature, as readers of Goncharov, Dostoevsky, Chernyshevsky, Tolstoy, and other writers will recall. Astafiev chose the symbolic content of his dream carefully: *ledokhod* 'the breakup of river ice in the spring' is perhaps the most important moment in the natural cycle and a leitmotiv of Village Prose. It is a sudden, powerful, elemental, and mysterious release of nature's energy that is almost always—as here— described by means of impersonal constructions. In the story "Predchustvie ledokhoda" (Signs of spring), Astafiev characterizes this annual event as something overwhelming that at first sounds like the end of the world (*svetoprestavlenie* 'the passing away of the world') but which is also an occasion for annual celebration.[29] The apocalyptic content of the dream matches Soshnin's sense that the bonds of time have been ruptured.[30]

When he awakens and sees his daughter safely asleep on an old peasant trunk that belonged to his Aunt Lina, Soshnin has more than a conventionally sentimental response. He sees this as both a sign of loss—she knows nothing of her rural forebears—and a restoration of one aspect of that loss—his immediate family is with him once again.

With village roots and family ties on his mind, he consults his well-worn edition of Dal and then faces a blank sheet of paper, ready to go on.

Soshnin is a writer-detective in search of his own past and, by extension, of the rural soul of modern Russia. Unlike Inspector Aniskin, the "sad detective" has lost his battle against crime; as a writer he launches another battle against historical and generational amnesia. In a passage about confiscated church property, on which a teachers' institute stadium has replaced a beautiful old pond, the narrator comments on such unsuccessful attempts to forget the past: "The cursed past made itself known—wearily, tenaciously, from underground, from under the trodden-down and rolled-out heart of the stadium, from tree stumps buried deep in the earth. Furtively and surreptitiously it sent heralds of spring into the bright-eyed present. The hardy branches of poplars and maple trees forced the well-developed future teachers jogging by to recall the past."[31]

The genre of *A Sad Detective* was the subject of extensive critical commentary, especially since the author seemed to be calling it both a detective story and a novel. Critics saw it as a family novel, a writer's diary, a bitter satire, a civic sermon, a confessional cri de coeur, a series of physiological sketches, an anti-intellectual diatribe, an anti-alcoholism tract, and a *detektiv* overloaded with serious material even by Soviet standards.

> At some point you begin to understand that the novel not only has many levels but also many genres; that it's no accident that the word "sad" acts as a corrective to the concept "detective story"; that we have before us a novel that is a satire, a memoir. . . . and a meditation.
>
> Several genres are intermingled in this contemporary book . . . by means of a remarkable synthesis of the realistic . . . the satirical and the philosophical.[32]

The language of this work was seen as almost too rich a mixture of stylistic levels, and on the narrative level it was difficult to separate out the reflections of the author, the narrator, and Soshnin.

Igor Zolotusskii found readers uncomfortable with some of the changes that were taking place in literature, which had—in many cases—brought fiction much closer to certain negative aspects of Soviet life that were at last being reported by the mass media. Overwhelmed by reality, they wanted less "stark realism" (*zhestkii realizm*), and more genres like the *detektiv* to function as an escape from their daily lives.

> Our reader is still riding detective stories: sitting astride the *action*, he's still galloping away into the unknown, into an unknown that doesn't

frighten anyone—where he's promised a bit of nervous tension, killing some time, and a happy ending. He'd like to wrap history, politics, and love in a detective story, to give them the energy of a detective story so that this energy will carry him away to God knows where—but not where things are bad.[33]

While the regular readers of detective stories were unhappy, the book was a big hit among professional criminologists.[34] Most reviewers noted that it was a very angry work, just a few of them questioning some of the objects of that anger, which include (along with criminals) women, mass culture, intellectuals, the literary establishment, and Jews.[35] It was acknowledged that Astafiev had transcended Village Prose issues by showing crime to be a phenomenon that touched city and countryside alike; still, there was a sense that the loss of a family-centered rural world is implied in all the other losses portrayed in the novel. Zolotussky said that while he was reading Astafiev's story and then writing about it, the village and the peasant were never far from his own thoughts; for him, this story is clearly part of the debate over the peasantry that has been going on in Russia for well over a century.[36]

A Village Detective and A Sad Detective are both deeply conservative, but in quite different ways. The Lipatov stories are oriented toward an orderly march to the radiant Communist future, while Astafiev looks back approvingly at the pre-Revolutionary rural patriarchy. Each writer chose the detektiv format to capture the attention of the readers, but both had agendas that involved more than conventional tales of crime detection.[37] Lipatov polemicizes against Village Prose, which had achieved its canonical form by the mid-1960s; two decades later Astafiev branches out from a mature, even declining, rural literature. In the end the "sad detective" is much more closely linked to Village Prose than his "country cousin."

Beyond Village Prose

Astafiev's A Sad Detective is one of the works that evolved from *derevenskaia proza* and appeared in the early period of glasnost (1985–1987). Two other controversial stories that are part of this same evolutionary process are Valentin Rasputin's "Pozhar" ("The Fire")—which has been called an "emblem" of the first years of the Gorbachev period[38]—and Vasilii Belov's *Vse vperedi* (*The Best Is Yet to Come*).[39] Neither of these works follows the *detektiv* format, but they are close in spirit to the "village" side of Astafiev's novel, especially to his theme of moral decline as a result of the loss of traditional rural values.[40]

In "The Fire" Rasputin fulfills the promise he made after *Farewell to Matyora* to "follow" his island characters to new settlements in order to see what their lives would be like there. Sosnovka—constructed around a logging camp that attracts a rowdy group of temporary workers—has become "home" to the uprooted inhabitants of six flooded villages.

Farewell to Matyora shows the old community at the moment of its dissolution, when all its traditional values and customs are seen in bold relief. It is in many ways a luminous, elegiac work. The islanders' future home on the mainland is obviously a poor substitute for what is being lost to the floodwaters of progress. In "The Fire," the apprehensions about the new life expressed in 1976 have become a reality. The former villagers can only look to a place in the river where Egorovka used to be. After twenty years in the new settlement, it is painfully clear that the old villages "died" twice: first they disappeared physically, and then the transplanted inhabitants forgot the old ways that had helped them cope with trials much worse than the fire sweeping through the Sosnovka warehouses. Unable to work the fields that were submerged with their old villages, they lost the whole way of life that accompanied agricultural work; after the move most did not even bother to plant gardens near their houses. Their new occupation encouraged an indifference toward nature and, eventually, toward the common good.

The absence of the old ways is experienced not as a luminous memory, but as a dark, angry pain. Such supportive structures as home (both *dom* 'house' and *rodina* 'homeland'), fulfilling work, a reverence for nature, and village solidarity, have all but disappeared; harmony (*lad*) has given way to disharmony (*razlad*).[41] One of the few righteous men from the past, Uncle Misha Khampo, is brutally killed by hooligans because of his failure to adapt to the new code of behavior. The evil atmosphere in Sosnovka is as thick as the acrid smoke that pours forth from the burning warehouses. There is no special satisfaction in saving most of the settlement from fire, because in a few years, when the surrounding forests are depleted, many of the residents will leave anyway. "Gorit selo, gorit rodnoe" (The village is burning, our dear, native village), the words from a Russian folk song that serve as an epigraph to the story have an ironic resonance; the settlement will never be *rodnoe*.

The hero, Ivan Petrovich Egorov, submitted to the inevitable when Egorovka was condemned, moving his *izba* to the new location.[42] In a sense, he lost more than the others because he lost the historical meaning of his last name, derived from the name of his former village.

Instead of being "Egorov of Egorovka" he was now "Egorov without Egorovka."[43] His name now meant as little as did Sosnovka (from *sosna* 'pine') as the name for a settlement whose sole reason for existence was to cut down trees. At least he still was able to look out at the water every day and think of his village, as he tried to maintain his closeness to the land. The critic Lobodov explains Egorov's feelings in the following way: "Let's say that you were born in the small village of Utkiny Dvoriki [Duck-yards], and there's no place on earth that's dearer to you, but suddenly it's declared to be 'not economically viable' and you have to move. Soon, this land where your great-grandparents and parents lie is wiped off the face of the earth."[44] He thinks of leaving to join a son who lives far away, but feels that this would be an abdication of his responsibility to preserve the memory of Egorovka.

At the end of the story, he walks through the spring forest, seeking to recapture his inner sense of *rodnaia zemlia* (native land) and *rodnoi dom* (one's own/family home). Like Soshnin, he cannot fight single-handedly against the disorder around him; he can only try to restore his own feelings of harmony, his own "inner village."

The difference between Socialist Realist Kolkhoz Literature and Village Prose was in part marked by a reversal of the positive and negative values put on such binary pairs as rural/urban, old age/youth and continuity/change. In "The Fire" there are mostly negatives; it has quite properly been called Rasputin's "bleakest" work.[45] One need only reread "Downstream" (1972) with its greater possibility of at least personal redemption to see how the treatment of rural themes had changed dramatically. Socialist Realism had a radiant future and Village Prose had a radiant past, but this post–Village Prose literature has only the dreary, violent "territory of the present."[46]

A more controversial example of "post–Village Prose" literature is Belov's ironically titled *The Best Is Yet to Come*, which has been called an "antiurban" novel. "Everything in the city is 'anti.' Anticoncord. Antiharmony. Antiattachment. Antifriendship. Antilove."[47] The characters are not former villagers, and the nearest the book comes to a rural setting is during periodic excursions to the Moscow suburbs. And yet the patriarchal village and "peasant Rus" loom large in this book as emblems of an idealized past in which men did manual labor, women had babies, and nobody went to France to see pornographic films (as several of the book's characters are rumored to have done).

If Ivan Petrovich and his wife are the only positive elements of "The Fire," the debilitated Dmitrii Medvedev (*medved'* means 'bear') is the rather modest source of hope for Belov. Formerly a successful urban *intelligent* who spent six years in prison after an accident at his institute, Medvedev, bearded and looking like a peasant, refuses to attempt a return to Moscow, preferring to live on the outskirts of the city. To his friend Ivanov he declares that he is proud to call himself not just a conservative but a reactionary. When Ivanov questions Medvedev's decision to live in a rural shack, the latter replies that "it is the peasant hut that has always been the salvation of Russia."[48]

Belov's novel rejects the illusion shared by several of its negative characters that "everything lies ahead." The danger in idealizing the past, we are told, cannot be compared with the danger of idealizing the future. "According to Belov, the past is not only a sacred object; it is also part of the present. It is part of the chain of 'continuity' that extends from centuries past. Only 'demons' can fail to respect the past. Only 'demons,' Belov says, are capable of looking at the present as an 'experiment.'"[49] An orientation toward the past is, of course, one of the most important characteristics of Village Prose, where the past is specific, almost palpable, brought to life in the stories of older villagers, in the chronotope of a rural childhood, in an affectionate examination of the inventory of traditional peasant life, and in the influence of rural speech on dialogue and narrative. Belov's turn to the past in *The Best Is Yet to Come* is a strictly ideological move.

Critics of the novel called it an artistic failure, in which the author's anger and prejudice distorted the portrayal of characters like Liuba and Brish.[50] Supporters rejected the notion of any aesthetic appraisal of a work of such high "truth" value and relevance to the problems of contemporary life. Several of them, forgetting that Misha Brish was Belov's own creation, went much further than the author in their attacks on Brish and the "evil forces" he represented.[51]

The fact that "The Fire," *A Sad Detective*, and *The Best Is Yet to Come* appeared within the space of just a year (from July 1985 to July/August 1986) was seen as more than a coincidence. The three most important living rural writers were clearly tired of what Lavlinskii calls the "offensive nickname *derevenshchik*," a term that was not only limiting but which implied that they were literary provincials. They were impatient to go beyond the boundaries of canonical Village Prose to create new works with a deeper "moral-philosophical" (*nravstvenno-filosofskii*) potential that would belong to an indivisible "big literature."[52] From the microcosm of the native village (*malaia rodina*) and an emphasis on the preservation of folk customs and objects, and the specific memories of past generations, they moved toward the macrocosm of the whole Russian nation (*narod*), taking on a role that Lavlinskii calls "nation-preserving" (*narodo-okhranitel'naia*). In their new setting they were "defending the village from the city and protecting it from being infected by urban culture."[53]

Village Prose writers simultaneously mourned the decline of their beloved villages and worried about the growing spiritual vacuum in the land. In their "post–Village Prose" works they wonder aloud about the virtual disappearance of the "simple laws of morality" that had held firm through so many generations.[54] The numerous wise old peasants of Village Prose have been reduced to a few isolated "righteous ones"—Ivan Petrovich, Soshnin, and Medvedev—who seem like cranks to their urban neighbors.[55] These men are the literary sons of Solzhenitsyn's Matryona, an obvious comparison that still could not be made in Soviet criticism during the years 1985 to 1987. The ending of "Matryona's Home" with its impassioned direct address to the reader is very close in spirit and style to these recent works of Astafiev, Rasputin, and Belov. They, too, are concerned with the unappreciated "righteous one without whom, as the proverb says, no village can stand. Nor any city. Nor our whole land."[56] The rhetorical line that Village Prose took with "Matryona's Home" in 1963 was not fully developed at the time (for reasons that have more to do with the repressive atmosphere of the mid-sixties than with art), although the affectionate portraits of older villagers that had begun to appear before Solzhenitsyn (in Kazakov and others) continued. It is with works like Rasputin's "The Fire" that we see the reappearance of this aphoristic, moralizing tone, which has been described—in Bakhtinian terms—as "monologic."[57]

The relaxation of censorship after spring 1985 encouraged writers to express their concerns more directly than would have been possible even a few years earlier. Rasputin declared that "the time has come for a direct, open, literary text," and one can in fact see in these works a high publicistic content and reduced distance between author, narrator, and characters.[58] Rasputin and other contemporary writers opt for "direct contact with the reader without elaborate metaphors, masks, or Aesopian language, but with a straightforward expression of the things that are most painful."[59] The tolerance and warm feelings that accompanied memoirs of the past virtually disappeared when the attention shifted to the present; nostalgia, sorrow, and acceptance were transformed into despair and anger. The optimistic endings of Socialist Realism and the bittersweet endings of Village Prose are a thing of the past. "Nowadays the ending is different; it has an anxious quality to it. It is *pregnant* with meaning."[60]

These former *derevenshchiki* went beyond the "literary village" in the 1980s but for the most part did not reach the artistic heights of their earlier writing. Their "post–Village Prose" works seem, like Shukshin's heroes, to be caught between the city and the village, awkward, unhappy, and nowhere completely at home, with no solace for their aching souls. Village Prose has ceased to exist as a unified movement, and writers have moved off in various directions, in search of the next stage in Russian literature. But wherever they go, some part of "village Russia" goes with them.

EIGHT

REWRITING AND REREADING

LITERARY HISTORY

And what we said of it became
A part of what it is . . .
(Wallace Stevens)[1]

T HE INFLUX of previously unpublished works into Soviet Russian literature in the second half of the 1980s has stimulated a revision of the canon and a reinterpretation of the course of modern Russian literary history. In this process, the legacy of Village Prose and the activities of several erstwhile *derevenshchiki* play important roles. Many rural writers had been involved in an ongoing, if largely unspoken, project of "rewriting" Soviet Russian literature since the 1950s. They had—during the post-Stalin thaws and into the period of "stagnation"—been deliberately writing "against" Socialist Realism, moving the story of life in the countryside closer to their own genuine rural experiences as children, and closer to the pre-Revolutionary canon; in addition, they made judicious use of traditional Russian folklore. A closer look at the literary process from the Khrushchev and Brezhnev years shows that "rereading" the literary landscape was an ongoing activity for critics as well as writers. The examination of previously unknown texts adds new depth to a picture that has been fragmented for many reasons; no one had access to or even knowledge of all literary texts, and, in the USSR, it was for many years impossible to speak about certain works and authors publicly.[2] It is the access to a wealth of new material, the coming of glasnost to literary discussion, and ideological and political developments at the end of the 1980s that make the evaluation of such literary directions as Village Prose even more complicated and interesting than it had been in the past.

Rereading Tendriakov

Vladimir Tendriakov provides an exemplary case of a talented writer mediating between the parameters of Socialist Realism and Village Prose and working under the constraints of censorship. "Den' na rodine" (A day in the old hometown, 1964) fits a pattern that was fairly common in the first half of the 1960s—the return trip to the writer's *rodnye mesta* 'native places'.[3] Such works combine a discussion of the continuing problems in collective-farm management with lyrical passages about the village of one's childhood and reflections on the *ukhodiashchaia derevnia*, the 'vanishing' Russian village.

Tendriakov's essay even divides neatly into halves, the first half leaning toward Village Prose, the second half closer to an Ovechkin-style *ocherk*, which was reformist in its intent, but fairly close to Socialist Realism in its setting, character, and language. "A Day" begins with the author's reminiscences of his return as a five-year-old to the village in which he was born and of how he spent a summer month there with his father. But there is a second narrative of return that "frames" the story—the day the author spent as a forty-year-old man in the same village, the first time he had been there since that distant summer. Much of the first half is by now familiar territory—the return, luminous childhood memories interwoven with fairy tales, family legends and fishing stories, colorful local place-names, the old peasant home and the proud profile of a white church, tearful aged neighbors and relatives, and a painful yearning for roots.

Halfway through "A Day," the orientation suddenly changes: a car appears in a cloud of dust carrying the kolkhoz chairman. Tendriakov brusquely interrupts his reverie with the comment "Enough about the past; this man personifies the present day in my native region."[4] What follows is a discussion of the harvest, agricultural technology, the salary scale for kolkhoz workers, and the building of a club; it ends with Tendriakov's evening appearance in one of the settlements.

How are we to read this essay? The author stresses the pro-Bolshevik, atheist, pro-collectivization sympathies of the men in his family and then with equal fervor describes the aesthetic and spiritual values represented by the local church. The juxtapositions are seemingly awkward; one is reminded of Sinyavsky's designation of a hybrid work as "a loathsome literary salad."[5] A second look at "A Day in the Old Hometown" makes it clear that there is more going on *podspudno* 'behind the scenes'; Tendriakov is in full control of his materials and he uses this essay to comment on various approaches to the rural theme.

At the beginning he is a gently ironic five-year-old, skeptical about his father's nostalgia for his hometown, his *malaia rodina*, deflating the fairy tale he had been told about the very special place called Makarovskaia.

> Alas, we had seen the same roofs and birches in dozens of similar villages. It couldn't be that the fairy-tale village of Makarovskaia was such an ordinary place. But father's eyes were sparkling and his voice was breaking—

there must be a reason, something that distinguished your own village from other places. And then it dawned upon me: "'Your hometown' means that everything is yours." I pointed to the roofs and asked:

"Are all these houses ours?!"

"No, just the one . . ."

That's odd; we already had one house of our own in the town we had moved to. So how did that differ from our "hometown"? I looked at the roofs of the village and was deeply perplexed.[6]

Tendriakov gives a comical account of how, as a forty-year-old, he was recognized by the people of Makarovskaia not by his face but by the shape of his body (*po korpusu*). The old villagers filled him with home-brewed beer at every house, and they all insisted that they had carried him in their arms when he was a small boy. The childhood stories he recalls are more amusing than sentimental: a peasant traded horses thirty-five times one winter and by the spring plowing had no horse at all; the author's great-grandmother, a concertina under her arm, took off for distant monasteries every time there was a family squabble; one peasant could only tell time by stating whether the clock hands pointed toward the floor or the ceiling.

These anecdotes and the pro-regime heroism of his family lessen the nostalgia and sense of loss that usually accompanies the narrative of return. Tendriakov was in his own way responding to—or at least taking into account—Solzhenitsyn's widely discussed story "Matryona's Home" (1963) with its final passage that made serious moral claims for the peasant heroine. The righteous old woman—or man— is not to be found in "A Day in the Old Hometown." Tendriakov's mother is hardly mentioned, his grandmother is simply a hardworking survivor, and his pious great-grandmother is so exultant at her son-in-law's death that the author remarks with some irony, "The old pilgrim-woman, alas, didn't have enough of Christ's meekness and all-forgiving nature."[7]

In the second half, the author parodies certain conventions of Socialist Realist Kolkhoz Literature. The arrival of the chairman's car in a cloud of dust is an oft-repeated scene in kolkhoz novels. At the height of Kolkhoz Literature in the late forties, the critic Makarov provided a distilled vision of the collectivized village drawn from these works: "Say the word 'village' to yourself and before you there arise tractors in the field, a truck raising dust along a country road, lines of poles with telephone and electrical wires stretching beyond the horizon, endless fields: people file by, their faces shining with the consciousness of their own worth. On some of their chests sparkle the stars of a Hero of Socialist Labor, which seem to absorb the living gold of ripe grain."[8]

Tendriakov says in his essay that when the chairman appears, one has no choice but to begin to discuss the harvest. The latest laborsaving machinery is described—but is never available—and a new club is called not so much a "temple of culture" as a "house of the dead."[9] Why is it, the author wonders, that the descendants of the people who built the magnificent churches of the Russian north with only an ax and trees cannot construct an attractive clubhouse?

Juxtapositions of dissimilar elements are much on Tendriakov's mind. His corrections of both Village Prose and reformist *ocherk* styles show that he does not force these two sets of conventions—or parameters—into the same work uncritically. He even complains about the introduction that he is given at the village club by the chairman of the rural soviet, who "tries to put together some not very compatible things: the chance appearance of a writer and the present level of production in the kolkhoz,"[10] an indication of the impoverished level of discourse in such situations that Yashin had so forcefully pointed out in his 1956 story "Levers." The very title of the journal in which "A Day in the Old Hometown" appeared—*Nauka i religiia* (Science and religion) is another such juxtaposition in which both concepts are weakened, if not compromised, by their proximity.

The essay ends with Tendriakov sitting in his Vologda hotel room, planning his next trip to the village, somewhat like Rasputin's writer-protagonist in "Downstream" (1972). But once again, on the verge of ending on a note of loss like canonical Village Prose, Tendriakov remarks that in his village the houses are not boarded up and the collective farmers are being paid every month; they are buying motorcycles, brewing beer, and still celebrating *troitsa* (the Trinity) though under the new secular name *festival'*.

Where does Tendriakov fit, based on this work? In a sense, where is he *placing himself* in a literary-political world that was being polarized by such provocative works as "Matryona's Home"? In the next few years the Village Prose canon would grow large, with the addition of major works by Belov, Mozhaev, Rasputin, Abramov, and others, and the movement would develop its own recognizable patterns, even its own clichés. Village Prose would have an army of critics discussing it and taking different positions in regard to the works themselves and the issues they raised. With his northern Russian village background, Tendriakov could easily have written himself "into" the Village Prose movement. Instead, he remained on the borderline between village and kolkhoz, as in a different way Shukshin would do: he was nostalgic for the village of his childhood summers, but he was not willing to dispense completely with the enthusiasm his family had for the opportunities that the Revolution had offered the poorer peasantry.

In the end Tendriakov chose to stay somewhere in the middle of the literary spectrum, closer to Village Prose than to the reformist branch of Socialist Realism, but committing himself completely to neither type of rural literature.[11] He took an ironic view of both extremes, worrying about the excesses of each in the name of "correct belief" (i.e., orthodoxy). Andrei Sinyavsky has said of irony that it is "the faithful companion of unbelief and doubt; it vanishes as soon as there appears a faith that does not tolerate sacrilege."[12] The price of appearing detached in a deeply committed literary context is that one is often not taken seriously.

Those readers and critics who undervalued Tendriakov must have been surprised by the previously unpublished autobiographical stories from 1969–1971 that surfaced in the March 1988 issue of *Novyi mir*. "Para gnedykh" (A pair of bays) takes place later in the summer of 1929, which was commemorated in "A Day," when the father had been sent on with his family to another village as a local official in charge of collectivization. It begins with a brief restatement of childhood pleasures but also mentions that the villagers were very anxious about the changes underway in the countryside. The single village street was filled with carts: Tendriakov's father had instructed the poor and the prosperous peasants to exchange houses. One clever kulak convinces a poorer neighbor to accept his two bay horses as a gift, conveniently reversing their status. Tendriakov's father is not amused and advises the poor peasant to refuse the offer.

> "Think of the honor of the poor peasant! It's not worth it!" Father's voice was cold and angry.
> "The honor of the poor? . . . Fedor Vasilevich, I've spent forty-eight years on this earth trying to reject that honor . . . To hell with the honor of being a poor peasant!"[13]

Rural life was changing very rapidly in 1929, and what was legal one week was dangerously illegal the next. Cows were even more confused than people; they would return each evening to their old homes, only to find that their masters had moved to another part of the village. The boy Tendriakov was torn in a very real way between love for his father, along with pride in his father's record in the Revolution and civil war, and a sense that villagers with two horses were not really "enemies." He secretly admires the kulak who got away.

"Khleb dlia sobaki" (Bread for a dog) picks up the story in 1933, when the author was nine and the family had been transferred to a settlement near a railroad station. He sees the victims of dekulakization, who have been reduced to mad, homeless, bark-eating skeletons, in transit only to death: "We would . . . watch them from behind a fence. There was no horror so great that it could stifle our tremendous—almost inhuman—curiosity. Frozen with fear and disgust, exhausted by the panic-filled sense of pity that we kept well-hidden, we watched the bark-eaters."[14]

The stationmaster wonders that the children do not go mad at the sight of these living corpses; by the end of the story he has shot himself. Tendriakov remembers that the horrors were introduced slowly, so that they became part of daily life. Besides, the children were repeatedly told that these people were enemies. They heard one such "enemy" who was lying helplessly on the ground ask a passing official:

"Tell me, before I die . . . why . . . why me? . . . Is it really because I had two horses? . . .

"Yes, it is," Dybakov responded calmly and coldly.[15]

This exchange ties the three stories together, referring to the crime of having two horses that was cleverly circumvented in "A Pair of Bays," and to the official named Dybakov, who will himself perish in the third story. It became increasingly difficult for the children—who instinctively resisted the devaluation of language—to fit slogans about "enemies" to these "living relics." Young Tendriakov decides to feed the very hungriest person from his own dinner but is overwhelmed by the crowds that begin to follow him everywhere. In the end he is reduced to the less complicated moral business of feeding a hungry but suspicious dog, who is also a victim of the times.

The third story, "Parania," is grotesque, on the order of Voinovich's *Pretender to the Throne* (the second of the Chonkin novels). It is summer 1937, one of the worst purge years. Life goes on in the railroad settlement. Against the background noise of the loudspeaker bellowing out enthusiastic songs about Stalin, victory, and the rapid improvement of Soviet life—the daily dose of Socialist Realism—the children observe the activities of the village *iurodivaia* (a type of holy fool thought to have a gift of prophecy), Parania. In response to constant teasing about her "fiancé"—formerly Jesus—she answers that she is now betrothed to Stalin himself. The crowd is struck dumb, afraid to be seen reacting in any way. Through the rest of the story, Parania walks around the village, pointing out potential "assassins" of Stalin, all of whom are arrested. The last of the accused kills her, wisely—in that context—preferring a charge of murder to that of treason.

These childhood memoirs are ironic, tragic, and grotesque.[16] Each story ends with what Tendriakov calls a "documentary comment" (some of the material courtesy of Roy Medvedev), a sort of historical coda. The cited figures are as harrowing as what the child saw. Despite the use of historical material at the end, the tone is never predominantly publicistic.

In "A Day in the Old Hometown" Tendriakov knowingly moves between the conventions of both Village Prose and Socialist Realism in an attempt to give a more balanced picture of his village past and present than he felt either method taken alone would provide. The latent strength one had often sensed in Tendriakov is confirmed by the three powerful stories about the countryside that appeared posthumously in 1988, where—both ideologically and aesthetically—he ranged much further afield. The critic A. Turkov, in reviewing these newly released works, used the image of "spliced wires" to describe what Tendriakov has done for the contemporary reader, rejoining disrupted lines of communication across the decades, healing with his realistic—almost surrealistic—vignettes from 1929–1937 some of the breaks in memory and the bonds of time that have tormented Astafiev, Rasputin, and other Village Prose writers.[17]

Tendriakov was one of a number of writers seen by Soviet and Western critics to be stranded at a crossroads. As we reread the literature of Soviet Russia, we can learn a great deal from those writers of talent and conscience who never arrived at a literary destination that can be mapped with utter precision, but who nonetheless made significant contributions to the revival of literature in the post-Stalinist period and who still contribute through the publication of long-delayed works. As efforts are made to establish canons precisely, works that fall just outside their parameters should be neither ignored nor misrepresented.

Village Prose in the 1980s

By the 1980s Village Prose no longer functioned as a viable literary movement in itself as it had during the previous two decades. The elegiacal period had peaked in 1976 with *Farewell to Matyora*, and, although Astafiev, Belov, Abramov, Mozhaev, and Lichutin all published major works between the years 1976 and 1980, the sense among critics was that Village Prose had run its course. Aitmatov's *The Day Lasts More Than a Hundred Years* (1980) may have drawn its inspiration from Village Prose, but it hardly added to that movement, coming hard upon its decline. Taking place as it does in a railroad settlement, Aitmatov's novel and his subsequent work *The Place of Execution* (*Plakha*, 1986) are more closely related to "post–Village Prose" works like Rasputin's "The Fire."

A number of older and younger writers continued to write on familiar themes, but their work simply did not have the same impact as it would have had during the previous two decades.[18] The only new rural writers who attracted much attention were Boris Ekimov and

Vladimir Krupin, both of whom were respected for their well-crafted stories.

Krupin's works—like those of Tendriakov—provide us with a reflection of a changing literary landscape. His semidocumentary piece "The Fortieth Day," which tells of a visit to his ailing parents in the countryside, was one of the more significant rural works of the early eighties.[19] Even though this *povest' v pis'makh* (epistolary tale) continues to display many of the attributes of Village Prose with its focus on LOSS, NATURE, FOLK LANGUAGE AND CULTURE, THE PAST, THE VILLAGE, THE PEASANT HOME AND FAMILY, and in general things that can be classified as *rodnoi* (native, one's own), it is already possible to see how the rural theme has evolved. It is not his native region or village that the narrator visits, but simply the place where his father's work as a forestry official has taken him. On the "parents' Saturday" (*pokrovskaia roditel'skaia subbota*) that occurs during this visit, he goes to the local cemetery as is the custom, but there is no relative to honor there.

It is not only the breakup of the traditional extended family that bothers Krupin. He is also experiencing a crisis of conscience and of confidence as a rural writer. He feels that much of his previous rural journalism has contained gaps, lies, and half-truths. He also senses that there is very little that he can add to what has already been said about the countryside: "We have Rasputin, who's about my age, and he's written about the old women so successfully that after him no one would dare attempt it . . . real talent can make it impossible for others to write about the same thing . . . it wouldn't make sense to try. But what if you don't have anything else to write about?"[20] Krupin, who was born in 1941, is already one of the last of the rural writers who were eyewitnesses to the end of traditional village life. The title "The Fortieth Day," with its meaning of a final commemoration and an acceptance of loss, was well chosen.[21]

During the years from 1980 to 1985 rural writers did not seem to have had a significant impact on the literary process, but that situation certainly changed in 1985, the year that brought Gorbachev to power.[22] And it was Valentin Rasputin, the very writer who saw canonical Village Prose to its dramatic conclusion in 1976, who offered in "The Fire" a powerful example of the new direction in literature that he had promised after writing *Farewell to Matyora*. Starting in 1985, offshoots of *derevenskaia proza* began to emerge in fairly rapid succession. What happened in the following five years can be best understood in terms of a complex rewriting and rereading of literary history.

As Village Prose fragmented, some of its most talented writers carried its themes into urban settings. New settlements (Sosnovka in "The

Fire"), provincial cities (Veisk in Astafiev's "The Sad Detective") and Moscow (in Belov's *The Best Is Yet to Come* and Lichutin's *The Demon*) became more important settings than the village itself.[23] The emphasis in these works is on the consequences not just of one uprooted person or village, but on the uprooting of the Russian peasantry, who had for so long been the largest single group in the Russian population. These works are not simply *pro-village*, they are also *anti-city*. In canonical Village Prose the city was far away, it was exciting and even forbidding for villagers, but it was not irredeemably evil, as it becomes in the 1980s. In *The Best Is Yet to Come* and other similar works, the city is a place of pernicious foreign trends, thoroughly "cosmopolitan" (a code word used to indicate what is thought to be under Jewish and foreign influence). Each work has at least one Matryona-like righteous person (*pravednik*). The Avvakum-Dostoevsky-Solzhenitsyn rhetorical line is revived in this literature. The luminous quality (*svetlost'*) of the elegy is gone, and all that is left is a destroyed past, a dark present, and a future that is discussed in apocalyptic tones.

Several rural writers were engaged in the second half of the eighties in finishing up long-term projects. Mozhaev and Belov published further volumes of, respectively, *Peasant Men and Women* and *The Eve*, the rural epics they had begun in the seventies. Both writers made certain changes in their narrative approach: while taking advantage of relaxed censorship, using newly accessible archival material, and relying less on their own or their families' stories, they—paradoxically— also began to express markedly chauvinistic feelings. The historical novel, whether distorted by prejudice or not, does not really belong to canonical Village Prose, but it is certainly linked to that movement in the minds of readers and critics by virtue of its setting and its authors. While one would naturally have expected a fuller account of collectivization in glasnost literature, in this kind of "post–Village Prose" work there is a collectivization of the Russian countryside without Russians—or Stalin—playing much of a role. This is a rereading not so much of literary history as of history itself. That Belov at least is going to pursue the story of collectivization—as he sees it—was clear from the November 1989 issue of *Nash sovremennik*, where under the title "The Open Wound," he introduced the reader to the kinds of letters he has received from readers telling him what they or their families experienced in this difficult period.[24] This is reminiscent of the gulag archive that Solzhenitsyn began to amass after the publication of *One Day in the Life of Ivan Denisovich*; there might, then, be long nonfictional volumes on this subject from Belov in the future. In this as in other ways, the Solzhenitsyn influence is beginning to make itself strongly felt.

Viktor Astafiev also published further installments of his massive rural memoir *The Final Bow*, including three chapters in the March 1988 issue of *Nash sovremennik*; these very interesting and well-written works did not follow the new Belov and Mozhaev line. Astafiev's apocalyptic and angry trio of stories in the same journal in May 1986 *were* controversial, especially the ill-tempered "Fishing for Gudgeon in Georgia," which, along with "The Sad Detective," triggered serious— and legitimate—criticism of the author, who fired off a venomous reply.

The literature that evolved from Village Prose was in general less lyrical and more publicistic than Village Prose had been, to such an extent that one critic asked whether the *derevenshchiki*—the very writers who had helped to cure Russian literature of an overdose of politics—had simply done so in order to make room for their own ideological agenda.[25] Leading rural writers began to speak directly to the public and to devote a greater percentage of their time to publicistic activities. Some of their essays were concerned with the environment, others were primarily ethnographic in character (Rasputin about Siberia, Belov and Lichutin about northern Russia), but often in their anger and anxiety for the state of the nation, they spoke as conservative ideologues. Readers of *Nash sovremennik* and *Literaturnaia Rossiia* have been regularly treated to the ideas and theories of Rasputin, Belov, Astafiev, Lichutin, and others. These statements range from deeply flawed, offensive, and potentially dangerous rereadings of the role of Jews in Russian history to cranky diatribes on mass culture— especially rock music—and eccentric digressions by Lichutin on the Russian pagan deities.

A final development in the 1980s involving the *derevenshchiki* is the publication of "delayed" works of Village Prose that were written in the 1960s, but kept in the drawer until recent years. The most interesting of these works to appear by the end of the decade were Soloukhin's "Stepanida Ivanovna's Funeral," the Tendriakov stories discussed above, and Abramov's "A Journey into the Past." These are wonderfully written, rich accounts of rural life, which greatly increase our estimation of these writers, and, by extension, of the possibilities of Village Prose. It gives the lie to the widely held assumption that the rural writers were free to publish everything they were capable of writing. More will certainly emerge from the drawers of rural writers: the Abramov archive may be especially large.[26] In Soloukhin's autobiographical *Laughter over the Left Shoulder*, another "delayed" work, the author basically rewrites his personal history, berating himself for what he sees as the lies and compromises of such works as *A Drop of Dew* (1960). Soloukhin has at least one other large work from the past to publish, something he calls "Posledniaia stupen'" (The final stage). He also wants to reissue his earlier works in their uncut form.[27]

Filling in some of the blank spots in the Soviet Russian literary picture are stories previously known only in samizdat and tamizdat, and also literature of whose existence nothing was known. Some works that reached the West in the three decades from the mid-1950s to the mid-1980s seemed like anomalies, relevant only to literature of the twenties, or further back, to Gogol and other nineteenth-century writers. But it is becoming increasingly clear that Voinovich, Sinyavsky, and other writers were not alone in their ability to express the absurdity of life under Stalin. It is also clear that there were more than just two ways—canonical Socialist Realism and canonical Village Prose—of depicting life in the countryside.[28] The Tendriakov stories published in 1988 draw a great deal from the child-as-eyewitness approach of Village Prose, but they are enriched by irony and artistic sophistication, and even by an orientation toward modernism.[29] Unlike the "post–Village Prose" chronicles of collectivization, these stories have no veneer of righteousness, and the writer is not driven to lay blame anywhere; readers are allowed to draw their own conclusions about the events described. Evaluations—both aesthetic and ideological—of the canon of Village Prose will be enriched and balanced by these long-delayed works.

The Legacy of Russian Village Prose

The initial literary-critical message of the glasnost years was *unity*; as the various threads (Soviet, émigré, samizdat, and literature "for the drawer") came together, critics began to take a longer view of the course of Russian literature in the Soviet period. At first, Village Prose benefited from this process, and the important role this movement played was openly acknowledged. Iurii Davydov wrote that wherever the "moral-philosophical 'nucleus'" of Russian literature resided in the decades after the Revolution, it definitely returned to Russia in the 1960s through the works of Soviet Russian Village Prose writers.[30] Nikolai Anastasiev called the *derevenshchiki* the "direct and legitimate heirs to the Russian classical tradition"; he reminded readers that these rural writers had bypassed the now openly derided Socialist Realist tradition and had looked to pre-Revolutionary literature for their inspiration.[31]

Neither the newly achieved unity of Russian literature nor the grateful acknowledgment of the positive role of Village Prose lasted for very long. By the end of the 1980s, the literary-critical communities of Moscow, Leningrad, and other cities were in turmoil, torn by major disputes and seemingly unbreachable chasms. Local branches of the Writers' Union divided, meetings of splinter groups were interrupted by hooligans, bitter fights for control of key journals erupted, new journals and newspapers were founded to voice the views of those who felt themselves to be disenfranchised, and in general it was literary "war." The Leningrad correspondent for the émigré paper *Russkaia mysl'* said that following the literary situation in that city was somewhat like observing a dying psychopath trying to compose a last will and testament.[32]

The image of a deathbed struggle captured the sense of a need for closure at the beginning of the 1990s; one phase of Russian literary history had to palpably come to an end before the next phase could begin. Viktor Erofeev sought to satisfy this need in his provocative article "Pominki po sovetskoi literature" ("A Funeral Feast for Soviet Literature").[33] But declaring the "death" of Soviet literature was not a simple task; there first had to be a working definition of *sovetskaia literatura*, especially for the postwar period. These definitions often took the form of polemical typologies—a number of them quite eccentric—in Erofeev's article and the many responses it provoked on the pages of *Literaturnaia gazeta* and other periodicals. Erofeev came up with three kinds of Soviet literature: official (or officious, *ofitsioznaia*) literature, Village Prose, and liberal literature. The first was beyond the pale, the second was gradually drawn into the orbit of official literature by the reward system for useful writers and later further degraded itself through its creators' post-1985 tirades, and the third type, liberal literature, with its Aesopian—but not particularly interesting—style, aged rapidly after the onset of glasnost. Other critics offered different typologies of works from the past and metaphors for the contemporary literary process and found different places for Village Prose within the post-Stalinist canon.

It is not surprising that in this literary struggle, in which ideology counts for much more than aesthetics—even among those critics who lobby for a more artistic prose—the legacy of Village Prose would be problematic. The main arguments that are used against Village Prose are that (1) it was the seedbed of Russian chauvinism, and that (2) by default, virtually everything published during the years of "stagnation" fails to tell the whole truth or is even dishonest; in aesthetic terms, all published literature is a form of Socialist Realism.

It is one of the ironies of Soviet literary development that during the "stagnation years" village prose was respected for its truth and honesty, whereas in the late 1980s, Rasputin, Belov, and Astaf'ev are regarded as conservatives harking back to patriarchal values and traditions. . . . the fact that they can be classed as conservatives . . . is doubly ironic in that their best works twenty years ago were in the best democratic traditions of Russian literature, deploring the plight of the common man and the hardships imposed on him by an uncaring government.[34]

The rise of Russian chauvinism in the latter part of the 1980s sent shock waves around more than just the Soviet Union. As I have explained at some length in this book, to identify Village Prose as the primary cause of this phenomenon is to ignore the facts at hand. That several erstwhile *derevenshchiki* have joined this activity does not make them its chief architects. Russian anti-Semitism has a long history; in the case of the outbreak of the 1980s, the immediate intellectual roots are more logically traced to the work of such urban figures as the mathematician Igor Shafarevich (who had an active role in samizdat in the 1970s, before he was able to publish his theory of "Russophobia" in the Soviet press) and a host of critics who transformed the metaphors of Village Prose into a conservative and nationalistic ideology on the pages of *Molodaia gvardiia*, *Nash sovremennik*, and *Literaturnaia Rossiia*.[35] An objective—and thorough—examination of the materials available makes it quite clear that the simplistic view of rural writers as the leading "Nazis" of a "Weimar" Russia does not hold. It is no more useful to look for a single scapegoat for Russian chauvinism than it is to look for a single scapegoat for the disastrous state of the Soviet economy. To put Village Prose in this position leads to the kind of thinking whereby Alexander Ostrovsky would be condemned because Dobroliubov saw a revolutionary message in Ostrovsky's play *The Storm*, and a revolution did in fact eventually take place. This is not careful analysis, but a reaction to ominous events.[36] It has to be said, though, that had Belov, Rasputin, and Astafiev *not* chosen to become involved in these kinds of activities, few people would have made this mistaken connection of cause and effect. One sometimes feels the need to defend the legacy of Village Prose from those who used to write it.

The other criticism of Village Prose—that the very fact of its publication in the USSR casts suspicion on its sincerity and honesty and brands the writers as craven opportunists—is a harder one to counteract. It poses, first of all, an unanswerable moral dilemma: is the best decision in times of oppression and censorship to emigrate (either physically or spiritually), to cultivate the "genre of silence" as Isaac Babel suggested in 1934, to risk prison for what you have said or what you have failed to say? Or should one publish the best possible works that can get past the censor, help keep literary traditions alive, and give the public something of value to read? Village Prose writers did not emigrate—the very move from the *malaia rodina* to the city was experienced as a kind of "emigration"—they did not go to prison, and with rare exception they did not speak out in defense of writers in trouble, not even to help Alexander Solzhenitsyn.[37] Even the most positive view of Village Prose cannot give them virtues that they do not possess. However, it is also clear that they were not the pampered darlings of the regime who could publish anything they wished with impunity. Beginning with Pomerantsev's essay on sincerity in literature, there are a number of cases in which rural writers, their critics, and the editors of the journals in which they appeared were chastised publicly and privately for works about rural life that were too critical for the time, or which presented too much of a challenge to canonical Socialist Realism. The publication of the first of the "delayed" works of Village Prose makes it clear that rural writers did not have a free hand in literature. They did indirectly benefit from the travails of other writers to the extent that once so many urban writers either were imprisoned or exiled, or had emigrated, and could no longer be read in gosizdat, the only large body of well-written literature available was Village Prose; it was good, popular with the reading public, and it conveniently filled a vacuum. Alexander Zholkovsky has expressed concern that the revision of the post-Revolutionary canon could cause published authors like Ilf and Petrov to lose "some of their luster in the wake of the rediscovery of Mikhail Bulgakov and Andrei Platonov, or, for that matter, the Russian Vladimir Nabokov."[38] This is a problem that affects the reputations of many writers who bear the "stigma" of having been published between 1925 and 1985, especially the large number of Village Prose writers.

As literature and criticism experience the throes of glasnost and perestroika—with a brief period of unification followed by a new disunity—the crucial role played by Village Prose in the post-Stalinist revival of literature may be temporarily lost from sight, and Village Prose may wind up being conflated with its antithesis, Socialist Realist Kolkhoz Literature. Along with the issue of the Village Prose writers' having been published rather than punished, and the problem posed by efforts to locate the sources of Russian chauvinism, there is the additional factor that works have appeared since 1985 that are more daring stylistically (e.g., Sokolov, the Erofeevs) and more far-reaching politically (e.g., Voinovich, Solzhenitsyn, Rybakov, Grossman) than virtually anything in Village Prose.

Vladimir Soloukhin has initiated criticism from *within* the ranks of the Village Prose movement itself. It began with the publication of *Laughter over the Left Shoulder*; not content with self-criticism, Soloukhin then sought to dismantle the accepted history of Village Prose, in which Ovechkin's "District Routine" and Pomerantsev's essay "On Sincerity in Literature" have stood as the "primary chronicles" of the new rural writing. In the February 1990 issue of *Moskva*, Soloukhin spoke of the Ovechkin-style *ocherk* as having been *not useful, but harmful* literature because its writers still accepted collectivization and were simply trying to expose the inefficient way collective farms were run. "On the one hand, these writers did some good in revealing the sorry state of our agriculture, but, on the other hand, they were looking for simple ways to improve our fundamentally flawed system of collectivization. So objectively speaking their literature is not useful, but harmful."[39] Soloukhin sees Fedor Abramov as a much more truthful—and therefore useful—writer. This is a major restatement of the development of rural literature in the post-Stalinist period.

The attempt to devalue Ovechkin in favor of Abramov is all the more ironic since, during the very same commemoration of Abramov on the occasion of what would have been his seventieth birthday (he died in 1983), the critic Igor Zolotussky wrote that the writer's diaries evidence Abramov's own feeling that his work had not been sufficiently truthful and that he was trying very hard to write only the truth, and to "teach" himself to be free.[40] For instance, we now know that in 1963, the year that Abramov published "Round and About" with its harsh criticism of kolkhoz management, he began the more artistically effective "Journey into the Past," which savaged the entire Soviet experience and was not to be published until 1989.[41]

With Russian chauvinists dividing "ethnically Russian" (*rossiiskii*) literature from that which is merely "Russian-language" (*russkoiazychnyi*), and other Soviet and émigré critics and writers castigating anyone who dared to publish before the Gorbachev era or who joined the Party in the Thaw years, the canon is more likely to undergo further fragmentation than to be unified. In this chaotic situation, there have been a few voices of reason who have tried to bring some perspective to the discussion. Galina Belaia warned of the harm done when past literary history is forgotten in the light of new developments.[42] Nikolai Anastasiev said that while he opposes the politics of Belov, Rasputin, and Astafiev, that does not cancel out in his mind their major contribution to Russian literature.[43] S. Frederick Starr has described canonical Village Prose as highly critical writing, which "encouraged public dialogue on reform" because it revealed the "poverty, aimlessness, and spiritual alienation in large parts of the population."[44] The most perceptive analysis, perhaps, was offered by émigré poet Naum Korzhavin, in answer to a questionnaire from the journal *Inostrannaia literatura*. Korzhavin wrote that Village Prose and all it has meant to Russian literature has been "unjustly forgotten" because the flowering of this movement coincided with the "period of stagnation." He went on to say, "No matter what factors allowed it to exist, no matter what strange statements some of its representatives have recently made . . . this is not stagnant, but genuine literature, which did much in that difficult period . . . to restore historical truth and develop social consciousness."[45]

We are accustomed to following the evolution of literary styles, themes, and genres, but are apt to forget that "codes of reading" change as well. The Village Prose that seemed an important and valuable development and a hopeful sign for literature and society from the 1950s through the 1970s may be read differently now by those who place the greatest value on bold political statement or on literary modernism. It may also be misappropriated by those who are looking for a nationalistic literature to buttress their ideology. However, in any thoughtful reading of the post-Stalinist period, Village Prose will continue to play a central role for having greatly contributed to loosening the grip of Socialist Realism and to returning Russian literature to its roots, and for having restored some of the dignity and value of Russian peasants, their traditions, and their folklore that had been lost in the first half of the Soviet period. Informed by both utopian and apocalyptic modes—and by memories of a rural childhood—*derevenskaia proza* stands as an accurate and artistically convincing reflection of life in the Russian countryside in the twentieth century. Whether such erstwhile *derevenshchiki* as Rasputin, Belov, and Astafiev ever return to the lyrical fiction that made them famous or whether they continue to exercise their—at times—pernicious influence as public figures, such past achievements as *Farewell to Matyora*, *Harmony*, and *The Final Bow* have permanently enriched Russian literature. These and many other Village Prose writers waged a battle against the Socialist Realist narrative of rural life, and they won that battle, one village at a time.

APPENDIX I

KONDYR

Aleksei Leonov

(Asterisked words and phrases are explained in the Annotations that follow the story.)

"Grandpa! We're moving tomorrow. The director loaned us a car."

When he heard his daughter-in-law's cheerful voice, Kondyr* called her a slut under his breath.

"She's jumping for joy," he muttered. "She hasn't got a brick to her name, and already she's running the new house."

His daughter-in-law rushed past the root cellar while calling out to someone down the road. It was always about the same old thing, the move. Kondyr began to straighten out the quilted jacket that he used as a pillow. He was uncomfortable and he began to curse his daughter-in-law.

August was really hot that year. It hadn't rained for a long time and everything had gotten overheated, dried out and brittle. Things were so flammable that if you were to strike a match, the flame would take a running start. The heat wore you out and took all your strength. Since noon the cattle had been lazily drifting away from their shed. The chickens flapped their wings a bit and then fell into a stupor. In the hilly pastures and on the roads the ground was cracked, and you had to lower the bucket deeper in the wells to reach water.

Kondyr was in his ninetieth year. He had outlived all his friends, everyone his age and even many who were younger. He was the oldest person around, but he really didn't feel all that old. He could still have shown his son and daughter-in-law how to stack up the rye in the field and how to thresh it properly if it weren't for all those machines, which, to his way of thinking, had spoiled both the people and the land.

In the root cellar, Kondyr could escape from the heat, lying on a pile of freshly cut straw that he had brought in from the rye-field. He threshed it a bit to get the grain out and then threw his quilted jacket on top of the pile. He was content to spend his days dozing. Time had slowed down, but that gave him the solitude that old people need in order to recall their lives and to put them in some kind of order that is good for the soul.

His long life passed before him, and now, just when Kondyr was taking in the sun's warmth and the coolness of the air and water for perhaps the last time, the day had come for him to see his roots torn away from Mother Earth. Their possessions would be loaded in the car and taken away, and the walls of their house would be broken up into bricks and dragged off to build a poultry-yard or pig-barn for the sovkhoz*. He had often felt pain for other people's houses, and for the thoughtlessness of people who moved to other villages or even to far-off places. Now it was his turn to experience this intense pain, which was so much like death.

"He loaned us a car," Kondyr mimicked his daughter-in-law. "The dee-rector will give you anything that will get you closer to him, you fool, and you think that you're going to build a nest by his side . . . Once you hatch a little chick, you won't be able to fill its belly just with cherries from the orchard."

Kondyr was transported back in time, and, one by one, his children passed before his eyes. He remembered that when the cherries were ripening they would walk around with mouths stained from the juice. An icon painter could have used them as models for angels. In raspberry season there would be a bowlful with milk for dinner and they'd all dig in with their wooden spoons. The berries grew all over the place. Some of their apples were dried and frozen, while others were kept fresh in a sandy part of the root cellar until Trinity Sunday. Now they've dreamed up this jam to spoil the children—once you've given them bread and jam during berry season they won't even look at the fresh fruit.

"Where are we moving to? She ought to come to her senses—that village is called Govorenki* for a reason—the only thing they're good at is talk . . . They've always been known as liars."

They were to move to Govorenki, which Kondyr hated with his whole being. The village had been built in Kondyr's lifetime on a stony hill above a small river. The houses were too close together as if there wasn't enough land, and, with only two northern windows looking out on the river, the sun never shone into them. People in Govorenki lived thoughtlessly and carelessly. It had always been the custom there for the men to be drinkers and brawlers. They would roll barrels, wheels, and even carts down into the river when they were drunk. The women didn't weave their own cloth but they did love to make clever conversation.

"In Govorenki we have pike that are five feet long! You throw a bucket of bleach into the water and a sackful of fish will float to the top!"*

You couldn't grow much grain on Govorenki land and the local people scoured the countryside looking for anyone who was willing to trade grain or potatoes for livestock. They lived from hand to mouth but they didn't lose their swaggering ways: they wore short sheepskin jackets, strange hats with no earflaps, and they were all light on their feet. If a man ran across a field waving a stick, everybody could see from afar that he was from Govorenki. "That liar's gone to pester people with his tall tales."

"So, go live with them since your own life is over," Kondyr muttered to himself as he fumbled with his quilted coat.

Kondyr sat down. The greenish daylight penetrated the cracks in the door and, hitting his eyes, blinded him in the darkness of the cellar. Kondyr took his walking stick from its customary place and stood up decisively. Bending down low to push the cellar door aside, he climbed out onto the road. All around him he saw lifeless peasant houses with smashed-in windows, doors left open, and chimneys that had gone cold. Keeping out of sight, he set off for his own place, which was condemned to the very same fate, but which still had life and warmth.

He sat down on the bench nearest the door. This corner of the table was his special place as head of the household and no one else dared to sit there. When he ran his hand along the edge of the table, he could feel a notch from where his grandfather used to cut homegrown tobacco. The knife's traces had worn down and the hole had turned black from tobacco and from the table's being washed. Next to it his father had cut tobacco. This place was fresher: it wasn't as dark and you could still see the cross-marks from the sharp edge of the blade. Up until quite recently Kondyr had also used his own tobacco. He stopped smoking about five years ago to help his breathing. No one else touched the table: his son smoked store-bought cigarettes. The corner of the table was rounded off from the preparation of bark for weaving bast shoes. Now that there were new, brightly varnished folding tables, black oak wouldn't do, and when the old tables turned dark they'd be thrown out.

"'Turn dark'—you birdbrain!"—Kondyr began once again to scold his daughter-in-law. "The tractor-driver stuck his dirty hand down your blouse and didn't darken it—but the table will turn dark!"

A week ago when they were harvesting the grain, Kondyr set out for the fields to get some newly mown rye for his bed. He went up to the idle combine to talk to the driver—and there he saw his daughter-in-law. The combine operator, with a grotesque smile on his face, was poking under her blouse. He would pour grain through his fingers and then check to see if it was still on her breasts. When she saw her father-in-law, she tore herself away and threatened the driver with her hand, but prior to that she had just lazily pushed him aside. Recalling that now, Kondyr was offended for his son's sake. The son had divorced his first wife after several childless years and had brought a much younger woman into the household. The fact that she was from Govorenki made Kondyr even angrier.

"The dee-rector loaned us a car! She talked her husband into building there. She wiggled her hips and lured him over to those gossips. Those people never did know how to behave . . . Our peasants would run two miles to their own fields when they had to go. But these loudmouths would leave a turd in their neighbor's furrow as a joke."

Kondyr rose from the bench and looked into the stove. He was struck by the smell of warm, meaty broth and his stomach growled. But he didn't want to have lunch because then they would come back and say that he hadn't waited for them but had dug in first. He closed the stove door and thought: "She didn't peel any potatoes. There's nothing to take along with me. Alyona would have left a whole panful for the day." Going up to the side of the stove, he ran his hand along the dark bricks that had been worn smooth by children's backsides and sighed. "They built a new-style house in Govorenki without a big stove. There's just something with open burners."

"Just you wait. When the flames shoot up and start a fire—you'll remember this dear old stove."*

Kondyr looked around and awkwardly crossed himself in the direction of the icon-corner, where a poster of cosmonauts hung in the icon's place. He took a piece of bread from the box on the table and went outside.

Everything was limp from the sun: burdocks and nettles were drooping and the trees gave off a stuffy heat. Kondyr went through the orchard towards the woods. The apple trees hadn't been cultivated for a long time—every year they said that the apples would be thrown out anyway—and as a result the trunks were overgrown with vines and nettles, the leaves looked like spiderwebs and the fruit was small. Kondyr couldn't take up a spade himself because in the fall and in the spring, when it was time to cultivate the trees he was often ailing, and by the summertime the dried-up earth was a mass of grass roots. And so the orchard fell into a state of neglect.

The woods began just on the other side of the vegetable gardens. A hawk circled high above, carefully surveying the edge of the forest. All the green foliage Kondyr had seen during his long lifetime had kept his eyes young, and he could still see everything on the ground and in the sky. Because his vision was so sharp, his soul hadn't aged, it was still eager about everything—and if it weren't for the constraints imposed by his weary body, he could still have kept a hold on things. He wouldn't have allowed them to act this way towards the house, the orchard, and the earth that had sustained him through his whole life.

The leaves of the potato plants had dried up before they were supposed to—they should all have stayed green and kept growing. They weren't allowed to mow their neighbors' abandoned gardens and so thorny weeds had taken over. The stalks of goosefoot got woody, and the seed pods would burst open, spilling out their seeds.

"They've abandoned the land!" Kondyr shook his head. "The deerector found the people here superfluous, so then there were no people and the land was abandoned."

The path through the woods was overgrown with grass. The branches of the hazelnut trees touched the ground and got tangled up with the grass, making it hard to walk. In the past Kondyr himself had cut back the branches and mowed the grass. The path was always bright and safe and he could get firewood and cattle feed without any loss to the forest. It was wonderful to walk along such a path: in the summer the nuts ripened on the bushes along the side—and you just had to stretch out your hand, pull one off, and crack it. In the winter, after the first snow, when hare tracks crisscrossed the path, his heart was filled with a rare kind of joy. In all this there was a feeling of boundless life; everything seen by itself and everything taken as a whole was there for human beings to enjoy. The old women used to gather fallen branches in the woods during the summer, but now people were cutting down whole living trees.

"People have changed," thought Kondyr, "they're wild and good-for-nothing. It used to be that when there was bad weather, and heavy rain washed away the boundary-markers, it was like a wound that you wanted to heal as quickly as possible. But now the gullies are turning into ravines and it's as if no one sees them. Life has gotten worse and things aren't done according to custom anymore—people are moving to other regions and to the city . . . "

The sun struck his eyes and the drought-green sky opened up before him. Kondyr emerged into a clearing near the forest pond and suddenly felt agitated. It was the way you feel when you hear a fairy tale with a happy ending: it's frightening and you really experience it and then there is a sense of joy because everything's worked out okay and you can relax.

The pond in the forest had been dug before there was a kolkhoz. A village pond had been planned before the revolution—the local barynia* had hired laborers from Troitsa and had even given them an advance, but the whole business fell through. Then the village assembly discussed it on a number of occasions and tried to collect money from each household, but it was argued that some people ought to contribute more and others less, which led to disagreements, and so the pond filled up with silt.

It was late at night in Govorenki. Kondyr went out of the brightly lit house onto the street. From the pig-barns by the river came the yelping of exhausted pigs, and through the curtained windows you could hear the sound of men's voices and women's shrill laughter. Songs were being played and the stamping of feet signaled that they had begun to dance.

"They're whirling around. What fun! They organized a house-warming. If only there were one elderberry bush growing under the windows but the only thing here is wormwood."

There were all sorts of vehicles in front of the house: a motorcycle that his son rode all over the countryside to arrange work for tractor-drivers and chauffeurs, and the director's jeep which had been parked by some logs left over from the construction. The bright moon was reflected in the window of a truck, and a tractor was parked on a pile of white woodchips.

"You can't go visiting on foot anymore but you have to make lots of noise when you arrive."

Kondyr walked onto the road and looking up at the moon that shone high above Govorenki, he crossed himself.

"I won't let them tear down the house. I'll stand at the threshold with a pitchfork. I have no business being here and I should never have agreed to move in the first place."

Kondyr walked for a long time on the road that led through the fields away from Govorenki. He sat down from time to time on straw scattered about by the combine, and thought about the remarks— most of which he hadn't agreed with—that he had heard during the long evening.

"Now I've returned to my homeland," rejoiced his daughter-in-law. "Thanks to you, Mikhail Ivanych, I've escaped from that hole."

"We will bring everyone together!" said the director. "It will be much more convenient for everyone to work in the same place."

His son had agreed. "This place will really be hopping now! We'll show what we can do!"

By the time Kondyr reached the pond it was almost sunrise. The birds were up and were feeding and calling to each other in the bushes. The water on the far side of the pond was rosy from the approaching dawn. Kondyr recalled his distant youth and it seemed possible to him to bring back that time, to enter into it and relive it. He dipped his hands in the water and splashed his face. "Another hot, dry day. I'll run over to the Dubrava* woods to stay cool—this may be my last chance to go there." Kondyr shook his stick threateningly in the direction of Govorenki . . .

The forest road went toward Bolshie Vyselki* where the mill had once stood. Country roads from Grinev, Popovka, and Bobrik met just beyond the pond where the forest path began. This used to be a lively thoroughfare—grain was carted along it to the mill at Bolshie Vyselki. The mill was gone, having burned down during the war. Grinev and Popovka didn't exist anymore, and a new mill had been built in Bobrik, so the forest road had fallen into disuse. Roots had twisted themselves into rings along the cart-tracks, and the aspens shot up and stretched out at full length. The middle and sides of the path were hidden by grass. In those places where the soil had washed away, there was a weblike network of tiny roots, and the hazelnut branches had grown out thickly over the sunlit path.

There were some trees near the pond, and an ancient, serenely quiet forest called Dubrava on the other side of the ravine, where long ago, when the trees still rustled youthfully, Kondyr and his friends had mowed grass in the meadows. Remembering this, Kondyr headed in the direction of Dubrava and the meadows, to see, probably for the last time, places that were very dear to him.

He and his father had been cutting hay in the Dubrava woods; on the next meadow, Savel from Grinevo, a man with lots of daughters, was mowing. One day Kondyr's father sent him out alone to turn the hay. He was annoyed because he didn't want to work all by himself. They had cut a lot of hay and he was feeling a little lazy. With his first stroke Kondyr broke the rake. Out of spite he threw the piece that had broken off into the woods. A girl's voice cried out from the bushes.

"Hey, you! Stop throwing things!"

Kondyr was startled; he hadn't thought that there was anyone nearby. One of Savel's daughters walked out onto the meadow. He didn't know which one she was. They all had the same proud faces and were very pretty.

"So, you broke your rake," she said as she approached him.

"Yeah, I broke it," Kondyr replied.

"Clumsy oaf."

Kondyr shrugged his shoulders, not knowing how to respond. He noticed that the ends of her apron were tucked up by her sash and he asked: "Have you been gathering mushrooms?"

"Toadstools" she said, winking. "Do you want to try one?"

Although Kondyr hadn't said yes, she was already cleaning off a mushroom. She cut off the cap and after she had taken a bite, she gave it to him.

"It's sweet, isn't it?"

"Give me another one," demanded Kondyr.

"That's enough. Go turn the hay."

"There's nothing to turn it with."

"I'll bring you a rake. We have some hidden nearby."

As she was walking away Kondyr looked at her as if she were some sort of miraculous being. She had already disappeared behind the trees and yet he could still see her. She alone existed. The road home was cut off—if only they could stay together in the forest forever, just as they were now.

Her name was Alyona and she was the fourth daughter. Two of her sisters were already married, another wedding was set for the fall, and now her turn had come. After turning the hay together, they set off for Grinevo. They talked about trifles—about their parents, about the livestock—but all the while they were thinking about each other, and secretly admiring each other. They parted just outside Grinevo. Kondyr hid behind a hazelnut tree at the edge of the woods and watched Alyona until she disappeared into the house.

They were married at Shrovetide. Together they mowed and turned the hay, and took it to be threshed. They worked for both family farms and Kondyr was considered a model son-in-law, always to be seated in the place of honor next to his wife's father.

The forest clearings had long ago been turned over to the jurisdiction of the forester and no one went by them anymore. The hay was given to strangers and taken by horse and cart to the district center. And only rarely did one chance to pass by this spot and remember the past.

The ravine was as bare and gloomy as ever. The roots of oak trees hung down into it like braids of twisted straw on a thatched roof. The road near the ravine went down and across the forest meadow and then rose again in the direction of Dubrava. Kondyr managed this difficult path but it really tired him out. He stopped to catch his breath, and looked all around him. There were bushes everywhere: hazelnuts, buckthorn, honeysuckle, and bird cherry, and islands of pale ferns that were useful for stomach problems but not to feed cattle. Aspens, oaks, and birches soared above him. The Dubrava road was very old—there were ruts a foot deep from horses, people, and carts. In some places the road was clayey, while in other places it was so ash-gray that even grass wouldn't grow.

Kondyr quietly wandered along the abandoned path. He came across some edible mushrooms on the road. He picked one up and a milky white liquid flowed from its roots and crumpled gills. "What a treasure! And there's no one to gather them." He remembered his daughter-in-law who had brought home a jar of mushroom soup from the store and thought it was pretty good. "It was so thin you could pour it into your shirt! You won't even find a mushroom there—just a sour taste."

Kondyr put the mushroom by the side of the road. Alyona was always one for grabbing a basket and heading for the woods. Before you had time to turn around she'd have already run home with the mushrooms and be frying them in sour cream. They weren't just mushrooms—they were a real feast.

Kondyr's strength was coming back to him. He raised his shoulders slightly, adjusted his cap, and went into the clearing, as if Alyona were waiting for him there. He walked a little crookedly, with his chest forward and his heavy head proudly thrown backward. He looked at the trees yellow from sunlight and at a perfectly clear blue sky. He was transformed—there was no old age, it had been swept away by the memories of the past and his vision of Alyona, and by the quiet of the Dubrava woods, where something of the former life was preserved.

But Kondyr's strength didn't last for long; his step slowed and there was a stabbing pain in his chest that took his breath away. His legs and lower back began to hurt him. A new path cut across the old road; tractors and cars had carved it straight through the bushes, which were crushed and torn and covered with motor oil. The tree trunks were splintered and their reddened bark was torn off in places. Wisps of hay hung from the lower branches.

He guessed that the new path led to the clearing and he decided that there was no reason for him to go there. If he were to go anywhere it would be to Alyona's grave, if they hadn't already plowed it under for the summer. But Kondyr didn't immediately turn in that direction; leaning on his walking stick, he continued to make his way to the clearing. All he could think about was that he was tired and wanted to sit down and catch his breath.

He stopped in a place where the sun was shining on the road because he had gotten chilled in the shade of the forest. Touching the ground with his crooked fingers, he sat down. The grass and the earth were warm. He trampled down the grass with all its new shoots and lay down; he was so tired that he fell asleep immediately . . .

The sun was moving over the trees to the side but still it warmed him. Flies rose from the earth on invisible wings, and tiny spiders descended to the earth from branches. The aspens awoke and then quieted down once again, and birds squawked in the distance.

Kondyr closed his eyes; he could hear how the voices of the birds changed as they flew further away. The sun darkened and began to disappear, and his anxiety had melted away when suddenly the sound of a voice that he never expected to hear made Kondyr leap to his feet.

"Hey! Why are you sleeping?"

Kondyr quickly looked around. There was no one near him, but still he heard that familiar, youthful voice from the past. "Alyona, let me see you. You haven't appeared in my dreams for years."

A cloud passed over the forest. The sun came out again and once more Kondyr fell asleep. Then he opened his eyes and felt anxious, sensing the trembling of the aspens nearby. An oriole cried out. The tree tops suddenly began to sway, not from side to side but bending downward and then rising toward the sky. He was having difficulty breathing. But then everything passed away—and Alyona appeared. She had brought him a fresh mushroom. He wanted to knock it out of her hand because he knew it was poisonous, but an unseen power held him back. Alyona raised the mushroom to her lips and was scorched by the bitter poison. He tried to cry out, to call for help (after all, he did still have a son), but everything got very noisy and no one heard him. And then he began to dream of a riotous holiday celebration.

In a large, familiar, peasant house the tables were piled high with food: roast lamb, pieces of goose meat in large bowls, bottles of home brew, steaming cabbage-soup, and kasha.* There were girls and women dressed up in coins and gold lace, and men and boys in red shirts with silken sashes. The girls and women had glistening lips and a diabolical power drew everyone to them.

A balalaika started playing and people began to whisper about something. Kondyr was pushed into the circle, towards Alyona. She moved away from him around the circle and a young fellow came up to her. He was stocky and bold and wore a very odd outfit—a large, bright peaked cap covered with red and white dots.

Kondyr was flushed with anger and went to cut off the newly arrived dancer and get him away from Alyona. Kondyr did one dance step after another, but the stranger, having won the contest, was walking away while people applauded him and laughed at Kondyr.

Everyone had left the table. It had grown dark in the house and the people outside looked at the dancing through the windows. The balalaikas went wild with dance tunes. Alyona whirled around so fast that you couldn't make out her face. The unknown dancer winked at her and laughed in Kondyr's face. When he had done every possible dance step, he began to carry Alyona away with him. People shouted: "Vaska, Kondyr, don't disgrace yourself!"

He stumbled and something tore at his chest. He felt dizzy, almost intoxicated, but he still had a little strength left. He caught up with them, pushed them back into the circle, and then, dancing on the tips of his boots, he did steps no one had ever done before. He even managed to knock the stranger's flashing-red, poison-mushroom cap from his head and crush it.

Suddenly the people and the sounds all disappeared. Kondyr was victorious, but something had picked him up like a leaf in the wind, and was carrying him off somewhere . . .

Annotations

"Kondyr" first appeared in *Khodiat devki* (Country girls stroll about) (Moscow: Sovetskaia Rossiia, 1971), a collection of Leonov's stories, and was reprinted in *Ptitsy pereletnye* (Birds of passage) (Leningrad: Sovetskii pisatel', 1983). I would like to thank Natalia Nikolaevna Leonova, who answered many of the questions that arose while I was translating this story.

Kondyr—"Kondyr'"is a nickname that assumes the place of a given name; we know from Kondyr's final dream that his real name is Vasilii (Vas'ka is a pejorative diminutive). Dal's dictionary defines *kondyr'* as a stiff collar or cuff or the peak of a cap. In the Orel region, the setting for Leonov's stories, it can be used to describe a stubborn, unyielding person. The name also suggests *kondovyi*, an adjective that refers literally to solid, close-grained wood, and figuratively to old Russia (*kondovaia Rus'*) and to old-fashioned people and places (*kondovye liudi, kondovyi krai*).

sovkhoz—a state farm, which was run differently from a *kolkhoz* 'collective farm'.

Govorenki—probably the pejorative nickname for the neighboring village. *Govorit'* is a verb meaning 'to speak, talk' so the nickname refers to the villagers' reputation as compulsive gossips, glib talkers, and outright liars.

bleach . . . top—Poachers violating fishing regulations would throw bleach into the water; the fish would die, float to the surface, and thus be easily collected.

matushka-pechka—'little-mother-stove'. Kondyr uses an affectionate diminutive that to some extent personifies the stove.

barynia—a female member of the landowning gentry.

Dubrava—*dub* is 'oak'; *dubrava* can be a leafy grove or a small oak wood. In this story it is a specific ancient forest with aspens and birches as well as oak trees.

Bolshie Vyselki—literally 'Big Settlement(s)'; here it is used as a proper name.

kasha—'buckwheat groats', or, any cooked grain.

APPENDIX II

"KONDYR": A PARAMETRIC ANALYSIS

Aleksei Leonov's "Kondyr" is a canonical work of Village Prose; while
not all the parameters of Village Prose are employed in every work
included in this category, the story certainly comes very close to com-
pleteness. The village, the peasant home, nature, generational and cyclical time, folklore, radiant and bitter nostalgia, and the chronotope
of an idyllic rural childhood/youth are all well developed here. Binary
pairs such as old age/youth, rural/urban, submitting to nature/ruling
nature, and past/present structure this story as they do so much of
rural literature. It is important to realize that the undying allegiance
in "Kondyr" is to the *malaia rodina* 'small homeland', that is, to one's
own village and the fields and forest that surround it. Not only is
"Kondyr" not chauvinist, it is not even nationalist. This is a universal
story of lonely old age and the decline of traditional rural life in the
modern world.

The idea of the VILLAGE is central to this story. The fact that Kondyr's native village, which he is forced to leave, remains unnamed does
not diminish its importance and may even enhance the universality of
the narrative. Rather than describe the virtues of this place, Leonov implies them by showing the faults of neighboring Govorenki.
Govorenki people are lazy, brawling gossips. Locating the settlement
on a stony hill was a poor choice, and the houses are placed too close
together with very few windows. The land cannot produce grain, and
the women have never woven their own cloth. Kondyr's daughter-in-
law personifies the thoughtless, careless inhabitants of Govorenki (to
which she is as loyal as Kondyr is to his village). When Kondyr moves
there, he finds that the new house is surrounded by vehicles instead of
bushes and trees.

Govorenki may objectively be a bad place, but more significantly, it
can be seen as being bad simply because it is *chuzhoi* 'another's, strange,
alien, foreign' and not *rodnoi* 'native, one's own'. It is the "other," the
next village over, which, according to Moshe Lewin, may by definition
be hostile territory. In the story, which is told from Kondyr's point of
view, only the pejorative nickname for this village is used. The whole
system of village nomenclature, with an official name, the name the
inhabitants used, and the nickname coined by the village's neighbors,
itself implies a distinction between "native" and "foreign."

Kondyr hates Govorenki "with his whole being" (*vsem nutrom*). It represents the antithesis of everything he stands for, like hard work, modest behavior, and a tender concern for nature, and to have to abandon his family home to move there is the greatest possible indignity, a negation of his whole life.

It is no surprise, then, that in Kondyr's final dream, the intruder who tries to take Alyona away from him is clearly a Govorenki boy. Characteristic of the inhabitants of that village, he is light on his feet, wears *nevidannyi* 'strange' (lit. 'not-normally-seen') clothing, and likes to show off. But this "neighborhood" rivalry is transformed in the dream into something much more ominous: the visitor is clearly connected to *nechistaia sila* 'evil, impure, unclean spirits' and death. His cap even looks like a poisonous mushroom, an image that has figured twice before in the story.

The intruder is called *zakhozhyi legok*, which can mean 'the newly arrived dancer' (i.e., a person "light" on his feet) but which is also used in the phrase *legok na pomine* 'speak of the devil'.[1] Even before his arrival, it is noted that there was a "diabolical power" present among the revelers. The newcomer outdances Kondyr, and winks and laughs triumphantly. Kondyr makes a heroic effort and with his last reserves of strength vanquishes the devil himself and knocks off his poison-mushroom hat, but at the cost of his own life, for he awakens from his dream of victory to die. Kondyr has visualized this playful "dancing death" as a brash young fellow from a nearby settlement; no stronger sense of the magic, almost sacred boundaries of the village could be expressed.

The final scene of "Kondyr" would appear on first reading to have definite "carnivalistic overtones": a noisy folk holiday observance, tables heavily laden with rich food and drink, an excited throng of gaudily dressed peasants, a celebration of the body ("The girls and women had glistening lips and a diabolical power drew everyone to them"), frenzied dancing, winking, laughter, a comical-menacing intruder, and an ending that erases clear boundaries between life and death.[2] The "carnival" character of this scene seems to emerge even more clearly when one realizes that it is a dream retelling of the time surrounding Kondyr's wedding, which is being celebrated during *maslenitsa*, literally at "carnival" time.

And yet a closer examination reveals that what is functioning in the story is not so much a carnival chronotope as a *carnival manqué*.[3] Carnival, as described by Bakhtin, "liberates the world from all that is dark and terrifying; it takes away all fears and is therefore completely gay and bright. All that was frightening in ordinary life is turned into amusing or ludicrous monstrosities."[4] "Dancing death" is one of these comical monsters, and the carnival feast celebrates a victory over the fear of death when everyone shares in the laughter and the only time experienced is the present.[5]

In "Kondyr," on the other hand, the death-figure is more frightening than funny. Rather than fitting organically into the feast, he is the blasphemous "other"; it is not a renewing death, but "a debased and trivialized Death that dances, a death from that fraudulent Govorenki" where nothing is done according to tradition.[6] In this *carnival manqué*, the orientation is toward an idyllic past and it is the present that is devoid of interest. But Kondyr's time is up, and he cannot escape his death in a return to the past; death both is defeated by him and defeats him.

Iurii Lotman and Boris Uspensky have demonstrated the ways in which such concepts as "carnival laughter," which Bakhtin draws from medieval European culture, cannot be applied wholesale to Russia. In the Russian context, laughter is not infectious, but terrifying and impure, not alternative behavior but *anti*-behavior.[7] "Kondyr" can be seen as proof of the essential correctness of the Lotman-Uspensky view; Leonov was exposed to folk traditions as a child and his vision of the wedding/holiday feast can be taken as an authentic expression of the Russian peasant worldview.

In Russian folk belief a wedding was a time of great danger from *porcha* 'spoiling' (the transfer of impersonal, harmful magic to people or objects). "Almost everywhere it was believed that if precautions were not taken, the young couple and sometimes the whole wedding party would suffer harm. The bride was especially vulnerable."[8] A holiday such as *maslenitsa* was itself an amalgam of Orthodox and pagan rituals (a situation referred to as *dvoeverie*, lit. 'dual faith'). A wedding during Shrovetide would thus be a natural occasion for the appearance of evil spirits in human form. In fact, as Likhachev and others have pointed out, *maslenitsa* was, among other things, a special time for couples who had been married just before the holiday began or indeed at any point during the preceding *miasoed* 'season when meat can be eaten' between the Epiphany and the beginning of Shrovetide. Many of the rituals, customs, and games for this holiday—sledding, riding in troikas, festive gatherings—focus on newlyweds. There is an element of competition in these celebrations, including attempts by still-unmarried local men to kiss the young brides or at least to scandalize them with dirty jokes.[9] From all this it is clear that in writing the dream scene Leonov draws on a folk culture that was still functioning at some level in rural Russia in the early part of the twentieth century when Kondyr was a young man.[10]

For ninety years, Kondyr's life has been linked in the closest possible way to NATURE. At the beginning of the story, he literally emerges from Mother Earth, i.e., from the root cellar where he has been keeping cool. The cause of his sorrow is not only the impending move but also the careless attitude toward nature that he sees among young people: abandoned orchards, overgrown paths, and a preference for store-bought food over that picked freely in the forest. Not only were people neglecting and destroying the environment and letting nature's gifts go to waste, but they no longer knew how to appreciate the magical, healing quiet of the forest. When Kondyr feels nostalgic, he goes to the Dubrava woods rather than to his wife's grave. It is in the woods that he can recall not only his dead, but a whole way of life of which he is the last representative, in which nature was central. Kondyr's own dying is presented in a very natural way: "something had picked him up like a leaf in the wind and was carrying him off somewhere into the unknown." In the natural cycle of life, his time had come. This echoes the death scenes of Tolstoy's peasants, who knew so much better than their educated masters how to live and die in harmony with nature.

Kondyr's family HOME is so dear to him that contemplating its being turned into building materials for a pig-barn is like anticipating the death of a loved one. All around him he sees the village "dead": "lifeless peasant houses with smashed-in windows, doors left open, and chimneys that had gone cold." The same fate awaits his house. He cherishes the simple objects in it, especially the table and stove, worn and marked by the generations of family members who used them daily. The new house in Govorenki would have a modern stove and a varnished folding table. Kondyr had moved slowly through time to his place at the head of his family's oak table; from this vantage point he could see the "chronicle in wood" (Fedor Abramov's term) of his grandfather's and his father's lives in the marks they made cutting homegrown tobacco and preparing *lapti* 'bast shoes'. To throw away the table was, for Kondyr, to discard the PAST and MEMORY itself.

Kondyr leaves the housewarming in Govorenki to head for his old village, where he plans to stand on the threshold with a pitchfork and defend his home. The "narrative of dangerous uprooting" so important in Village Prose is central to "Kondyr." Like a number of older rural characters, Kondyr dies when his ROOTS (*rodovoi koren'*) are torn from Mother Earth.

The young people in "Kondyr" love any kind of vehicle that allows them to move easily from one place to another in the rush toward a more comfortable and pleasant future. Kondyr, by contrast, has been slowed down by age and the summer heat, but he is content. "Time had slowed down, but that gave him the solitude that old people need in order to recall their lives and put them in some kind of order." Clocks and calendars mean little to him; nature has always provided all the means for gauging TIME that he requires. Like Rasputin's Anna, he is living on "borrowed time," living out his last summer and making final visits to his favorite places in the nearby forests and fields. Kondyr is not merely oriented toward the PAST, he *is* the living past, ninety years of it (ca. 1880–1970) that saw the face of rural Russia emerge from an almost medieval existence directly into the modern world.

There are in "Kondyr" both kinds of NOSTALGIA—a radiant sadness and a "black" nostalgia (Coe's term). The former sees the past through a golden haze, for example, when Kondyr's walk through the forest triggers memories of his magical first meeting with Alyona. The latter reflects a bitterness that "things aren't done according to custom anymore." He is the last person around who knows and cares about the old ways, and when he dies, they will die with him. The way people live now seems to go against both tradition and nature, and that is painful for him to observe. The combination of these two poles of nostalgia creates a lyrical work with a great deal of implied criticism, especially of the abandonment of *neperspektivnye* 'unpromising, not economically viable' villages.

The LANGUAGE of "Kondyr" is atypical in the sense that there is relatively little dialogue. The story is told in the third person from Kondyr's viewpoint in a narrative language that is enriched but not controlled by the rural idiom. Leonov makes judicious use of *nesobstvenno-priamaia rech'* 'indirect interior monologue' to present Kondyr's thoughts; this can be seen in the following example, where the old man comes upon edible mushrooms in the forest and recalls how his wife loved mushroom picking.

> Alena, byvalo, shchustro soberetsia, pokhvatit pletushku—i v les. Ne uspeesh' obernut'sia—bezhit s gribami da tut tebe i podzharit v smetane. Ne griby—ob"edenie.[11]

> Alyona was always one for grabbing a basket and heading for the woods. Before you had time to turn around she'd have already run home with the mushrooms and be frying them in sour cream. They weren't just mushrooms—they were a real feast.

Leonov uses impersonal constructions and indefinite forms (*chto-to* 'something', *kakoi-to* 'some sort of', *kuda-to* '[to] somewhere') to convey Kondyr's worldview in which human life is subject to the power of invisible, unnamed forces. Such examples as "Kondyria poneslo v davnee" (lit. 'There was a carrying of Kondyr into the past') and "chto-to podkhvatilo ego, slovno vetrom listok, i poneslo kuda-to" (lit. 'something picked him up like a leaf in the wind and carried him off somewhere') give a sense of Kondyr's being swept first into the past and then gently but inexorably into oblivion. The whole context of the story with its acceptance of nature's rules and its anger at contemporary man's attempts to ignore those rules supports these linguistic-stylistic devices. Rasputin's Darya comes to mind with her comment about her son Pavel: "svoim shagom malo kto khodit" (it is a rare person who sets his own pace).[12]

Not only folk language, but folk genres, primarily the *skazka* 'fairy tale', also influence the narrative. When Kondyr emerges into a clearing near the forest pond and the sunny sky opens up before him, he feels a sudden excitement. "It was the way you feel when you hear a fairy tale with a happy ending: it's frightening and you really experience it and then there is a sense of joy, because everything's worked out okay and you can relax." Kondyr's final walk through the forest, which makes up the second half of the story, borrows from the *skazka* a sense of magic, of an expansion of the possible. In the fairy-tale world of the forest, Alyona can return from the dead to speak to him, a poisonous mushroom can turn into the hat of a suspicious stranger, and a wedding/holiday celebration can become a dancing contest with the devil himself. The "real" world of government-run farms and five-year plans is very far away, in another "kingdom."

The most important chronotope in "Kondyr" is that of idyllic youth, a variation on the chronotope of Childhood.[13] While the forest bears some signs of contemporary life, at its center it is still the primordial setting that Kondyr knew as a young man. When he reaches the forest pond it is a rosy dawn and the birds are calling out to each other. "Kondyr recalled his distant youth and it seemed possible to him to bring back that time, to enter into it and relive it." The subsequent remembered scene of Kondyr's first meeting with Alyona is presented as vividly as if it were happening in the present. Walking along, the old man feels as if Alyona might be waiting for him beyond the next turning in the sunlit path. "He was transformed—there was no old age, it had been swept away by the memories of the past and his vision of Alyona, and by the quiet of the Dubrava woods, where something of the former life was preserved." When he lies down to rest in this ancient place, he is immediately carried off into a fairy-tale dreamworld where he and Alyona are young again, but where he must face a dangerous rival.

This chronotope of youth is made more powerful by Kondyr's death upon awakening. He has so successfully returned to this sphere that his life in the present can no longer be sustained. We are not presented with a conventional death scene; rather, Kondyr is "carried off somewhere" into that "other" world where he and Alyona will always be young. It is this powerful chronotope of rural youth that keeps the story from having an atmosphere of tragedy. Kondyr successfully escapes from old age and his uprooted state into an eternal youth in the depths of the forest.

In a book about central Russian rural literature, Aleksandr Logvinov referred to "Kondyr" as a story that seems to have been created "in one breath."[14] Behind the author's superficially calm and restrained manner there is a "hidden lyricism, which is the more powerful for being so unexpected."[15] And, while there is no Rousseauistic (or Tolstoyan) call for a simpler life or praise of the patriarchal past, it is made clear that much has been lost in the rapid transition from the old village to the new consolidated settlement, and from a life based in nature to one centered on machines. Kondyr's death signifies "the natural and irreversible departure of the old way of life."[16] Leonov does not weep for the disappearing village, but he does note its passing with "laconic simplicity" and "subtle lyricism."[17] Another critic echoed these comments and noted that "Kondyr" was "a conscientious eyewitness account" of rural decline.[18]

Aleksei Danilovich Leonov (b. 1929) is a native of the central Russian Orel region that is associated with the works of writers such as Turgenev, Leskov, Fet, Tiutchev, Bunin, and Prishvin.[19] In his autobiographical stories for children and young adults, Leonov describes a rural childhood typical of his generation, with boyhood pleasures intermingled with wartime hardships, especially the loss of a father and older brother at the front. His semiautobiographical trilogy "I ostalis' zhit'" (And they came through it alive), "Po letnim i zimnim dorogam" (Along summer and winter roads), and "Dolgie meteli" (The long winter storms) sheds further light on the difficulties of occupation, evacuation, and return to a village that is officially abandoned soon after the war is over.

Leonov was a brigadier in his kolkhoz and then served in the army for three years, when for the first time he began to seriously consider becoming a writer. He moved to postwar Leningrad where he worked on reconstruction projects by day and studied and met with other writers in the evenings. His literary debut came in 1960 with the story "Glukhaia" (The deaf woman), and he was admitted to the Writers' Union in 1969 after the publication of his first book, Iabloki padaiut (The apples are falling, 1968). He has since published six story collections and numerous children's books.[20]

The typical Leonov plot is one common to Village Prose: a person, usually in the postwar period, is on the borders of the village, at the edge of its "magic circle," either trying to return and reintegrate himself into the community after a long absence, or attempting to leave the village for the unknown future of urban life. Leonov emphasizes a sense of LOSS (of home, health, youth, ties to other people, traditional ways) and displacement. Like Shukshin's characters, Leonov's younger protagonists are nowhere completely at home and his older villagers are in danger of being uprooted.

In "The Widowed Well" ("Vdovii kolodets," 1971), a recently widowed man returns with his son to his native village in hope that there he will find a way to tell the boy that his mother died in the hospital. In "The Flood" ("Navodnenie," 1980), a young writer, whose birth was the result of a wartime romance between a Tartar woman and a Russian man, looks for his roots in his father's village, and in finding himself, also finds death. "Along Summer and Winter Roads" ("Po letnim i zimnim dorogam," 1971) focuses on Tatiana Averkina as she struggles to save her family during the war. In "Ukhan and Kriazhik" ("Ukhan i Kriazhik," 1968) the last old people in a village are cut off from the outside world by a fierce snowstorm; in contrast to "Kondyr," it shows what life was like for those who chose to stay on alone after their children and the kolkhoz moved away. The setting for many of Leonov's stories is not so much Soviet Russia or even the patriarchal countryside as it is the village against the background of impersonal nature and history.

Critics have found Leonov's stories to be a sincere, finely written, nondogmatic account of the countryside in transition, clearly based on the author's own experiences and observations. Leonov does not idealize the village or the peasant, but he does care deeply about their fate in an increasingly urban world. Most often he is compared to Kazakov and to the early Belov, all three of whom are better at conveying the poetry of *byt* 'everyday routine' than the drama of *sobytiia* 'events'.

Leonov's style is the most striking feature of his stories; it is original, laconic, and unaffected, written in a minor key. A number of critics have stated that while the author's themes and characters are common to Village Prose, his voice is unique, not to be confused with other rural writers. It is a style that requires patience because it reads slowly. "Aleksei Leonov's prose isn't meant to be read on mass transit, when it's only possible to grasp major plot developments. It's also not good to use as an 'emotional release' during breaks in a hockey game. This prose demands a serious effort on the part of the reader."[21]

In "Aleksei Leonov and His Heroes" Nikolai Panteleimonov wondered why such a fine writer as Leonov received relatively little attention.[22] In the 1970s his early prose was judged to be among the best in the rural school, worthy of serious attention and analysis, but his work does not fit neatly into any of the divisions within Village Prose, e.g., reform essay, childhood memoir, or nationalistic elegy. In a literary context in which righteous anger has sometimes been equated with talent, Leonov's narrative voice is quiet and precise. He does not claim in his fiction that the Russian peasants have suffered more than anyone else, or that they are superior to others morally or in their appreciation of beauty.[23] He thinks that life is tough, and he sees that happiness comes through work and a closeness to nature, but that all happiness is fragile. It is a sure sign of the depth of the Russian Village Prose movement that there are such finely wrought stories as "Kondyr" still waiting to be discovered.

A. D. Leonov: A Select Bibliography

Works by Leonov

Iabloki padaiut (The apples are falling). Leningrad: Sovetskii pisatel', 1968.
Khodiat devki (Country girls stroll about). Moscow: Sovetskaia Rossiia, 1971.
Dolgie meteli (The long winter storms). Leningrad: Sovetskii pisatel', 1975.
I ostalis' zhit' (And they came through it alive). Moscow: Sovremennik, 1976. Leningrad: Lenizdat, 1984.
Navodnenie (The flood). Leningrad: Sovetskii pisatel', 1980.
Ptitsy pereletnye (Birds of passage). Leningrad: Sovetskii pisatel', 1983.
Za povorotom perekrestok (The crossroads around the bend). Leningrad: Detskaia literatura, 1984.
Chei sovet dorozhe? (Whose advice is best?). Leningrad: Detskaia literatura, 1985.
[Under the name Andrei Zushin.] *Muzyka d'iavola* (The Devil's band). Leningrad: Leningradskaia panorama, 1989.

Criticism

Kutuzov, Evgenii. "Potrebnost' souchastiia." *Avrora*, no. 5 (1976): 64–68.
Logvinov, Aleksandr. *Priokskie rodniki*. Moscow: Sovremennik, 1977.
Ninov, Aleksandr, et al. "Priniato edinoglasno." *Avrora*, no. 1 (1969): 61–63.
Panteleimonov, Nikolai. "Aleksei Leonov i ego geroi." Afterword. *I ostalis' zhit'*. By A. D. Leonov. Leningrad: Lenizdat, 1984. 400–414.
Pogodin, Radii. "Kto ty, vlastelin zemli?" *Avrora*, no. 10 (1978): 154–59.
Protchenko, V. I. "Sovremennaia povest' o derevne (K probleme narodnogo kharaktera). *Russkaia literatura*, no. 2 (1970): 62–79.
———. "Nekotorye voprosy razvitiia 'derevenskoi prozy.'" *Problemy russkoi sovetskoi literatury (50–70-e gody)*. Ed. V. A. Kovalev. Leningrad: Nauka, 1976. 58–107.
Solov'ev, V. "Nedaleko ot Moskvy." *Novyi mir*, no. 1 (1969): 230–32.
Starikova, E. "Sotsiologicheskii analiz sovremennoi 'derevenskoi prozy.'" *Voprosy literatury*, no. 7 (1972): 11–35.

NOTES

The following abbreviations have been used in the notes for frequently cited periodicals:

CDSP   *Current Digest of the Soviet Press*
LG   *Literaturnaia gazeta*
LR   *Literaturnaia Rossiia*
NM   *Novyi mir*
NS   *Nash sovremennik*
NYRB   *New York Review of Books*
NYT   *New York Times*
SEEJ   *Slavic and East European Journal*
SEER   *Slavonic and East European Journal*
SR   *Slavic Review*
SSL   *Soviet Studies in Literature*
VL   *Voprosy literatury*
WSJ   *Wall Street Journal*

PREFACE

1. The Voznesensky quatrain is from "Krony i korni. Pamiati L. N. Tolstogo" (Leaves and roots. To the memory of L. N. Tolstoi). Written in 1960, it is thought to refer as much to Boris Pasternak as to Tolstoy. "Lesa roniaiut krony. / No moshchno pod zemlei / Vorochaiutsia korni / Koriavoi piaternei." Trans. by Stanley Kunitz in Andrey Voznesensky, *Antiworlds and "The Fifth Ace,"* ed. Patricia Blake and Max Hayward (Garden City, NY: Anchor, 1967), 120–23.

2. Jurij Lotman and Boris Uspenskij, "New Aspects of Early Russian Culture," trans. N.F.C. Owen, in *The Semiotics of Russian Culture*, ed. Ann Shukman, Michigan Slavic Contributions, no. 11 (Ann Arbor: Department of Slavic Languages and Literatures, University of Michigan, 1984), 38.

3. Geoffrey Hosking, "The Twentieth Century: In Search of New Ways, 1933–80," in *The Cambridge History of Russian Literature*, ed. Charles Moser (Cambridge: Cambridge University Press, 1989), 565–66.

4. *Skandal* has been defined as "a conflict which brings to the surface deep and wounding feelings"; ibid., 565.

5. Gary Saul Morson, "Dostoevsky's Anti-Semitism and the Critics: A Review Article," *SEEJ* 27:3 (1983). Soviet critics have begun to use analogies with the nineteenth century to explain the contemporary situation; see, for example, D. Zatonskii, "Vynos krivykh zerkal," *Inostrannaia literatura*, no. 3 (1989): 248–49. On Solzhenitsyn and anti-Semitism, see Daniel Rancour-Laferrière, "Solzhenitsyn and the Jews: A Psychoanalytic View," in *Russian Literature and Psychoanalysis*, ed. D. Rancour-Laferrière (Philadelphia: John Benjamins, 1989).

6. Katerina Clark, *The Soviet Novel: History as Ritual*, 2d ed. (Chicago: University of Chicago Press, 1985).

CHAPTER ONE
THE PARAMETERS OF VILLAGE PROSE

1. John Berger, *Pig Earth* (New York: Pantheon, 1979), 8. The Rubtsov couplet ("Tikhaia moia rodina / Ia nichego ne zabyla") is from "Tikhaia Rodina" (My quiet homeland).

2. The "Ovechkin-style" essay is a relatively short piece of publicistic writing—often part of a series—that dates back to the first installment of Valentin Ovechkin's "District Routine" ("Raionnye budni") in the journal *Novyi mir* in September 1952. Ovechkin's work was loyal to the Party, but at the same time it was very critical of collective-farm administration and of the way rural Russia fared in the postwar period. "District Routine" was discussed in detail in the influential essay "On Sincerity in Literature" ("Ob iskrennosti v literature") by Vladimir Pomerantsev that appeared in December 1953 in the same journal. Numerous essays of a similar nature—and with varying amounts of bold statement and artistry—followed in the 1950s; among the better-known *ocherkisty* (essayists) were Sergei Zalygin, Fedor Abramov, Efim Dorosh, Vladimir Tendriakov, and Gavriil Troepolsky.

3. See, for example, Edward Brown, *Russian Literature since the Revolution*, rev. ed. (Cambridge: Harvard University Press, 1982), 293; V. Kardin, "Sekret uspekha," *VL*, no. 4 (1986): 102; E. A. Shubin, *Sovremennyi russkii rasskaz. Voprosy poetiki zhanra* (Leningrad: Nauka, 1974), 63–65; Dubravka Ugresic, *Nova ruska proza* (Zagreb: Hrvatsko Filolosko drustvo, 1980), 51–52; Gleb Zekulin, "Aspects of Peasant Life As Portrayed in Contemporary Soviet Literature," *Canadian Slavic Studies* 1:4 (Winter 1967): 552–65; Yves Perret-Gentil, "Der Kolchosbauer in der heutigen russischen Dorfliteratur," *Osteuropa*, no. 9 (1978): 794–810; N. N. Shneidman, *Soviet Literature in the 1970s: Artistic Diversity and Ideological Conformity* (Toronto: University of Toronto Press, 1979), 16–20, 75, cites differing uses of the term "Village Prose" and concludes that it can be seen as either arbitrary or flexible; L. Terakopian, *Pafos preobrazovaniia. Tema derevni v proze 50–70-x godov* (Moscow: Khudozhestvennaia literatura, 1978), adheres to the thematic approach, using it to try to keep this type of literature within the realm of Socialist Realism. Lily Daetz sees the difference between *Bauerliteratur* and *Dorfprosa* in an acceptance of the Revolution and collectivization by the former, and a rejection by the latter; "Die bäuerliche Literatur und ihre Traditionen," in *Sowjetliteratur heute* (Munich: Beck, 1979), 120. There are dozens of other slight variations on the theme/location/ writer's origin approach to this body of writing.

4. Geoffrey Hosking, "The Politics of Literature," in *The Soviet Union Today*, ed. James Cracraft, 2d ed. (Chicago: University of Chicago Press, 1988), 273; and, by the same author, "The Russian Peasant Rediscovered: 'Village Prose' of the 1960s," *SR* 32:4 (Dec. 1973): 710, and *Beyond Socialist Realism: Soviet Fiction since "Ivan Denisovich"* (New York: Holmes and Meier, 1980), 52. See also Deming Brown, *Soviet Russian Literature since Stalin* (Cambridge: Cambridge University Press, 1979), 218–52; Katerina Clark, *The Soviet Novel: His-*

tory as Ritual, rev. ed. (Chicago: University of Chicago Press, 1985), 241–46; Philippa Lewis, "Peasant Nostalgia in Contemporary Russian Literature," *Soviet Studies* 27:4 (Oct. 1976): 548; Rosalind J. Marsh, *Soviet Fiction since Stalin: Science, Politics and Literature* (London: Croom Helm, 1986), 191.

5. Lewis, "Peasant Nostalgia," 552.

6. Galina Belaia, "Pol'za intuitsii. Proza 70-kh godov v zhurnal'nykh stat'iakh 1980 goda. Opyt problemnogo obzora," *Literaturnoe obozrenie,* no. 9 (1981): 9–14; and, by the same author, "O 'vnutrennei' i 'vneshnei' teme," in *Literatura v zerkale kritiki. Sovremennye problemy* (Moscow: Sovetskii pisatel', 1986), 158, 170–71.

7. Shubin, *Sovremennyi russkii rasskaz,* 64–66; Liliia Vil'chek, "Derevenskaia proza," in *Sovremennaia russkaia sovetskaia literatura,* Part 2, ed. A. Bocharov and G. Belaia (Moscow: Prosveshchenie, 1987), 52–53; V. A. Apukhtina, *Sovremennaia sovetskaia proza. 60–70-e gody,* rev. ed. (Moscow: Vysshaia shkola, 1984), 77; G. A. Tsvetov, *Tema derevni v sovremennoi sovetskoi proze* (Leningrad: Znanie, 1985), 6; A. P. Petrik, "'Derevenskaia proza': Itogi i perspektivy izucheniia," *Filologicheskie nauki,* no. 1 (1981): 65; Wolfgang Kasack, *Dictionary of Russian Literature since 1917,* trans. M. Carlson and J. Hedges (New York: Columbia University Press, 1988), 446–47.

8. Vil'chek, "Derevenskaia proza," 52–53; and, by the same author, "Vniz po techeniiu derevenskoi prozy," *VL,* no. 6 (1985): 35, 72. It has been said that writers like Rasputin, Abramov, and Belov created not merely a literary style but a "mode of thought"; Petr Vail and Aleksandr Genis, *Sovremennaia russkaia proza* (Ann Arbor: Hermitage, 1982), 93; Georg Witte warned against seeing the evolution from Kolkhoz to Village Prose as merely a change of themes: *Die sowjetische Kolchos- und Dorfprosa der fünfziger und sechziger Jahre: Zur Evolution einer literarischen Unterreihe* (Munich: Otto Sagner, 1983), 1.

9. Clark, *The Soviet Novel,* chapters 7 and 8; and, by the same author, "'Boy Gets Tractor' and All That: The Parable Structure of the Soviet Novel," in *Russian and Soviet Literature,* ed. R. Milner-Gulland et al. (Cambridge, MA: Slavica, 1976), 359–75.

10. Witte, *Die sowjetische Kolchos- und Dorfprosa,* 15. Tsvetov, *Tema derevni,* lists the following contrasts: "city-village, new-old, young-old people, life-death, progress-stagnation" (26). In the phrase "progress-stagnation," his placement of the first term of comparison is itself a hierarchical gesture, as is his use of the word *kosnost'* 'stagnation'; for "progress," the environmental activists among the Village Prose writers might have substituted "unrestrained growth" or "the destruction of rural traditions and the environment," and instead of "stagnation" they would have said "moderate growth," "preservation of the environment," or Likhachev's term, "the ecology of culture." Dmitrii Likhachev, "Ekologiia kul'tury," in *Zametki o russkom,* 2d ed. (Moscow: Sovetskaia Rossiia, 1984), 54–61.

11. G. S. Morson, *The Boundaries of Genre: Dostoevsky's "Diary of a Writer" and the Traditions of Literary Utopia* (Austin: University of Texas Press, 1981), 4.

12. *Derevenskaia proza* has also been translated as 'rural' or 'country' prose, but these translations do not notice or capture the importance of the village to this literature. Kolkhoz Literature also has a rural setting.

13. Vladimir Lichutin, *Poslednii koldun* (Moscow: Sovremennik, 1980), 142.

14. This is from an ethnographic report about the Russian north, as quoted by Vladimir Lichutin, "Divis'-gora—v ozhidanii chuda," in *Divis'-gora* (Moscow: Sovremennik, 1986), 42.

15. Moshe Lewin, *The Making of the Soviet System: Essays in the Social History of Interwar Russia* (New York: Pantheon, 1985), 54.

16. Clark, *The Soviet Novel*, 242.

17. The words *bol'shaki* and *proselki* also acquired a symbolic resonance in Village Prose and in the criticism it engendered. One of the earliest works of Village Prose is Vladimir Soloukhin's *Vladimirskie proselki* (Vladimir country roads). A long-running critical discussion of Village Prose in *Literaturnaia gazeta* was called "Bol'shaki i proselki" (Highways and cart-tracks). In the essay "On Literature, Revolution, Entropy and Other Matters" (1923), Zamiatin spoke of the "highways" and "cart-tracks" of Russian literature.

18. Berger, *Pig Earth*, 8–9. The rest of this paragraph is a paraphrase of Berger.

19. Ibid., 11.

20. Emmet Kennedy, *A Cultural History of the French Revolution* (New Haven: Yale University Press, 1989), 27–33.

21. Lewin, *The Making of the Soviet System*, 56.

22. Georges Nivat, "Le paysage russe en tant que mythe," *Rossiia/Russia*, 1987: 7–20.

23. Tsvetov, *Tema derevni*, 28.

24. In a description of his childhood in the Missouri countryside, Terrence Des Pres' view of nature is one that prevails in Russian Village Prose as well, and which may be a universal quality of prose by rural-born writers. "In the Missouri I knew as a boy, nobody called fishing a sport. Life was rooted in the land and fishing was mainly for food. . . . Fishing was brutal, savage, cruel, but none of that was the point. Joy was what counted, the rush of deep delight that came, I think, from rites that for a million years kept men living and in touch with awe." Terrence Des Pres, "Memory of Boyhood," in *Writing into the World: Essays 1973–1987* (New York: Viking, 1991), 287, 295.

25. On the subject of nature in Village Prose, see also Renate Schäper, *Die Prosa V. G. Rasputins. Erzählverfahren und ethisch-religiöse Problematik* (Munich: Otto Sagner, 1985), 142–63.

26. There is no adequate word in English for the Russian *izba* or *khata*, which have been translated as 'hut', 'shanty', 'cabin', and 'cottage'. The "unmarked" word for 'house' in Russian is *dom*, but in the rural context that indicates a more elaborate structure on two levels. On the importance of the village and the peasant home to this literature, see Witte, *Die sowjetische Kolchos- und Dorfprosa*, 216–39.

27. Vasilii Belov, *Lad. Ocherki o narodnoi estetike* (Moscow: Molodaia gvardiia, 1982), 134.

28. For example: *rod* (family, clan), *rodimyi* (own, native, dear), *rodovoi* (ancestral), *rodina* (native land), *roditeli* (parents), *rodnia* (kinsfolk), *rodstvennyi* (kindred), *rodstvo* (kinship, relationship), *rodit'* (to give birth to). *Rodnoi* and *rodina* often appear in phrases that are very rich in meaning, but difficult to translate into English. On this subject, see Igor' Dedkov, "Vozvrashchenie k sebe," *NS*,

no. 7 (1975); and Svetlana Semenova, "Preobrazhit' sebia i zhizn'. O Tvorchestve Valentina Rasputina," *NS*, no. 3 (1987): 172–80.

29. Vladimir Tendriakov, "Den' na rodine," *Nauka i religiia*, no. 11 (1964): 44.

30. Tsvetov, *Tema derevni*, 28.

31. Fred Davis, *Yearning for Yesterday: A Sociology of Nostalgia* (New York: Free Press/Macmillan), 1979), 8–10.

32. Ibid., 73, 77.

33. Ibid., 80–81.

34. "Na kholmakh Gruzii lezhit nochnaia mgla; / Shumit Aragva predo mnoiu. / Mne grustno i legko; pechal' moia svetla; / Pechal' moia polna toboiu." The poem is known by its first line and was written in 1829.

35. Davis, *Yearning for Yesterday*, 16.

36. From vol. 6 of the diary; as quoted by Davis, ibid., 51.

37. Vladimir Nabokov, *Speak, Memory: An Autobiography Revisited* (New York: G. P. Putnam's Sons, 1966), 153–54, 223.

38. Richard Coe, *When the Grass Was Taller: Autobiography and the Experience of Childhood* (New Haven: Yale University Press, 1984), xii, 35, 62–63, 131–33.

39. Davis, *Yearning for Yesterday*, 15–16.

40. Coe, *When the Grass Was Taller*, 64. Coe looked at hundreds of texts from a number of different national literatures, including Russian, but his Russian material goes only as far as Kataev and he is clearly not familiar with Russian Village Prose, hence his incorrect statement—in an otherwise superb book—that there is no "black nostalgia" in Soviet literature because it would not be allowed (65).

41. Ibid.

CHAPTER TWO
THE QUESTION OF GENRE

1. Katerina Clark, *The Soviet Novel: History as Ritual*, 2d ed. (Chicago: University of Chicago Press, 1985), xii. Clark focused on the novel because it is "*the* privileged genre of Soviet Socialist Realism, occupying the same structural slot as the opera does in China" (xiii).

2. Wolf Schmid contends that the use of retrospective narration of a character's life allowed the *derevenshchiki*—modeling themselves on Chekhov—to condense a great deal of material into a short story; "Thesen zur innovatorischen Poetik der russischen Gegenwartsprosa," *Wiener Slawistischer Almanach*, no. 4 (1979): 85.

3. Andrew Durkin, "Two Instances of Prose Pastoral: Nemcova and Aksakov," in *American Contributions to the Ninth International Congress of Slavists*, Kiev, Sept. 1983, vol. 2, ed. Paul Debreczeny (Columbus, OH: Slavica, 1983), 126.

4. Glushkov uses the term *bezrazmerna* 'elastic'; N. I. Glushkov, *Ocherkovye formy v sovetskoi literature* (Rostov: Izdatel'stvo Rostovskogo universiteta, 1969), 92.

5. V. Kantorovich, *Zametki pisatelia o sovremennom ocherke* (Moscow: Sovetskii pisatel', 1962), 46; as quoted by Glushkov, *Ocherkovye formy*, 92.

6. With the exception of other specifically annotated sentences, the rest of this paragraph is a paraphrase of L. Vil'chek, "Vniz po techeniiu derevenskoi prozy," *VL*, no. 6 (1985): 41–43, 82.

7. Valentin Ovechkin, "Raionnye budni," in O. S. Liauer, ed. *Derevenskii dnevnik. Sel'skie ocherki 50–60kh godov* (Moscow: Sovetskii pisatel', 1984), 47. Ovechkin later came to regard his cycle of "District Routine" sketches as something approaching a novel, and he expressed resentment at being relegated to the sphere of journalism by many critics (though certainly not by Pomerantsev); as quoted by Hans Elveson, *The Rural Ocherk in Russian Literature after the Second World War* (Thesis, Slavic Institute of the University of Goteborg, 1975), 69.

8. The poem is from the collection entitled *Gorodskaia vesna*; as quoted in Elveson, *The Rural Ocherk*, 67.

9. Elveson sees the *rasskaz* and *povest'* as being "ill-defined" as well; he says that the rural *rasskaz*, for instance, "is a category where one can pile anything that is too short to be a povest and that is not an ocherk" (*The Rural Ocherk*, 113).

10. Margaret Lane, introduction to Flora Thompson, *A Country Calendar and Other Writings*, ed. M. Lane (New York: Oxford University Press, 1984), 3.

11. Ibid., 3–4.

12. Ibid., 10, 29.

13. Gary Saul Morson and Caryl Emerson, *Mikhail Bakhtin: Creation of a Prosaics* (Stanford: Stanford University Press, 1990), 282.

14. Ibid., 282–83. This concept is discussed in Mikhail Bakhtin, *Problems of Dostoevsky's Poetics*, ed. and trans. Caryl Emerson (Minneapolis: University of Minnesota Press, 1984), chapter 3.

15. Elveson, *The Rural Ocherk*, adds to this list the *ocherkovaia povest'* (essay-like story), *ocherkovyi rasskaz* (essay-like short story), and *roman v novellakh* (novel in novellas), 56–57, 99, 107, 116. Belov called *Lad* (Harmony) *ocherki*; reviewers labeled it a *povest'-khronika* (story-chronicle), *liricheskii dnevnik* (lyrical diary), and a *roman-issledovanie* (novel–research work). Zolotussky mentions that Abramov may have called "Around and About" a *povest'*, but it was universally read as an *ocherk*; Igor' Zolotusskii, *V svete pozhara* (Moscow: Sovremennik, 1989), 246.

16. Fedor Abramov, "Trava-murava," in *Trava-murava. Povesti i rasskazy* (Moscow: Sovremennik, 1983), 548. This section contains many colorful, pithy sayings, e.g., "The mosquitoes here are really big eaters—they even do blood transfusions" (550).

17. Fedor Abramov, "Dom v Verkole," ed. L. V. Krutikova, *NS*, nos. 3–4 (1986); Krutikova's comments on genre appear in no. 4:71.

18. Viktor Astaf'ev, "Ot avtora," the foreword to "Zatesi," in *Padenie lista. Roman, rasskazy, ocherki* (Moscow: Sovetskii pisatel', 1988), 133.

19. Belov used the word *zatesi* for incisions made in birch trees; the scarred wood was considered to be ideal for rakes. This process took many years, and the cuts that a peasant made were for the benefit of the next generation. Vasilii Belov, *Lad. Ocherki o narodnoi estetike* (Moscow: Molodaia gvardiia, 1982), 135.

20. Astaf'ev, "Zatesi," 351.

21. Alexander Solzhenitsyn, "A Journey along the Oka," in *Matryona's House and Other Stories*, trans. Michael Glenny (Harmondsworth, Middlesex: Penguin, 1975), 203. The Russian text ("Puteshestviia vdol' Oki") is in Aleksandr Solzhenitsyn, *Sobranie sochinenii v shesti tomakh*, 2d ed., vol. 5 (Frankfurt: Possev, 1971), 231–32.

22. This was said of Belov in a review of *Harmony* but is true of many Village Prose writers; see Evgenii Osetrov, "Rodnoe, zavetnoe, vynoshennoe," *LG*, March 19, 1980: 4.

23. I have used the term "the image of the author" (*obraz avtora*) somewhat differently from Vinogradov, for whom it was a central problem of the structure of artistic works, the essence of a work that unites all of its levels (style, plot, ideas, and genre). See V. V. Vinogradov, *O teorii khudozhestvennoi rechi* (Moscow: Vysshaia shkola, 1971), which includes useful commentary by D. S. Likhachev.

24. Durkin, "Two Instances of Prose Pastoral," 128–31.

25. Wolf Schmid analyzed narrative patterns in Village Prose with reference to the perceiving subject and the time frame; "Thesen," 59–64.

26. Nikolai Zhdanov, "Poezdka na rodinu," in M. I. Aliger et al., ed., *Literaturnaia Moskva*, vol. 2 (Moscow: Khudozhestvennaia literatura, 1956), 407. Trans. as "A Trip Home" in *The Year of Protest, 1956*, trans. and ed. Hugh McLean and Walter Vickery (New York: Random House, 1961), 214.

27. Boris Ekimov, "Pastush'ia zvezda," *NM*, no. 2 (1989): 5–32.

28. Richard Coe, *When the Grass Was Taller: Autobiography and the Experience of Childhood* (New Haven: Yale University Press, 1984), 1; see also xi–xiv, 8–9. Coe advises readers of Childhoods to look for patterns—especially the cyclical pattern of the year—and not plot (6–7, 189).

29. Andrew Wachtel also lists Andrei Bely's *Kotik Letaev* (1922) and Konstantin Paustovsky's *The Story of a Life* (1945–1963). The rest of this paragraph is a paraphrase of Wachtel's comments; see Andrew Wachtel, *The Battle for Childhood: Creation of a Russian Myth* (Stanford: Stanford University Press, 1990), especially chapter 4, "M. Gorky: Anti-*Childhood*," 135–37, 145.

30. Ibid., 131. In a similar vein, Anton Hiersche identifies two types of literature and painting on rural themes from the nineteenth century, the 1920s, and the post-Stalinist period: the first type is a poetic idealization, and the second is a critical analysis. See A. Hiersche, "Die russische sowjetische Dorfprosa. Fragen ihre Traditionen," *Zeitschrift für Slawistik* 27:4 (1984): 568–75.

31. Wachtel, *The Battle for Childhood*, 145.

32. Quoted in ibid., 147.

33. Valentin Rasputin, "Proshchanie s Materoi," in *Povesti* (Moscow: Sovetskaia Rossiia, 1978), 346 (chapter 18); *Farewell to Matyora*, trans. Antonina Bouis (1979; Evanston: Northwestern University Press, 1991).

34. Vladimir Lichutin, "Drevo pamiati," in *Divis'-gora* (Moscow: Sovremennik, 1986), 3–10. By "gaining language," Lichutin means that he had tried to speak like an urban Russian in order to fit in, but as a result he had lost access to what Abramov referred to as the "treasure chest" of the Russian folk lan-

guage. When Lichutin reconstructed his childhood, he gained the narrative of himself and the authentic words with which to relate it. Coe describes all Childhoods as "re-creations": "Childhood revisited is childhood *recreated*, and recreated in terms of art" (*When the Grass Was Taller*, 84).

35. Georgii Tsvetov, *Tema derevni v sovremennoi sovestskoi proze* (Leningrad: Znanie, 1985), 12.

36. "The chronotope of Childhood" is my term, a synthesis of Coe's "Child-hood" and Bakhtin's "chronotope." In Goncharov's novel *Oblomov*, for exam-ple, Oblomovka is obviously a chronotope of Childhood. In Iurii Trifonov's story "Games at Dusk," the tennis court on the hill in the summer settlement is where the first-person narrator places his childhood. For a basically Bakh-tinian approach to Village Prose—which is interesting but not entirely success-ful in its execution—see Georg Witte, *Die sowjetische Kolchos- und Dorfprosa der fünfziger und sechziger Jahre: zur Evolution einer literarischen Unterreihe* (Munich: Otto Sagner, 1983).

37. Clark, *The Soviet Novel*, 241. She took this phrase from the title of a 1948 novel by Vasilii Azhaev.

38. Katerina Clark, "Political History and Literary Chronotope: Some So-viet Case Studies," in *Literature and History: Theoretical Problems and Russian Case Studies*, ed. G. S. Morson (Stanford: Stanford University Press, 1986), 243; see also 238–42.

39. Clark, "Political History and Literary Chronotope," 243.

40. "The forgotten chronotope of the traditional village" is also my term.

41. M. M. Bakhtin, "Forms of Time and Chronotope in the Novel," in *The Dialogic Imagination: Four Essays*, trans. Caryl Emerson and Michael Holquist (Austin: University of Texas Press, 1981), 225.

42. Vladimir Lichutin, "Obrabotno—vremia svadeb," the first part of *Pos-lednii koldun* (Moscow: Sovremennik, 1980), 19–20.

43. Vladimir Soloukhin, "Kaplia rosy," in *Sobranie sochinenii v 4-kh tomakh*, vol. 1 (Moscow: Khudozhestvennaia literatura, 1983), 434.

44. Ibid., 456.

45. Ibid., 457–58.

46. Nikolai Rylenkov, "Skazka moego detstva," *Znamia*, nos. 6–7 (1962); this quotation is from no. 7:70; "Skazka moego detstva" was written between 1957 and 1960. Coe's description of first memories is in *When the Grass Was Taller*, 97.

47. Coe speaks of the importance of the detailed inventory of objects in the Childhood, and this is borne out in Russian Village Prose; *When the Grass Was Taller*, xii, 205–39.

48. Rylenkov, "Skazka," *Znamia*, no. 6 (1962): 75.

49. Coe, *When the Grass Was Taller*, 158, 77.

50. Rylenkov, "Skazka," *Znamia*, no. 7 (1962): 148.

51. It is not at all unusual for a Village Prose "childhood" to be followed by a "boyhood" and "youth" as it was in Tolstoy's work.

52. Nikolai Rylenkov, "Mne chetyrnadtsat' let," *Znamia*, no. 1 (1965): 107; written 1963–1964.

53. Ibid., 112.

54. Vladimir Soloukhin, *Smekh za levym plechom* (Frankfurt: Possev, 1988). It was subsequently published in the Soviet journal *Moskva* (1 [1989]). An English translation appeared, minus the first chapter; Vladimir Soloukhin, *Laughter over the Left Shoulder*, trans. David Martin (London: Peter Owen, 1990). References are to the Possev Russian edition.

55. Ibid., 89.

56. This justifies to some extent Mal'tsev's criticism of the *derevenshchiki* for avoiding the tough questions concerning the countryside; Iurii Mal'tsev, "Promezhutochnaia literatura i kriterii podlinnosti," *Kontinent*, no. 25 (1980): 285–321.

57. Soloukhin, *Smekh*, 189.

58. Vil'chek, "Vniz po techeniiu," 50. For instance, Soloukhin mentions that his wife accompanied him on his stroll through Vladimir, and then ignores her presence and her reactions for the rest of the book.

59. This description is a paraphrase of L. Vil'chek, "Derevenskaia proza," in *Sovremennaia russkaia sovetskaia literatura*, Part 2, ed. A. Bocharov and G. Belaia (Moscow: Prosveshchenie, 1987), 50, 65.

60. Vladimir Tendriakov, "Den' na rodine," *Nauka i religiia*, no. 11 (1964): 43–50.

61. For an elaboration of Tendriakov's two views of childhood, see chapter 8.

62. Vasilii Subbotin, "Proshchanie s mirom," *Oktiabr'*, no. 6 (1988): 86–138.

63. I. Sobolev, "Po zakonu pamiati," *LG*, Aug. 31, 1988: 4.

64. Subbotin, "Proshchanie," 106.

65. Coe, *When the Grass Was Taller*, 1.

66. In his book Coe speaks at length about the innate "magic" in the story of childhood.

CHAPTER THREE
THE POETICS OF VILLAGE PROSE

1. Anatolii Lanshchikov, as quoted in "Iz literaturnoi zhizni. Na seminare literaturnykh kritikov," in *Politicheskii dnevnik 1964–1970*, vol. 1 (Amsterdam: Alexander Herzen Foundation, 1972), 506. This is the transcript of a meeting that took place in April 1969.

2. A. P. Petrik, "'Derevenskaia proza': Itogi i perspektivy izucheniia," *Filologicheskie nauki*, no. 1 (1981): 66–67.

3. Vladimir Pomerantsev, "Ob iskrennosti v literature," *NM*, no. 12 (1953): 218, 229, 232.

4. Fedor Abramov, "Liudi kolkhoznoi derevni v poslevoennoi proze," *NM*, no. 4 (1954): 220–21. The rest of this paragraph and the following one summarize the most important points made about the style of rural literature, culled from dozens of critical essays written between 1953 and 1956.

5. Ovechkin even proposed Avvakum as a model for style, advice that was taken up by Belov, Rasputin, and other writers in the late 1970s and 1980s but probably not in the way that Ovechkin had hoped; Valentin Ovechkin, "Kolkhoznaia zhizn' i literatura," *NM*, no. 12 (1955): 136.

6. "Takaia tema bezuslovno dissertabel'na" (This would make a good dissertation topic); Sergei Zalygin, "Tochka zreniia pisatelia," in *Zhizn' kol'khoznoi derevni i literatura (tvorcheskaia diskussiia v Soiuze Pisatelei SSSR)*, ed. K. I. Bukovskii (Moscow: Sovetskii pisatel', 1956), 230.

7. Sergei Zalygin, "The Reader Will Judge," *CDSP* 38:46 (Dec. 17, 1986): 14, 17; this is a translation from *Izvestiia*, Nov. 16, 1986: 3.

8. Valentin Rasputin, "Byt' samim soboi," *VL*, no. 9 (1976): 148; as quoted by G. A. Tsvetov, *Tema derevni v sovremennoi sovetskoi proze* (Leningrad: Znanie, 1985), 32. A translation of the Rasputin article has appeared as "To Be Oneself," in *SSL* 14:1 (Winter 1977–1978).

9. Tsvetov, *Tema derevni*, 32. For an interesting discussion of dialect, jargon, and folkloric elements in the language of Rasputin's prose fiction, see Teresa Polowy, *The Novellas of Valentin Rasputin: Genre, Language and Style* (New York: Peter Lang, 1989), chapter 5.

10. Fedor Abramov, "Iazyk na kotorom govorit vremia," *LG*, Nov. 22, 1972; also in Abramov, *Sobranie sochinenii v 3-kh tomakh*, vol. 3 (Leningrad: Khudozhestvennaia literatura, 1982), 583.

11. Iurii Kazakov, "Pomorka," in *Osen' v dubovykh lesakh* (Moscow: Sovremennik, 1983), 184. Marietta Chudakova felt that while this story has merit as providing an early example of an old village woman as a central character, "the author did not so much listen to her as pose . . . questions dictated by literature. . . . and without waiting for her to answer, the author replied to those questions himself, masterfully preserving the tone of Bunin or Chekhov"; see her "Zametki o iazyke sovremennoi prozy," *NM*, no. 1 (1972): 230. Trans. as "Notes on the Language of Contemporary Prose," *Soviet Studies in Literature* 9:1 (Winter 1972–1973): 79. Further citations of this highly influential text will refer, respectively, to the Russian and English versions.

12. Like that of a number of rural writers, Leonov's education was interrupted by the war and postwar military service.

13. Aleksei Leonov, letter to the author, Nov. 29, 1984.

14. Abramov, "Iazyk," 581.

15. Vasilii Belov, *Lad. Ocherki o narodnoi estetike* (Moscow: Molodaia gvardiia, 1982), 244.

16. Abramov, "Iazyk," 581.

17. *Skomorokhi* were itinerant folk entertainers with roots that went back to Kievan Russia; they were increasingly marginalized from official culture and finally exiled to the north in the seventeenth century. It is probably due to them that the epic song tradition was preserved longer in the north than elsewhere in Russia. On the *skomorokhi*, see Russell Zguta, *Russian Minstrels: A History of the Skomorokhi* (Philadelphia: University of Pennsylvania Press, 1978).

18. Belov, *Lad*, 245. *Chastushki* are featured for example in the first volume of Belov's *Kanuny* (The eve), and in the film "Proshchanie" (Farewell), which is based on Rasputin's *Farewell to Matyora*.

19. Abramov, "Iazyk," 582.

20. Aleksandr Solzhenitsyn, "Matrenin dvor," in *Sobranie sochinenii v shesti tomakh*, vol. 1 (Frankfurt: Possev, 1970), 197. Alexander Solzhenitsyn, "Ma-

tryona's Home," trans. H. T. Willetts, *Twentieth Century Russian Reader*, ed. Clarence Brown (New York: Penguin, 1985), 424.

21. Aleksandr Iashin, "Rychagi," in *Literaturnaia Moskva*, vol. 2, ed. M. Aliger et al. (Moscow: Khudozhestvennaia literatura, 1956), 502–13; Aleksandr Yashin, "Levers," trans. Hugh McLean and Walter Vickery, in *The Year of Protest, 1956* (New York: Vintage, 1961), 193–210.

22. See, for example, A. Tvardovskii, "O Bunine," introduction to Ivan Bunin, *Sobranie sochinenii v deviati tomakh*, vol. 1, ed. A. S. Miasnikov et al. (Moscow: Khudozhestvennaia literatura, 1965), 10; L. Nikulin, "I. A. Bunin," introduction to Ivan Bunin, *Sobranie sochinenii v piati tomakh*, vol. 1 (Moscow: Ogonek, 1956), esp. 30; and a survey of writers conducted in 1968–1969 about Bunin's influence on their work, "Iz otzyvov sovetskikh pisatelei o Bunine," *Literaturnoe nasledstvo* 84, pt. 2: 365–74. Among the respondents are Dorosh, Belov, and Kazakov, the latter indicating his intention to write a book about Bunin. Bunin's bittersweet portrayals of the declining village and the impoverished gentry class have been as important an influence on Village Prose as his style.

23. Vladimir Dal', *Tolkovyi slovar'*, 4 vols. (Moscow: Gosudarstvennoe izdatel'stvo inostrannykh i natsional'nykh slovarei, 1955). Vladimir Ivanovich Dal' (1801–1872) studied and recorded fairy tales, proverbs, superstitions, folk songs and other examples of folk culture. Along with his dictionary—especially useful for regional and dialect forms—which first appeared in 1863–1866, he attracted the attention of writers and critics from Pushkin and Belinsky on for his books of literary fairy tales and of Russian proverbs. This favorite of the Russian nationalists is, ironically, of Danish-German background. See A. M. Babkin's introduction to the 1955 edition of the dictionary, iii–x; also Joachim Baer, "Dal," in *Handbook of Russian Literature*, ed. Victor Terras (New Haven: Yale University Press, 1985), 92–93. The 1955 reprint of Dal' was of the 1880 edition; the expanded 1906 edition, edited by Baudouin de Courtenay, included "four-letter" words, which were still not acceptable in the early post-Stalin years. My thanks to an anonymous reader for this last observation.

24. Tsvetov, *Tema derevni*, 31.

25. Ibid.

26. Chudakova, "Zametki," 232/81–82.

27. Ibid., 220–31/56–81. Chudakova obviously felt strongly about the deficiencies and excesses of Likhonosov's eclectic style, since she uses him at great length as a negative example for other writers.

28. Vasilii Belov, "Privychnoe delo," in *Izbrannye proizvedeniia v trekh tomakh*, vol. 2 (Moscow: Sovremennik, 1983), 4; "That's How It Is," trans. Eve Manning, *Soviet Literature*, no. 1 (1969): 3. I have made some changes in the translation. Belov's "post–Village Prose" novel *Vse vperedi* (The best is yet to come) speaks out strongly against alcohol, complaining that "outside forces" have encouraged excessive drinking in Russia.

29. Abramov, "Iazyk," 579–81.

30. Fedor Abramov, "Puti-pereput'ia," in *Sobranie sochinenii v 3-kh tomakh*, vol. 3 (Leningrad: Khudozhestvennaia literatura, 1982), 129. In Abramov's

story "Al'ka," the more urbanized characters explain what bikinis are and what it means to live together before marriage. On "the distortion of foreign words either through mispronunciation or a lack of comprehension" in Rasputin's works, see Polowy, *The Novellas of Valentin Rasputin*, 125–35.

31. Hugh McLean, "Skaz," in *Handbook of Russian Literature*, 420. Literary theorists such as Eikhenbaum, Tynyanov, Vinogradov, and Bakhtin have all written on skaz; Russian examples are found in the works of Gogol, Leskov, Babel, Zoshchenko, and other writers.

32. Vasilii Shukshin, "Raskas," in *Okhota zhit'* (Kazan: Tatarskoe knizhnoe izdatel'stvo, 1977), 181; trans. James Nelson, in Vasily Shukshin, *Snowball Berry Red and Other Stories*, ed. Donald M. Fiene (Ardis: Ann Arbor, 1979), 36. Further citations will be to the Russian and English texts, respectively.

33. Ibid., 182/37.

34. Vasilii Belov, "Bukhtiny vologodskie," in *Izbrannye proizvedeniia v trekh tomakh*, vol. 2 (Moscow: Sovremennik, 1983), 148. This first appeared in *NM*, no. 8 (1969).

35. Heide Wüst has also noted that "skaz seldom appears in modern Village Prose in its pure form": *Tradition und Innovation in der sowjetrussischen Dorfprosa der sechziger und siebziger Jahre. Zur Funktion, Darstellung und Gehalt des dörflichen Helden bei Vasilij Šukšin und Valentin Rasputin* (Munich: Otto Sagner, 1984), 27. See also Galina Belaia, "Rozhdenie novykh stilevykh form kak protsess preodoleniia 'neitral'nogo' stilia," in *Mnogoobrazie stilei sovetskoi literatury. Voprosy tipologii*, ed. N. K. Gei et al. (Moscow: Nauka, 1978), 460–85; and N. A. Kozhevnikova, "O sootnoshenii rechi avtora i personazha," in *Iazykovye protsessy sovremennoi russkoi khudozhestvennoi literatury. Proza*, ed. A. I. Gorshkov (Moscow: Nauka, 1977), 7–98.

36. Chudakova, "Zametki," 237/93. For another useful survey of the poetics of this period, see Wolf Schmid, "Thesen zur innovatorischen Poetik der russischen Gegenwartsprosa," *Wiener Slawistischer Almanach*, no. 4 (1979): 67–68.

37. Chudakova, "Zametki," 244–45/109–12

38. *Zaum* 'trans-sense language' involved the creation of words whose effect did not depend on an exact meaning but on sound symbolism or on the imaginative use of Slavic roots; it was a hallmark of the Russian avant-garde (ca. 1912–1930) and a bête noire of traditionalists.

39. Abramov, "Iazyk," 582–83. On the "interference" of the narrator's and hero's speech, see Schmid, "Thesen," 67–68.

40. The comments on interior monologue in this paragraph are a paraphrase of G. Schaarschmidt, "Interior Monologue and Soviet Literary Criticism," *Canadian Slavonic Papers* 8 (1966): 143–52. Schaarschmidt mentions Aksenov and Bondarev but no *derevenshchiki*, which is not surprising since urban writers took up this device before the ruralists. See also Schmid, "Thesen," 71–73.

41. On interior monologue in Rasputin, see Polowy, *The Novellas of Valentin Rasputin*, 143–50.

42. Vladimir Lichutin, "Obrabotno—vremia svadeb" (the first part of *Poslednii koldun*), in *Poslednii koldun* (Moscow: Sovremennik, 1980), 21–22.

43. Vasilii Belov, response to a survey of Soviet writers in "Literatura i iazyk," *VL*, no. 6 (1967): 98–99.

44. Chudakova, "Zametki," 234–35/86–89.

45. I. Borisova, "Privichnoe delo zhizn'," *LG*, Dec. 3, 1966; quoted in Chudakova, "Zametki," 235/88–89.

46. By "masking," I mean incomplete, indefinite reference to the agent of an action, the result being a disorienting effect on the reader. Masking can be used, for example, when the author wants to hesitate between a natural and supernatural explanation of unusual events or characters, a situation that Todorov calls the "fantastic." In Russian, masking can be accomplished through the use of anaphoric pronouns without referents, e.g., *ona* and *ono* (the feminine and neuter pronouns) used in Tolstoy's works to refer to *smert'* 'death' (a feminine noun), indefinite pronouns like *chto-to* 'something' and *kto-to* 'someone', and impersonal verbal constructions. By impersonal constructions I mean not only verbs that usually appear without a subject, like *morozilo* '[it] was freezing', but also—and more importantly—verbs that are usually personal, like *shumelo* 'there-was-a-noise'. The first have been called "absolutely" impersonal and the second "relatively" impersonal. I have used the term "depersonalized" for this second group, which are deliberate grammatical stylistic devices that serve to "mask" the agent of the action named. For more on grammatical masking, see my articles on Tolstoy's use of this device: "Masking the Fantastic and the Taboo in Tolstoy's 'Polikushka,'" *SEEJ* 25:1 (1981); "Death Masks in Tolstoy," *SR* 41:2 (1982); "The Metamorphosis of Death in Tolstoy," *Language and Style* 18:2 (1985); and "Tolstoy and the Geometry of Fear," *Modern Language Studies* 15:4 (1985).

47. Ronald Blythe, *Akenfield: Portrait of an English Village* (New York: Dell, 1973), 80.

48. Fedor Abramov, "Al'ka," in *Posledniaia okhota* (Moscow: Sovetskaia Rossiia, 1973), 125.

49. Ibid., 129.

50. Ibid., 151.

51. Valentin Rasputin, "Vasilii i Vasilisa," in *Izbrannye proizvedeniia v 2-kh tomakh*, vol. 2 (Moscow: Molodaia gvardiia, 1984), 395; trans. Alan Myers, in Valentin Rasputin, *You Live and Love and Other Stories* (New York: Vanguard, 1986), 149–50.

52. Valentin Rasputin, "Vniz i vverkh po techeniiu," in *Vniz i vverkh po techeniiu* (Moscow: Sovetskaia Rossiia, 1972), 252; "Downstream," trans. Valentina Brougher and Helen Poot, in *Contemporary Russian Prose*, ed. C. and E. Proffer (Ann Arbor: Ardis, 1982), 384. Further citations are to the Russsian and English texts, respectively. I have put the impersonal forms in italics.

53. Ibid., 253/386.

54. Viktor Astaf'ev, "Predchuvstvie ledokhoda," *NS*, no. 6 (1988): 15–16. This is one of the supplementary chapters to his lengthy memoir *Poslednii poklon* (The final bow).

55. For more on this scene and on the phenomenon of dual faith, see chapter 4.

56. Valentin Rasputin, "Proshchanie s Materoi," in *Povesti* (Moscow: So-

vetskaia Rossiia, 1978), 214; *Farewell to Matyora*, trans. Antonina Bouis (1979; Evanston: Northwestern University Press, 1991), 15. Further references are to the Russian and English texts, respectively; italics are mine.

57. Ibid., 274/91–92
58. Ibid., 317/145.
59. Ibid., 347/182.
60. Richard Coe, *When the Grass Was Taller: Autobiography and the Experience of Childhood* (New Haven: Yale University Press, 1984), 205–39.
61. Abramov, *Puti-pereput'ia*, 80–81.
62. Emmet Kennedy, *A Cultural History of the French Revolution* (New Haven: Yale University Press, 1989), 32.
63. Boris Ekimov, "Pastush'ia zvezda," *NM*, no. 2 (1989): 10.
64. Rasputin, "Vniz," 260/393.
65. Vladimir Soloukhin, *Smekh za levym plechom* (Frankfurt: Possev, 1988), 185.
66. Since the late 1980s there has been extensive lobbying for the renaming of towns, cities, neighborhoods, and streets. Sometimes this reflected a desire to remove honors previously awarded to leaders like Brezhnev; at other times—and this started as a grassroots movement—it stems from the desire to go back to the pre-Revolutionary name. Many of Moscow's streets have regained their old names, Kalinin became Tver' once again, and Leningraders in 1991 voted to return to "St. Petersburg." Sergei Zalygin and other rural writers have supported this movement, which seems so far to have been a mostly urban phenomenon. Villages themselves have not been subject so much in the Soviet period to renaming; more often they were combined under a kolkhoz title or abandoned.
67. Vladimir Krupin, "Sorokovoi den'. Povest' v pis'makh," *NS*, no. 11 (1981): 80. These names are often made up of linguistically meaningful components: Chernyi Voron is 'Black Raven', Krasnyi Iar is 'Red/Beautiful Ravine', etc. I have chosen to leave them unglossed because they are proper names.
68. Solzhenitsyn, "Matryona's Home," 425.
69. Ibid.
70. Viktor Astaf'ev, "Konchina," *NS*, no. 6 (1988): 22.

CHAPTER FOUR
TIME, BACKWARD!

1. Valentin Kataev, *Time, Forward!* trans. C. Malamuth (1933, 1961; rpt. Bloomington: Indiana University Press, 1976), 69.
2. Valentin Katayev, *The Grass of Oblivion*, trans. Robert Daglish (London: Macmillan, 1969), 183. Mayakovsky was in the midst of reciting his poem "The March of Time" ("Marsh vremeni") when he made this suggestion to Kataev. See also Dodona Kiziria, "Four Demons of Valentin Kataev," *SR* 44:4 (Winter 1985): 648, and Victor Terras, "Majakovskij and Time," *SEEJ* 13:2 (1969): 151–63. Dmitrii Moldavskii saw "Time, Forward!" as an appropriate epigraph for a dozen novels from the period of the first Five Year Plan. See D. Moldavskii, *V nachale tridtsatykh* (Leningrad: Sovetskii pisatel', 1984), 23–24.

3. Moshe Lewin discusses the sense of "frenzy" in the late 1920s as various plans for urban and rural change were being formulated, in *The Making of the Soviet System* (New York: Pantheon, 1985), 27, 51; Richard Stites analyzes at length the sense of accelerated time in the early years of the Soviet state, in *Revolutionary Dreams: Utopian Vision and Experimental Life in the Russian Revolution* (New York: Oxford University Press, 1989).

4. V. Ilyenkov, *Driving Axle* (New York: International Publishers, 1933), 10 [no trans. listed].

5. Geoffrey Hosking, *The Awakening of the Soviet Union* (Cambridge: Harvard University Press, 1990), 49.

6. John Berger, *Pig Earth* (New York: Pantheon, 1979), 204–5. I have paraphrased Berger's presentation of these concepts.

7. Vladimir Lichutin, "Divis'-gora. V ozhidanii chuda," in *Divis'-gora* (Moscow: Sovremennik,1986), 103.

8. The images of "highways" and "country roads" (*bol'shaki* and *proselki*) were prominent in critical debates as they seemed to symbolize the contrasting orientations of Socialist Realism and Village Prose.

9. Consider, for example, Natalia Baranskaia's story "Nedelia kak nedelia" ("A Week Like Any Other"). Iurii Trifonov is a notable exception to this general rule; he admitted feeling closer to the *derevenshchiki* than to urban writers, as is evident, for example, in the story "Igry v sumerkakh" ("Games at Dusk").

10. Berger, *Pig Earth*, 201.

11. L. Vil'chek, "Derevenskaia proza," in *Sovremennaia russkaia sovetskaia literatura* (in 2 parts; ed. A. Bocharov, G. Belaia), Part 2 (Moscow: Prosveshchenie, 1987), 84. Of course, writers continued to produce Socialist Realist works on contemporary rural life without interruption; these are not to be confused with the move by Rasputin and other Village Prose writers from the past into the present in the second half of the 1970s.

12. Geoffrey Hosking, "The Russian Peasant Rediscovered: Village Prose of the 1960s," *SR* 32:4 (Dec. 1973): 724 n. 26.

13. Aleksei Leonov, "Po letnim i zimnim dorogam," in *Khodiat devki* (Moscow: Sovetskaia Rossiia, 1971), 69.

14. Leonov, "Po letnim i zimnim dorogam," 8–9. This way of telling time is, of course, a feature of premodern rural life in general. Cf. the following entry in a parish register in Staffordshire, England for 1657: "Robert Stud and Tobey Dean his born in nuting time. Sara Dean his born in cucumber time." As quoted by G. E. Evans, *Ask the Fellows Who Cut the Hay* (London: Faber and Faber, 1956), 149–50.

15. Viktor Perepelka, "Starinnyi kalendar'," in *Lastochka nad gorodom* (Leningrad: Sovetskii pisatel', 1973), 201–2.

16. Ibid., 201.

17. Ibid., 208.

18. Linda J. Ivanits, *Russian Folk Belief* (Armonk, NY: M. E. Sharpe, 1989), 29–30. Vasilii Belov says that at least one literate person in each village possessed such a calendar: Vasilii Belov, *Lad. Ocherki o narodnoi estetike* (Moscow: Molodaia gvardiia, 1982), 151.

19. For a translation of this story see Appendix I.

20. A literal translation of the title is "A premontion/presentiment of the

annual breaking-up and floating downstream of the ice in the river." Viktor Astaf'ev, "Predchustvie ledokhoda," *NS*, no. 6 (1988). For other examples of dual faith, see Lichutin, "Divis'-gora," 40–47.

21. Astaf'ev, "Predchustvie," 16–17; Astaf'ev also mentions the springtime activities of the fertility god Iarilo, but this comment could be more of an addition on the author's part than a reflection of the villagers' worldview. Lichutin discusses Iarilo in a 1989 essay "Tsep' nezrimaia," *Druzhba narodov*, no. 8 (1989): 232.

22. Valentin Rasputin, "Vasilii i Vasilisa," in *Izbrannye proizvedeniia v 2-kh tomakh*, vol. 2 (Moscow: Molodaia gvardiia, 1984), 391; "Vasili and Vasilisa," trans. Alan Myers, in *You Live and Love and Other Stories*, foreword by Richard Lourie (New York: Vanguard, 1986), 144. Further references are to the English translation.

23. Ibid., 169.

24. Vasilii Belov, "Privychnoe delo," in *Izbrannye proizvedeniia v 3-kh tomakh*, vol. 2 (Moscow: Sovremennik, 1983), 142; Vasilii Belov, "That's How It Is," trans. Eve Manning, *Soviet Literature*, no. 1 (1969). I have adjusted Manning's translation as necessary.

25. Ibid., 146.

26. Valentin Rasputin, "Proshchanie s Materoi," in *Izbrannye proizvedeniia v 2-kh tomakh*, vol. 2 (Moscow: Molodaia gvardiia, 1984), 208; *Farewell to Matyora*, trans. Antonina W. Bouis (1979; Evanston: Northwestern University Press, 1991), 1. Further references are to the English translation.

27. Belov, *Lad*, 7.

28. The term dates from the time when the local church would supply rye from its stores for beer; ibid., 215, 261.

29. Berger, *Pig Earth*, 200–201.

30. Vladimir Lichutin, "Babushki i diadiushki," *Druzhba narodov*, no. 6 (1976): 50.

31. Goncharov, *Oblomov*, trans. David Magarshak (Baltimore: Penguin, 1967), 130.

32. Zinaida Gippius, "Outside of Time: An Old Etude" (first published in *Alyi mech. Rasskazy*, 1906), in *A Russian Cultural Revival: A Critical Anthology of Emigré Literature before 1939*, ed. and trans. Temira Pachmuss (Knoxville: University of Tennessee Press, 1981), 44.

33. Belov emphasizes that peasants knew the day of the week and the proximity of holidays and fasts; each day had its own set of activities, practices, characteristics, and folk sayings. Belov, *Lad*, 151.

34. I. A. Bunin, *Izbrannoe* (Moscow: Khudozhestvennaia literatura, 1970), 52.

35. Vladimir Lichutin, "Drevo pamiati," in *Divis'-gora*, 3. *Rodovaia pamiat'* should not be confused with *geneticheskaia pamiat'* (genetic or racial memory), a polemical concept advanced by chauvinist literary critics. See Vladimir Bondarenko, "Obratenie rodstva," *V mire knig*, no. 7 (1989): 12.

36. Lichutin, "Drevo pamiati," 5.

37. Rasputin has written about *dukhovnaia pamiat'* 'spiritual memory'; see, for example, Gerald Mikkelson and Margaret Winchell, "Valentin Rasputin

and His Siberia," introduction to Valentin Rasputin, *Siberia on Fire* (Dekalb: Northern Illinois University Press, 1989), xx.

38. Lichutin, "Divis'-gora," 54; see also 8–10.

39. Vladimir Krupin, "Sorokovoi den'," *NS*, no. 11 (1981): 111, 115.

40. Feodor Abramov, "Poezdka v proshloe," with extensive notes and variants provided by L. Krutikova-Abramova, *NM*, no. 5 (1989): 11.

41. Ibid., 20. In a variant of this scene, Miksha sees the living and the dead standing together in the church, and he marches to meet them as some of them sing "The International" and others sing church hymns (35).

42. David Gillespie, "Ironies and Legacies: Village Prose and Glasnost'," *Forum for Modern Language Studies* 27:1 (1991): 80–81.

43. Viktor Astaf'ev, *Poslednii poklon* (Leningrad: Lenizdat, 1982), 182; this chapter has been translated by Robert Daglish as "Granny's Day," in Viktor Astafiev, *The Horse with the Pink Mane* (Moscow: Progress, 1978), 137. I have altered the translation where necessary.

44. On the concept of *rod* in Rasputin, see Teresa Polowy, *The Novellas of Valentin Rasputin* (New York: Peter Lang, 1989), 110–15.

45. Rasputin, *Farewell to Matyora*, 105.

46. Ibid., 55. On the Master's role in the novel, see Heide Wüst, *Tradition und Innovation in der sowjetrussischen Dorfprosa der sechziger und siebziger Jahre* (Munich: Otto Sagner, 1984), 198–202, and Renate Schäper, *Die Prosa V. G. Rasputins. Erzählverfahren und ethisch-religiöse Problematik* (Munich: Otto Sagner, 1985), 157–58. See also my introduction to the 1991 reprint of *Farewell to Matyora*, xiii–xiv.

47. Rasputin generally liked the film but thought it would have been even better had Shepitko and the scriptwriter lived to make it. Source: conversation in Amsterdam, May 31, 1988.

48. See Donald Fanger, "The Peasant in Literature," in Wayne S. Vucinich, ed., *The Peasant in Nineteenth-Century Russia* (Stanford: Stanford University Press, 1968), 255–56. See also my articles "The Metamorphosis of Death in Tolstoy," *Language and Style* 18:2 (1985), and "Death Masks in Tolstoy," *SR* 41:2 (1982).

49. E.g., "In Nadezhda Pavlovna's vivid dreams, she saw all her relations, long dead, as if they were young and full of life"; Vladimir Lichutin, *Liubostai* (Moscow: Sovetskii pisatel', 1987), 86. See also Lichutin, "Divis'-gora," 52.

50. Viktor Astaf'ev, "Oda russkomu ogorodu," in *Povesti* (Moscow: Khudozhestvennaia literatura, 1984), 85–86.

51. Lichutin, "Divis'-gora," 20, 49.

52. Vladimir Nabokov, *Speak, Memory* (New York: G. P. Putnam's Sons, 1966), 73. The Russian version was first published abroad: *Drugie berega* (New York: Chekhov Publishing House, 1954), and only much later in the Soviet Union: *Drugie berega* (Moscow: Knizhnaia palata, 1989).

53. Vladimir Vasil'ev, "Slovo o rodine," introduction to Evgenii Nosov, *Izbrannye proizvedeniia v 2-kh tomakh*, vol. 1 (Moscow: Sovetskaia Rossiia, 1983), 6.

54. "What remained was not a memory, but the memory of a memory, a distant, much-weakened reflection and echo of what had been." Aleksandr

Prokhanov, "Svetlei lazuri," *Oktiabr'*, no. 9 (1986): 3. This statement at the beginning of Prokhanov's story expresses the sense of the past that prevails as well in much of Village Prose.

55. Viktor Astaf'ev, *Poslednii poklon* (Leningrad: Lenizdat, 1982), 274.

56. Lichutin, "Divis'-gora," 21.

57. Vladimir Tendriakov, "Den' na rodine," *Nauka i religiia*, no. 11 (1964): 43.

58. Valentin Rasputin, "Vniz i vverkh po techeniiu," in *Vniz i vverkh po techeniiu* (Moscow: Sovetskaia Rossiia, 1972), 254; "Downstream," trans. Valentina Brougher and Helen Poot, in *Contemporary Russian Prose*, ed. C. and E. Proffer (Ann Arbor: Ardis, 1982), 387.

59. On Rasputin's treatment of time, see David Gillespie, *Valentin Rasputin and Soviet Russian Village Prose* (London: Modern Humanities Research Association, 1986), 27–51.

CHAPTER FIVE
BORROWED TIME: METAPHORS FOR LOSS IN VILLAGE PROSE

1. The first epigraph is from Igor' Zolotusskii, "Proza Feodora Abramova," *LG*, Feb. 28, 1990: 5. The second is from Vladimir Lichutin, "Divis'-gora. V ozhidanii chuda," in *Divis'-gora* (Moscow: Sovremennik, 1986), 123.

2. See also Vasilii Subbotin, "Proshchanie s mirom" (Farewell to the world), *Oktiabr'*, no. 6 (1988); V. Potanin, "Poslednie koni" (The Last horses); A. Petukhov, *Posledniaia okhota* (The last hunt); F. Abramov, "Posledniaia strada" (The final harvest); and V. Goncharov, "Posledniaia zhatva" (The final harvest). Vladimir Soloukhin announced in 1990 that he would soon publish a "delayed" work from 1976, a five-hundred-page manuscript called *Posledniaia stupen'*, in the journal *Moskva*; see "Idti po svoei trope. Interv'iu pered publikatsiei," *LG*, May 30, 1990: 4.

3. Vladimir Soloukhin, "Bol' ego i nadezhda," *Ogonek*, no. 13 (1987): 2–3. On the theme of "last things" see Zolotusskii, "Proza Feodora Abramova," 5. On relevant folk beliefs, see Natalie Moyle, "Mermaids (*Rusalki*) and Russian Beliefs about Women," in *New Studies in Russian Language and Literature Presented to Bayara Aroutunova*, ed. A. Crone and C. Chvany (Columbus, OH: Slavica, 1987), 232–35.

4. Enthusiastic, upbeat names for collective farms and new settlements such as "Friendship" and "Victory" are contrasted to the colorful old names for Russian villages.

5. Siegfried Melchinger, *Anton Chekhov*, trans. Edith Tarcov (New York: Frederick Ungar, 1972), 153.

6. It also shows the gentry's at times tragically careless attitude toward the peasants. Rayfield mentions Chekhov's "Svirel'" (Panpipes), where the panpipe sound broods on the destruction of the world of gentry and peasants and introduces an entire catalog of loss; Donald Rayfield, *Chekhov: The Evolution of His Art* (New York: Barnes and Noble, 1975), 71. Chekhov's plays have a number of plot elements in common, including the loss of estates by the gentry. The breaking string is heard again in Rasputin's story "Downstream."

7. James B. Woodward, *Ivan Bunin: A Study of His Fiction* (Chapel Hill: University of North Carolina Press, 1980), 39.

8. I have to a certain extent simplified the role of the peasant in nineteenth-century Russian literature, but there were relatively few works that were focused accurately and at length on changes in peasant life, while also achieving high artistic quality. In Fanger's excellent survey of the peasant in nineteenth-century Russian literature, he said at the outset that he was struck by "the almost complete absence of works depicting peasant life from the inside"; the Golden Age of the novel in Russia "shows us not a single significant novel of peasant life." Donald Fanger, "The Peasant in Literature," in *The Peasant in Nineteenth-Century Russia*, ed. Wayne S. Vucinich (Stanford: Stanford University Press, 1968), 231. Irving Howe remarked that "Dostoevsky's peasant was as much an idealized figure as the proletarian of the cruder Marxists"; Dostoevsky's work touches little on peasant life while implying "an exalted vision of the peasants." Irving Howe, "Dostoevsky: The Politics of Salvation," in *Politics and the Novel* (New York: Horizon Press, 1957), 57. Rose Glickman has shown that Fanger's generalizations ignore *raznochintsy* writers of the 1860s like N. V. Uspensky and F. M. Reshetnikov (both the sons of village clergy), who in the interval between gentry idealization (in the cause of ending serfdom) and Populist idealization (which saw the peasant as proto-Socialist) described Russian peasant life in authentic, if depressing, stories. She does not, however, claim that these were works of enduring artistry, and sees them as primarily of interest to intellectual historians; see Rose Glickman, "An Alternative View of the Peasantry: The *Raznochintsy* Writers of the 1860s," *SR* 32:4 (Dec. 1973): 693–704.

9. On peasant writers see John Glad, "Peasant Writers and Poets," in *Handbook of Russian Literature*, ed. Victor Terras (New Haven: Yale University Press, 1985), 334–35.

10. Sergei Esenin, "Ia poslednii poet derevni" (1920), in *Sobranie sochinenii v piati tomakh*, vol. 2 (Moscow: Khudozhestvennaia literatura, 1966), 95–96; on this theme, see Gordon McVay, *Esenin: A Life* (Ann Arbor: Ardis, 1976), 131–48.

11. See also *Hatred* (I. Sukhov), *Sons* (V. Smirnov), "Dawn" (Iu. Laptev), and *The Sons' Revolt* (Babaevskii).

12. V. Ilyenkov, *Driving Axle* (New York: International Publishers, 1933), 454.

13. Katerina Clark, *The Soviet Novel: History as Ritual*, 2d ed. (Chicago: University of Chicago Press, 1985), 242.

14. Zolotusskii, "Proza Feodora Abramova," 5.

15. Vladimir Lichutin, "Babushki i diadiushki," *Druzhba narodov*, no. 6 (1976): 15.

16. Georgii Tsvetov, *Tema derevni v sovremennoi sovetskoi proze* (Leningrad: Znanie, 1985), 12.

17. Esenin contrasts the train to a horse—which symbolizes the dying village—running alongside it; McVay, *Esenin*, 139–40.

18. Evgenii Nosov, "Domoi za mater'iu," in *Izbrannye proizvedeniia v 2-kh tomakh*, vol. 1 (Moscow: Sovetskaia Rossiia, 1983), 146; the story originally appeared in *Literaturnaia Rossiia*, May 19, 1967.

19. This anticipates by a few years a somewhat similar theme in Iurii Trifonov's powerful story "Obmen" (*The Exchange*).

20. V. Rakhmanin, "I ostanetsia berega," *LR*, Oct. 17, 1975.

21. Boris Ekimov, "Posledniaia khata," in *Za teplym khlebom* (Moscow: Sovremennik, 1986), 383.

22. Aleksei Leonov, "Kondyr'," in *Khodiat devki* (Moscow: Sovetskaia Rossiia, 1971), 144.

23. Viktor Perepelka, "Poslednii den' v svoem dome," in *Lastochka nad gorodom* (Leningrad: Sovetskii pisatel', 1973), 70–71.

24. Vladimir Lichutin, *Poslednii koldun* (Moscow: Sovremennik, 1980), 278, 341.

25. Ibid., 211.

26. Vladimir Soloukhin, "Pokhorony Stepanidy Ivanovny," *NM*, no. 9 (1987): 137; Vladimir Soloukhin, "Stepanida Ivanovna's Funeral," trans. Diane Nemec Ignashev, in *The New Soviet Fiction*, ed. Sergei Zalygin (New York: Abbeville Press, 1989), 291.

27. Viktor Astaf'ev, "Konchina" (one of the supplementary chapters to *The Final Bow*), *NS*, no. 6 (1988): 26.

28. Fedor Abramov, "Brevenchatye mavzolei," in *Trava-murava* (Moscow: Sovremennik, 1983); trans. Eve Manning as "Wooden Mausoleums," in *The Swans Flew By* (Moscow: Raduga, 1986). Viktor Astaf'ev, "Slepoi rybak," *NS*, no. 5 (1986): 114.

29. For a discussion of the theme of "home" in Abramov's work, see Vladimir Bondarenko, "Beregi svoi dom," in *Sverstniki 1982*, ed. V. Dement'ev (Moscow: Sovremennik, 1982), 124–31. See also Anton Hiersche, *Sowjetische Dorfprosa. Geschichte und Problematik* (Berlin: Akademie-Verlag, 1985), 183–86. In the distant past an animal, usually a horse, was sacrificed to protect a new house and its occupants; this evolved—for practical reasons—into the use of a wooden representation of a horse's head.

30. The fear is that the *domovoi* will refuse to move to the new dwelling and will harm rather than help the family. For an excellent discussion of the *domovoi*, see Linda Ivanits, *Russian Folk Belief* (Armonk, NY: M. E. Sharp, 1989), chapter 4 and narratives 41–43. By the late nineteenth century, the house-spirit had evolved from the pagan ancestor cult in which it represented a "former head of the family" to the stage at which it represented a relative who had died before his time and had therefore been incorporated into the ranks of impure forces (*nechistaia sila*); traditional house-blessing ceremonies became not just a commemorative occasion but also a "rite of protection" (52, 62).

31. W. R. S. Ralston, *The Songs of the Russian People* (2d ed. 1872; New York: Haskell House, 1970), 126. The rest of this paragraph is a paraphrase of Ralston's remarks on 126 and 135–39. Ralston's work seems to be based largely on Aleksandr Afanas'ev, *Poeticheskie vozreniia Slavian na prirodu*, vol. 2 (1868; The Hague: Mouton, 1969).

32. For a discussion of boundary crossing and place-spirits, see Natalie Moyle, "Spacey Soviets and the Russian Attitude towards Territorial Passage," *New York Folklore* 7:1–2 (Summer 1981): 88.

33. Valentin Rasputin, "Vek zhivi—vek liubi," in *Izbrannye proizvedeniia v*

2-kh tomakh, vol. 1 (Moscow: Molodaia gvardiia, 1984), 347; "You Live and Love," trans. Alan Myers, in *You Live and Love and Other Stories* (New York: Vanguard, 1986), 14. Further references are to the English translation.

34. Valentin Rasputin, "Vniz i vverkh po techeniiu," in *Vniz i vverkh po techeniiu* (Moscow: Sovetskaia Rossiia, 1972), 262; "Downstream," trans. Valentina Brougher and Helen Poot, in *Contemporary Russian Prose*, ed. C. and E. Proffer (Ann Arbor: Ardis, 1982), 394. Further references are to the translation. This project is the same one treated enthusiastically in Evtushenko's 1964 poem "Bratskaia GES" ("The Bratsk Hydroelectric Station").

35. Rasputin, "Downstream," 415.

36. On the destruction of the cyclical pattern of rural life in this work, see Heide Wüst, *Tradition und Innovation in der sowjetrussischen Dorfprosa der sechziger und siebziger Jahre* (Munich: Otto Sagner, 1984), 185–92.

37. These new settlements are an important setting in Village Prose, e.g., Aleksei Leonov's "Kondyr'," and in post–Village Prose, e.g,. Rasputin's "The Fire." They make a contrast—as the kolkhoz itself did—to the traditional village.

38. Valentin Rasputin, "Proshchanie s Materoi," in *Povesti* (Moscow: Sovetskaia Rossiia, 1978), 346; *Farewell to Matyora*, trans. Antonina Bouis (1979; Evanston: Northwestern University Press, 1991), 181. A more extensive analysis of *Matyora* can be found in "Master of the Island," my introduction to the 1991 reprint. Further references will be to the translation. In a similar vein, Lichutin said, "He who loses the past, loses the future": see V. Lichutin, "Tsep' nezrimaia," *Druzhba narodov*, no. 8 (1989): 247.

39. Rasputin, *Farewell to Matyora*, 191.

40. Soloukhin, "Bol' ego," 3.

41. The movie *Farewell* ends with Pavel behind a glass door in the boat calling out "Matyo-o-ra!" in despair.

42. Vladimir Lichutin, "Babushki i diadiushki," *Druzhba narodov*, no. 6 (1976).

43. Valentin Rasputin, "Ne mog ne prostit'sia s Materoi," *LG*, March 16, 1977; trans. as "I Had to Say Goodbye to Matera," in *SSL* 14:3 (Summer 1978): 43.

44. Igor' Dedkov, "Prodlennyi svet," afterword to Rasputin, *Vek zhivi—vek liubi*, 537.

45. Rasputin, "You Live and Love," 12.

46. Viktor Astaf'ev, "Pechal'nyi detektiv," *Oktiabr'*, no. 1 (1986): 73.

47. Ibid., 73.

48. Aleksei Leonov, "Po letnim i zimnim dorogam," in *Khodiat devki*, 68.

49. Astaf'ev, "Konchina," 25.

50. Lichutin, "Divis'-gora," 103.

51. Lichutin complains that a whole range of folk genres lose their "magic power" in printed collections; see "Divis'-gora," 107.

52. Fyodor Sologub, *The Petty Demon,* trans. S. D. Cioran (Ann Arbor: Ardis, 1983), 109–10.

53. Evgenii Nosov, "I uplyvaiut parakhody, i ostaiutsia berega," in *Izbrannye proizvedeniia v 2-kh tomakh*, vol. 2 (Moscow: Sovetskii pisatel', 1983), 284.

54. Ibid., 338.

55. Fedor Abramov, "Dereviannye koni," in *Posledniaia okhota. Povesti i rasskazy* (Moscow: Sovetskaia Rossiia, 1973), 15–43; "Wooden Horses," trans. Eve Manning, in *The Swans Flew By*, 17–44. This story is analyzed in some detail in Hiersche, *Sowjetische Dorfprosa*, 178–81.

56. Vladimir Krupin, *Zhivaia voda, Roman-gazeta*, no. 15 (1985): 21.

57. On Yashin's story, see Deming Brown, *Soviet Russian Literature since Stalin* (London: Cambridge University Press, 1978), 233.

58. Vasilii Belov, "Plotnitskie rasskazy," in *Izbrannye proizvedeniia v 3-kh tomakh*, vol. 2 (Moscow: Sovremennik, 1983), 266; "Carpenter Yarns," trans. Eve Manning, in Vasily Belov, *Morning Rendezvous: Stories* (Moscow: Raduga, 1983).

59. Aleksei Leonov, "Vdovii kolodets," in *Khodiat devki*, 184.

60. Valentin Rasputin, "Ekh, starukha," in *Krai vozle samogo neba. Ocherki i rasskazy* (Moscow: Izvestiia, 1985), 537; "The Old Woman," trans. Alan Myers, in *You Live and Love and Other Stories* (New York: Vanguard, 1986), 176–77.

61. Lichutin, *Poslednii koldun*, 346, 362–63, 385, 390–91. On the death of sorcerers, see Ivanits, *Russian Folk Belief*, 95–96, 119–20, and S. V. Maksimov, *Nechistaia, nevedomaia i krestnaia sila* (St. Petersburg: Golike and Vil'borg, 1903), 125–27. Ivanits points out that shamans must pass on their knowledge to another person in order to free their souls at death (95–96, 119).

62. The apocalyptic tone of their statements—and those of other conservatives—has many sources, one of which must be Village Prose.

63. Candles were often placed in the hands of corpses, and it was believed that the dead walk with candles at night; see Lichutin, "Divis'-gora," 120.

64. Fedor Abramov, "Poezdka v proshloe," ed. L. Krutikova-Abramova, *NM*, no. 5 (1989): 20, 35.

CHAPTER SIX
THE VILLAGE PROSE WRITERS AND THEIR CRITICS

1. This was said to Turgenev by someone who met him on Nevsky Prospekt shortly after the publication of *Fathers and Sons* in the spring of 1862, when the city was plagued by a rash of fires attributed to revolutionaries; quoted by Avrahm Yarmolinsky in *Turgenev: The Man, His Art and His Age* (New York: Orion, 1959), 204.

2. Rosalind Krauss, "Poststructuralism and the Paraliterary," in *The Originality of the Avant-Garde and Other Modernist Myths* (Cambridge: MIT Press, 1985), 292–93; as quoted by Catherine R. Stimpson, "Woolf's Room, Our Project," in *The Future of Literary Theory*, ed. Ralph Cohen (New York: Routledge, 1989), 131.

3. A. P. Petrik, "'Derevenskaia proza': Itogi i perspektivy izucheniia," *Filologicheskie nauki*, no. 1 (1981): 66.

4. Deming Brown discusses the distortion of rural fiction by critics, "Nationalism and Ruralism in Recent Soviet Russian Literature," *Review of National Literatures* 2:1 (Spring 1972): 191. See also Philippa Lewis, "Peasant Nostalgia in Contemporary Russian Literature," *Soviet Studies* 28:4 (Oct. 1976):

548–69. Lewis notes that a number of critics "strongly defended the view of the moral superiority of the village . . . often distorting the works reviewed so as to fit their own scheme"(558).

5. M. Lobanov, one of the nationalistic critics who has written about Village Prose, complained, with no sense of self-irony, about Dobroliubov's misuse of Ostrovsky; S. Kaltakhchian, "Kuda stremitsia 'edinyj potok'?" *Sovetskaia kul'tura*, March 17, 1987: 6.

6. Perhaps Babaevsky hoped to take advantage not only of the popularity of Village Prose but also of the fact that when *The Wide-Open Spaces* appeared in the journal *Moskva* (nos. 9, 10, and 11 [1979]), canonical Village Prose was under attack by orthodox Party critics for having strayed too far from Socialist Realism. Katerina Clark discusses this novel in "Zhdanovist Fiction and Village Prose," in *Russian Literature and Criticism*, Selected Papers from the Second World Congress for Soviet and East European Studies, Garmisch-Partenkirchen, Sept. 30–Oct. 4, 1980, ed. Evelyn Bristol (Berkeley: Berkeley Slavic Specialities, 1982), 36–48.

7. Fedor Abramov, "Liudi kolkhoznoi derevni v poslevoennoi proze," *NM*, no. 4 (1954); Sergei Zalygin, *Zhizn' kolkhoznoi derevni i literatura. Tvorcheskaia diskussiia v Soiuze Pisatelei SSSR* (Moscow: Sovetskii pisatel', 1956), 230; Valentin Ovechkin, "Kolkhoznaia zhizn' i literatura," *NM*, no. 12 (1955).

8. On the early years of the Village Prose movement, see Anton Hiersche, *Sowjetische Dorfprosa. Geschichte und Problematik* (Berlin: Akademie-Verlag, 1985), 36–71.

9. Even less popular is *derevenshchina* 'country bumpkin, rustic'. "It's not surprising that writers unanimously . . . tried to disown such a tag." G. A. Tsvetov, *Tema derevni v sovremennoi sovetskoi proze* (Leningrad: Znanie, 1985), 4. Rasputin used the term *derevenshchik* at a conference in Amsterdam over Mozhaev's objections, saying that he needed it to discuss the subject at hand. Mozhaev denied the existence of Village Prose, Urban Prose, and War Prose, saying that these are examples of divisions created by critics. He resents the fact that it puts talented (Rasputin, Belov) and mediocre (M. Alekseev, Proskurin) writers together in one group. "The Topicality of Contemporary Soviet Literature," a conference at the University of Amsterdam, May 31–June 2, 1988. This discussion took place on June 1. It was announced at the conference that the proceedings would be published in English by Reidel, Dordrecht.

10. V. Kardin, "Diskussionaia tribuna. Sekret uspekha," *VL*, no. 4 (1986): 102–3. See also V. Kardin, "Dvoe protiv goroda," *Literaturnoe obozrenie* 6 (1986): 92–101, trans. by J. L. Hellie as "Two against the City," *SSL* 23:2 (Spring 1987): 58–87. And see Anatolii Lanshchikov, "Ostorozhno—Kontseptsiia! (polemicheskie zametki)," *Molodaia gvardiia*, no. 2 (1969).

11. Tsvetov, *Tema derevni*, 5.

12. Petrik, "'Derevenskaia proza,'" 65–68; Tsvetov, *Tema derevni*, 5, 6, 31; L. Vil'chek, "Vniz po techeniiu derevenskoi prozy," *VL*, no. 6 (1985): 34–35.

13. Vil'chek, "Vniz po techeniiu," 35; Tsvetov, *Tema derevni*, 5.

14. There are a number of interesting and useful discussions of these critical battles. See, for example, Geoffrey Hosking, *Beyond Socialist Realism: Soviet*

Fiction since "Ivan Denisovich" (New York: Holmes and Meier, 1980), especially chapter 3, "Village Prose: Vasily Belov, Valentin Rasputin"; Lewis, "Peasant Nostalgia," 548–69; Deming Brown, *Soviet Russian Literature since Stalin* (Cambridge: Cambridge University Press, 1979), chapter 8, "The Village Writers"; Georg Witte, *Die sowjetische Kolchos- und Dorfprosa der fünfziger und sechziger Jahre* (Munich: Otto Sagner, 1983), 80–85; Katerina Clark, "The Centrality of Rural Themes in Postwar Soviet Fiction," in *Perspectives on Literature and Society in Eastern and Western Europe*, ed. Geoffrey Hosking and George Cushing (London: Macmillan, 1989), 76–100; Tsvetov, *Tema derevni*, 4. The dynamics and implications of these and other literary-political controversies will be the subject of my next book.

15. Lev Anninskii and V. Kozhinov, "Kriticheskii dialog. Moda na prostonarodnost'," *Kodry*, no. 3 (1971): 132. Two decades later, the Village Prose writers were again compared unfavorably to Zlatovratsky, Engelgardt, and other Populist literary figures. See Aleksandr Genis, "Vzgliad iz tupika," *Ogonek*, no. 52 (Dec. 22–29, 1990): 17–19.

16. Fedor Abramov, "O khlebe nasushchom i khlebe dukhovnom," *Sobranie sochinenii v 3-kh tomakh*, vol. 3 (Leningrad: Khudozhestvennaia literatura, 1982), 631; this essay also appeared in *NS*, no. 9 (1976).

17. Iu. Prodan, "Podvig narodnyi i proza voiny," *Kuban*, no. 2 (1977): 122.

18. Ibid.

19. Conversations with Village Prose writers have confirmed that war scenes were scrutinized very carefully by editors. Writers were asked not only to make cuts but also to add scenes showing Soviet partisans behind enemy lines in occupied areas of the USSR.

20. The remarks about the Village Prose hero up until Gusev's observation are a paraphrase of Viktor Kochetkov, "Ekskursiia v stranu detstva. Zametki o molodoi proze," *Moskva*, no. 6 (1973): 200–208.

21. Ibid., 208.

22. Vladimir Gusev, *V predchustvie novogo* (Moscow: Sovetskii pisatel', 1974), 197–98; as quoted by Tsvetov, *Tema derevni*, 4.

23. Igor' Shaitanov, "Reaktsiia na peremeny (Tochka zreniia avtora i geroia v literature o derevne)," *VL*, no. 5 (1981): 59.

24. E. Shklovskii, "Eto slozhnoe vremia ... Beseda s Viktorom Astaf'evym," *Literaturnoe obozrenie*, no. 3 (1986): 70.

25. Abramov, "O khlebe nasushchom," 628–33, and Dmitrii Likhachev, *Zametki o russkom*, 2d ed. (Moscow: Sovetskaia Rossiia, 1984), 54–61.

26. Andrei Voznesenskii, *Iverskii svet. Stikhi i poemy* (Tbilisi: Merani, 1984), 34–35; reference from Robert Porter, *Four Contemporary Russian Writers* (New York: Berg, 1989), 50–51. Another version of this poem has been translated by William Jay Smith and Vera Dunham as "Technology," in Andrei Voznesensky, *An Arrow in the Wall: Selected Poetry and Prose*, ed. W. J. Smith and F. D. Reeve (New York: Henry Holt, 1987), 138–41. In a 1987 visit to the United States, Voznesensky spoke of the decline of Village Prose, which had, he felt, simply become a reaction to the westernized city and had "outlived itself" (courtesy of Anna Tavis).

27. Daniil Granin, "Obratnyi bilet," *NM*, no. 8 (1976): 6.

28. Boris Pankin, "Proshloe, kotoroe vsegda s toboi," in *Strogaia literatura: Literaturno-kriticheskie stat'i i ocherki* (Moscow: Sovetskii pisatel', 1982), 237, 241. This article has been translated by Michel Vale as "The Past That Is Always with You," *SSL* 28:1 (Winter 1981–1982): 44, 48. The whole book was translated by Ruth English as *Demanding Literature: Soviet Literature of the Seventies and Early Eighties* (Moscow: Raduga, 1984).

29. George Gibian, "Forward Movement through Backward Glances (Soviet Russian and Czech Fiction: Hrabal, Syomin, Granin)," *Fiction and Drama in Eastern and Southeastern Europe*, Proceedings of the 1978 UCLA Conference, ed. Henryk Birnbaum and Thomas Eekman (Columbus, OH: Slavica, 1980), 161–75. Pankin, "Proshloe," 225, 241, 242.

30. Vsevolod Kochetov, *Chego zhe ty khochesh'*, *Oktiabr'*, no. 9 (1969): 50. This work was mentioned by Katerina Clark in *The Soviet Novel: History as Ritual*, 2d ed. (Chicago: University of Chicago Press, 1985), p. 243. Vladimir Krutikov remembers that there were, in turn, parodies of the Kochetov work.

31. I would like to thank Wallace Sherlock for bringing this story to my attention; it was clearly published in an émigré journal, but an extensive search has failed to reveal either the exact place or date of publication. Sorokin received high praise for his other parodies of Soviet writers; see Genis, "Vzgliad iz tupika," 18.

32. Joseph Brodsky, *Less Than One: Selected Essays* (New York: Farrar, Straus, Giroux, 1986), 294–95.

33. Vladimir Voinovich, *Tribunal. Sudebnaia komediia v trekh deistviiakh* (London: Overseas Publications Interchange, 1985), 69–70; the play was broadcast to the USSR in 1984 over the BBC Russian Service. Voinovich's work began to be published again in the USSR in the late 1980s.

34. Nancy Condee and Vladimir Padunov, "The *Soiuz* on Trial: Voinovich as Magistrate and Stage Manager," *The Russian Review* 46 (1987): 318.

35. Vladimir Voinovich, *The Fur Hat*, trans. Susan Brownsberger (New York: Harcourt Brace Jovanovich, 1989), 34.

36. Petr Vail and Aleksandr Genis, *Sovremennaia russkaia proza* (Ann Arbor: Hermitage, 1982), 93–95; and, by the same authors, "Nobelevskii argument," *Panorama*, Oct. 30–Nov. 6, 1987: 20. Carl Proffer here, as elsewhere, shared the "third wave" writers' view of Soviet literature; see Proffer, "Russian Writing and Border Guards: Twenty-five Years of the New Isolationism," in *The Widows of Russia and Other Writings* (Ann Arbor: Ardis, 1987), 142–59.

37. Vail and Genis, *Sovremennaia russkaia proza*, 94; Proffer, "Russian Writing," 142–59.

38. Vasilii Aksenov, "Arestovan pisatel'," *Novoe russkoe slovo*, Dec. 20, 1981: 3. For speculation on Fedor Abramov's possible role as an executioner of suspected deserters for SMERSH (the Soviet military's counterintelligence service; from *smert' shpionam* 'death to spies'), see C. and E. Proffer, "Introduction: Abramov's Real Life," introduction to Fyodor Abramov, *Two Winters and Three Summers*, trans. D. B. and D. C. Powers (Ann Arbor: Ardis, 1984), vii–x; see also Vladimir Maksimov, "Kolonka redaktora," *Kontinent*, no. 37 (1983): 383–86. Igor' Zolotusskii referred in passing to Abramov's wartime activities: "They beat the freedom out of him in school, in the Komsomol, in SMERSH,

in the Party, and on the job." Zolotusskii concluded that, given this context and this kind of training, it is "commendable" that Abramov recognized—especially in the last five years of his life—that his writing was not as truthful and free as it could have been; see I. Zolotusskii, "Tropa Fedora Abramova. K 70-letiiu so dnia rozhdeniia," *LG*, Feb. 28, 1990: 5.

39. David Joravsky, "Glasnost Theater," *NYRB*, Nov. 10, 1988: 34.

40. Iurii Mal'tsev, "Promezhutochnaia literatura i kriterii podlinnosti," *Kontinent*, no. 25 (1980): 285–321.

41. Vladimir Soloukhin, *Smekh za levym plechom* (Frankfurt: Possev, 1988), 160.

42. Ibid., 161, 167.

43. In 1976 Philippa Lewis ("Peasant Nostalgia," 562–63) did connect "many" *derevenshchiki* to the "All-Russian" movement that developed after 1965 for the purpose of preserving historical and cultural monuments. This movement, in Moscow at least, was later infiltrated and used as a base by extreme chauvinists.

44. While discussions of this subject take place mainly at conferences and in conversation with Soviets, émigrés, and Western scholars, the reader may wish to consult the following: "On Gorbachev: A Talk with Andrei Sakharov," *NYRB*, Dec. 22, 1988: 28–29; Kathleen Parthé and Sergei Kovalyov, "Village Prose: An Exchange," *NYRB*, Feb. 2, 1989: 44; Adrian Karatnycky, "The Secret of Pamyat's Success," *WSJ*, April 3, 1989; Julia Wishnevsky, "The Emergence of 'Pamyat' and 'Otrochestvo,'" *Radio Liberty Research Paper* 342/87 (Aug. 26, 1987): 1–17; Esther Fein, "For Moscow Jews, Fear of Prejudice Is Stirring," *NYT*, Aug. 5, 1988; Bill Keller, "New Moscow: More Hymns to Old Russia," *NYT*, Feb. 22, 1989: 5; Esther Fein, "Soviet Conservatives Try to Turn Back the Clock on Gorbachev's Policies," *NYT*, Feb. 27, 1989: 3; G. Alimov and R. Lynev, "Kuda uvodit 'Pamiat'," *Izvestiia*, June 3, 1987: 3; E. Losoto, "V bespamiatstve. Kuda vedut rukovoditeli tak nazyvaemogo ob"edineniia 'Pamiat'," *Komsomol'skaia pravda*, May 22, 1987: 4; V. P., "Zashchita russkoi kul'tury ili bor'ba s 'zhido-masonami'? Antisemitskie vystupleniia v TsDX," *Russkaia mysl'*, May 15, 1987; Aleksandr Ianov (Yanov), *Russkaia ideia i 2000-i god* (New York: Liberty, 1988), 366–72; George Gibian, "Beneath Communism, There Is Russia," *WSJ*, March 4, 1988.

45. Geoffrey Hosking, *The Awakening of the Soviet Union* (Cambridge: Harvard University Press, 1990), 110.

46. Those who wish—for positive and negative reasons—to see Village Prose as highly nationalistic literature push the starting date up to 1963, so that it will seem as if everything proceeded from Solzhenitsyn's "Matryona's Home," and place the finishing date well into the 1980s. This alternative dating does not hold up under rigorous analysis of the movement from an aesthetic, thematic, or ideological point of view.

47. A. Yakovlev (who was one of Gorbachev's top advisors) objected in the early seventies to the conservative and nationalistic tendencies of some Village Prose, the way it revived what he saw as a false idyll of rural life. The "mournful sobbing" of this literature had, according to Yakovlev, little effect on the contemporary collective farmer, who wanted his life to be more comfortable and more modern: A. Iakovlev, "Protiv antiistorizma," *LG*, Nov. 15, 1972.

48. George Gibian, "Reviving Russian Nationalism," *The New Leader*, Nov. 19, 1979: 13–14.

49. Petrik,"'Derevenskaia proza,'" 66.

50. Catharine Theimer Nepomnyashchy, "The Search for Russian Identity in Contemporary Soviet Russian Literature," *Ethnic Russia in the USSR: The Dilemma of Dominance*, ed. Edward Allworth (New York: Pergamon, 1980), 95–96; see also George Gibian's commentary on this and other articles, "Comment—Beyond Soviet Categories of Literary Ethnocentrism," in the same volume, 98–101; and Lewis, "Peasant Nostalgia," 558–69. Deming Brown made some important distinctions between different levels of Russian nationalism in literature and criticism during the 1950s and 1960s in "Nationalism and Ruralism in Recent Soviet Russian Literature," 183–209.

51. Lewis, "Peasant Nostalgia," 552; Brown, "Nationalism," 252.

52. Hosking, *Beyond Socialist Realism*, 82. The first section of Belov's *Kanuny* appeared in journal form in *Sever* in 1972 (nos. 4 and 5). A number of chauvinistic passages were removed for the 1976 book version; see David Gillespie, "Ironies and Legacies: Village Prose and Glasnost'," *Forum for Modern Language Studies* 27:1 (1991): 74.

53. Vil'chek, "Vniz po techeniiu," 72.

54. Shukshin, Dorosh, Ovechkin, and Rubtsov died between 1968 and 1974; Solzhenitsyn had been forced to leave the country and no longer wrote about rural Russia.

55. Katerina Clark, foreword to Chingiz Aitmatov, *The Day Lasts More Than a Hundred Years*, trans. John French (Bloomington: Indiana University Press, 1988), v–xv. It is Clark more than anyone else who has made the connection between Village Prose and Aitmatov. See also Clark, "The Centrality of Rural Themes," 87–97.

56. *Evreichata*; this was changed in some editions—probably at the instigation of editors—to the innocuous *veichata* 'residents of the city of Veisk'. See Sheila Kunkle, "Nationalism, Chauvinism, and Viktor Astaf'ev's *Pechal'nyi Detektiv*," *Graduate Essays on Slavic Languages and Literatures* (University of Pittsburgh, Dept. of Slavic Languages and Literatures), 2 (1989): 96–97.

57. Ekaterina Starikova, "Kolokol trevogi," *VL*, no. 11 (1986): 87; trans. as "The Alarm-bell" in *SSL* 24:4 (Fall 1988): 18–19. There are two other articles in this forum in *Voprosy Literatury* titled "'Pechal'nyi detektiv' V. Astaf'eva: mnenie chitatelia, otkliki kritikov," both of which voice similar objections to Astaf'ev's use of this ethnic slur: Aleksandr Kucherskii, "Pechal'nyi negativ," 80; and Vadim Sokolov, "Moi drug Soshnin," 108–9. These two articles were translated in the same issue of *SSL* as the Starikova essay.

58. V. Lakshin, "Po pravde govoria: Romany, o kotorykh sporiat," *Izvestiia*, Dec. 3, 1986: 3, continued on Dec. 4, 1986: 3. Excerpts from this article were translated as "New 'Open' Criticism Hits Aitmatov, Belov," in *CDSP* 38:51 (Jan. 21, 1987): 7–9, 14. The most amusing (unintentionally) juxtaposition in the novel is of the healthy Russian perspiration coming from the hero Medvedev and the foul "international sweat" that Medvedev is exposed to in the tourist-filled Tretyakov Gallery where he goes to meet his "faithless" ex-wife.

59. Vasilii Belov, *God velikogo pereloma*, *NM*, no. 3 (1989): 6. For an understanding of the extent to which Belov's tone has changed—despite some of the

earlier stereotyped characters—it is helpful to look at the beginning passages of Parts 1–3 of *The Eve*. Michael Scammell reports that Sergei Zalygin and others at *Novyi mir* tried to get Belov to tone down such comments in *God velikogo pereloma*, but that Belov resisted their pressure.

60. Valentin Rasputin, "Zhertvovat' soboiu dlia pravdy. Protiv bespamiatstva (Vystuplenie na V s"ezde vserossiiskogo obshchestva okhrany pamiatnikov istorii i kul'tury—g. Gor'kii)," *NS*, no. 1 (1988): 169–72. At the conference in Amsterdam, Rasputin spoke on June 1, 1988, about the importance for all Russians of the "recovery of memory," while at the same time he acknowledged the presence of extremists in Pamyat.

61. N. Eidel'man and V. Astaf'ev, "Perepiska iz dvukh uglov," *Sintaksis*, no. 17 (1987): 80–87. In a "Posleslovie" to this exchange, P. Rostin comments that, unlike Eidelman, he (Rostin) never considered Astaf'ev an honest writer (88–89).

62. "Pis'ma pisatelei Rossii. V Tsentral'nyi komitet KPSS," *LR*, March 2, 1990. More than two hundred people subsequently wrote to the paper in March and April 1990 to express their full agreement with the contents of the letter and to add their signatures; among these additional names the only rural writer known to me is Vasilii Belov (*LR*, March 23, 1990). The March 2 letter was translated in *CDSP* 42:19 (June 13, 1990): 11. Rasputin had his name removed from the list of signatories when it was published elsewhere. See also Liah Greenfield, "The Closing of the Russian Mind," *New Republic*, Feb. 5, 1990: 30–34.

63. Transcripts of the RSFSR Writers' Union meetings are published regularly in *Literaturnaia Rossiia* and frequently in *Ogonek*; the latter periodical wants readers to see for themselves just how illogical, mean-spirited, and potentially dangerous the chauvinists are.

64. See, for instance, Rasputin's remarks to a *New York Times* reporter in Bill Keller, "Russian Nationalists: Yearning for an Iron Hand," *New York Times Magazine*, Jan. 28, 1990: 48, 50. Rasputin answered negative reaction by a number of Leningrad writers to this interview by explaining that some of the remarks attributed to him in Keller's interview were either mistranslated or taken out of context: see V. Rasputin, "O moem interv'iu 'N'iu-Iork Taims Megezin,'" *Izvestiia*, July 14, 1990: 6. In a lengthy account of a summer 1990 trip with Rasputin and others to Lake Baikal, Peter Matthiessen quoted sections of the original Keller interview that did not appear in the *New York Times*, as well as the text of his own discussions with Rasputin: see Peter Matthiessen, "The Blue Pearl of Siberia," *NYRB*, Feb. 14, 1991: 37–47. Matthiessen was both impressed by Rasputin as a writer and environmentalist and yet troubled by what he heard firsthand and read about the author's political views. Soloukhin, who generally stays within the bounds of a less extreme kind of nationalism, is reported by Hedrick Smith to share the chauvinist idea that the Revolution of 1917 was "Jewish" and not "Russian"; this information comes from Smith's July 18, 1989, interview with Soloukhin as reported in Hedrick Smith, *The New Russians* (New York: Random House, 1990), 405. Soloukhin has sparred with the anti-Stalinist group Memorial for dating the purges from 1934, and not 1929, when collectivization and dekulakization began; see "Pochemu ia ne podpisalsia pod tem pis'mom," *NS*, no. 12 (1988):

186–89. Village Prose writers have been included in a satire of Russian chauvinism by Tatiana Tolstaia, in which she begins with the statement "Pushkin was a Jew" and then goes on to demonstrate how all Russian writers were Jewish and to reveal their "real" names (Belov is "in fact" Baruch Weisman, and Rasputin is Rabinovich); "Ne mogu molchat'," *Ogonek*, no. 14 (1990).

65. Vasilii Aksenov, "Ne vpolne sentimental'noe puteshestvie," *Novoe Russkoe Slovo*, March 16, 1990: 10–11; trans. by Moira Ratchford and Josephine Woll in the *New Republic*, April 16, 1990: 215. Aksenov sees these writers, under Belov's leadership, as being worse than the leaders of Pamyat. His condemnation of Village Prose writers for their Party membership is somewhat surprising, considering that Aksenov and a number of other urban writers came from solid Party families, who suffered during the purges, but not because of a loss of faith in communism. I am grateful to Vladimir Krutikov for bringing this article to my attention.

66. The label *pochvenniki* refers to a group of Russian intellectuals in the 1860s whose leaders were Dostoevsky, Nikolai Strakhov, and Apollon Grigoriev; they held many beliefs in common with the Slavophiles and stressed a return of educated Russians to their roots in the Russian people as a whole.

67. The council itself was dissolved in December 1990.

68. For an excellent analysis of Russian chauvinism and the literary process, see Josephine Woll, "Russians and 'Russophobes': Antisemitism on the Russian Literary Scene," *Soviet Jewish Affairs* 19:3 (1989): 3–21. On the varieties of nationalism, see Yitzhak M. Brudny, "The Heralds of Opposition to Perestroyka," *Soviet Economy* 5:2 (1989). Another interesting and witty analysis is provided by Walter Laqueur, "From Russia with Hate," *New Republic*, Feb. 5, 1990: 21–25.

69. Alexander Solzhenitsyn, "The Smatterers," in *From under the Rubble*, trans. A. M. Brock et al. (New York: Bantam, 1976), 248–49.

70. Ibid.

71. The samizdat material is discussed in "The Debate over the National Renaissance in Russia," *The Political, Social and Religious Thought of Russian "Samizdat"—An Anthology*, ed. Mikhail Meerson-Aksenov and Boris Shragin, trans. Nicholas Lupinin (Belmont, MA: Nordland, 1977), 345–448. Of special interest are Mikhail Agurskii's discussion "The Intensification of Neo-Nazi Dangers in the Soviet Union" (414–19) and the two appendixes that follow. See also David Shipler, *Russia: Broken Idols, Solemn Dreams* (New York: Penguin, 1984), 323–46. Igor' Shafarevich's essay "Russophobia" appeared in two installments in the June and November 1989 issues of *Nash sovremennik*. On Pamyat and the Soviet press, see Vladislav Krasnov, "Pamyat: A Force for Change?" *Nationalities Papers* 19:2 (Fall 1991).

CHAPTER SEVEN
TWO DETECTIVES IN SEARCH OF VILLAGE PROSE

1. "Vot i poiavliaiutsia pod rubrikoi 'detektivov' ves'ma somnitel'nye sochineniia"; Nataliia Il'ina, "'Palitra krasok,' ili avtor i kritik sovremennogo detektiva," *VL*, no. 2 (1975): 129.

2. "Detektiv—eto zhanr. No eto eshche i tema. Tochnee, kombinatsiia togo

i drugogo"; A. Vulis, "Poetika detektiva," *NM*, no. 1 (1978): 248. For a stimulating discussion of the properties of detective fiction, see also V. Kardin, "Sekret uspekha," *VL*, no. 4 (1986): 102–50.

3. David Gillespie, "History, Politics, and the Russian Peasant: Boris Mozhaev and the Collectivization of Agriculture," *SEER* 67:2 (April 1989): 184.

4. The trilogy has been reissued in Boris Mozhaev, *Tonkomer* (Moscow: Sovremennik, 1984).

5. *Znamia*, nos. 8, 10, 11, 12 (1967); nos. 1, 2 (1968); also published as a separate edition, *Derevenskii detektiv* (Moscow: Molodaia gvardiia, 1968); and in *Sobranie sochinenii* (Moscow: Molodaia gvardiia, 1983), vol. 2. English translation, *A Village Detective*, trans. Raissa Bobrova, Fainna Glagoleva, Avril Pyman, and Vladimir Talmy (Moscow: Progress, 1970); further references will be to the Russian and English versions, respectively. A movie was made of the title story in 1969, directed by A. Roitman. Sinel'kov mentions several television and movie adaptations of the stories. The cycle was very popular with both readers and viewers, and critics even referred to this as the "Lipatov era" in *Znamia*. Mikhail Sinel'kov, introduction to *Sobranie sochinenii*, vol. 1, 19.

6. Introduction to *A Village Detective*, 10–11.

7. Matvei Medvedev, "Sherlok Kholms po-derevenski," *VL*, no. 12 (1968): 226–67.

8. This is Bukharin's term; it refers to Russian versions of Pinkerton serials and other Western crime novels that were translated and sold in Russia in the early twentieth century. Robert Russell, "Red Pinkertonism: An Aspect of Soviet Literature of the 1920s," *SEER* 60:3 (July 1982): 390–412. See also Kardin, "Sekret uspekha," 108. Boris Mozhaev has said that while he read Pinkertons in his youth, his grown daughter reads Agatha Christie: remarks at the "The Topicality of Contemporary Soviet Literature" conference, University of Amsterdam, May 31–June 2, 1988, June 1 discussion period.

9. See the debate between Natalya Ilyina and Arkadii Adamov, "Detective Novels: A Game and Life," *Soviet Literature*, no. 3 (1975): 142–50, trans. Peter Mann.

10. Science fiction, another component of *prikliuchencheskaia literatura*, had already begun to drift toward speculation on problems of freedom in totalitarian states, while detective fiction still stressed order. Science fiction changed in response to scientific and technological progress much more than *detektivy*; Kardin, "Sekret uspekha," 109.

11. Lipatov, "Derevenskii detektiv," 284/409. In a critical article devoted to Lipatov's writing up to 1966, Aleksandr Makarov stressed the importance of the collective in educating and forming individuals and the dangers of separating oneself from the collective; Aleksandr Makarov, "Ostrota sotsial'nogo zreniia," introduction to Vil' Lipatov, *Sobranie sochinenii*, vol. 2, 5–18.

12. E. Safronova, "Derevenskii detektiv," *Sovetskaia Litva*, Sept 7, 1969: 3; F. Nikolaev, "Skuchno takomu kritiku (kommentarii neobkhodimy)," *LR*, March 14, 1969: 16–17; I. Rodnianskaia, "K sporam vokrug Aniskina," *NM*, no. 12 (1968): 235–41; K. Shcherbakov, "Na svoem meste," *Komsomol'skaia pravda*, June 6, 1968; G. Ermakova, "V zashchitu chelovechnosti," *Zvezda*, no. 2

(1969): 210–12; Vadim Kovskii, "'Ja nadeius', chto kniga khoroshaia.' (Snova o detektive)," *VL*, no. 7 (1975): 109; Vulis, "Poetika detektiva," 248.

13. L. Fomenko, "Revoliutsii posviashchaetsia," *LR*, Nov. 12, 1967: 16; M. Korallov, "Litso i profil'," *VL*, no. 5 (1968): 46–51.

14. Lipatov, "Derevenskii detektiv," 102/157.

15. Russell, "Red Pinkertonism," 399, 409.

16. I. Grinberg, "Shirokoe dykhanie rasskaza," *Neva*, no. 8 (1968): 158–64; L. Tevekelian, "Est' s chem sravnit'," *LG*, April 10, 1968: 5.

17. Vladimir Bakhtin, "Kto ubil Stepana Murzina (Dve mneniia ob odnoi knige)," *LG*, March 20, 1968: 5; Ermakova, "V zashchitu chelovechnosti," 5.

18. Lipatov, "Derevenskii detektiv," 268/387.

19. Ermakova, "V zashchitu chelovechnosti," 5.

20. Vladimir Bakhtin, "Kto ubil Stepana Murzina," 5. Max Hayward said that Lipatov, along with Chakovsky, Mikhail Alekseev, and others, was on the conservatives' "approved list" at the June 1971 Fifth Congress of Soviet Writers: Max Hayward, "The Decline of Socialist Realism," *Survey* 18:1 (Winter 1972): 93.

21. Aleksandr Kogan, "Iz literaturnoi zhizni (Na seminare literaturnykh kritikov)," rpt. from *Politicheskii dnevnik*, no. 55 (April 1969) in *Politicheskii dnevnik 1964–1970*, vol. 1 (Amsterdam: The Alexander Herzen Foundation, 1972), 497.

22. *Oktiabr'*, no. 1 (1986): 8–74. The title can also be translated as *A Sad Detective Story*, an ambiguity that confused and disturbed Soviet critics who reviewed the work. Anatolii Lanshchikov suggests *Semeinoe schast'e* (Family happiness) as an alternative title in "Sem'ia (Po povodu romana Viktora Astaf'eva 'Pechal'nii detektiv')," *Ishchu sobesednika (O proze 70–80kh godov)* (Moscow: Sovetskii pisatel', 1988), 254. See also A. Khvatov, "Znaki podlinnosti (Zametki o sovremennoi literature)," *Zvezda*, no. 3 (1987): 193.

23. Astaf'ev, "Pechal'nyi detektiv," 26.

24. Dmitrii Moldavskii, "Sarkazm i bol' Leonida Soshnina (Eshche raz o romane Viktora Astaf'eva *Pechal'nyi detektiv*)," *Ural*, no. 1 (1987): 173.

25. Astaf'ev, "Pechal'nyi detektiv," 27. There are clear references to *Crime and Punishment, The Devils, The Brothers Karamazov*, and other works by Dostoevsky. In a devastating and ironic anecdote, we are told of a couple who left their youngest child to die at home while they read voraciously in the F. M. Dostoevsky Regional Library (53). The use of Dostoevsky as an aesthetic, ideological, and rhetorical model—whether alone or linked with such figures as Avvakum, Gogol, and Solzhenitsyn—has been especially important in literature and criticism since 1986. In light of this, Kariakin's reexamination of Dostoevsky may be of interest to readers of contemporary Russian literature as well: Iurii Kariakin, *Dostoevskii i kanun XXI veka* (Moscow: Sovetskii pisatel', 1989).

26. Moshe Lewin, *The Making of the Soviet System* (New York: Pantheon, 1985), 55.

27. Astaf'ev, "Pechal'nyi detektiv," 13.

28. Iurii Kariakin et al., "Khudozhnik ili publitsist—kto prav? (Nekruglyi stol)," *LG*, Aug. 27, 1986: 2.

29. Viktor Astaf'ev, "Predchustvie ledokhoda," *NS*, no. 6 (1988): 11–22.

30. At the beginning of the story, the narrator mentions that there has been an unusual December *ledokhod*. Igor' Zolotusskii sees the dream as symbolic of the breaking-up of the values that society has been built on, such as family, duty, and conscience. "Donkikhot iz Veiska," *NM*, no. 7 (1986): 248.

31. Astaf'ev, "Pechal'nyi detektiv," 31. This passage is reminiscent of the quatrain from Voznesensky that serves as an epigraph to the Preface.

32. Moldavskii, "Sarkazm i bol'," 173. Kardin, "Sekret uspekha," (somewhat tongue-in-cheek) sets up the following categories for the *detektiv* genre: "When a detective tries to catch a criminal—it's a canonical detective story, when a counterespionage agent hunts for a spy—it's a political detective story. If the agent and the spy read newspapers and speak out on contemporary issues—we have before us a political novel" (114). Astaf'ev's book certainly is most closely linked to the third category. It also has some of the moralistic characteristics of what Kardin calls "anti–detective fiction" (137–38). Lanshchikov, *Ishchu sobesednika*, sees the composition of this novel as being based on the "skewer" principle, where separate episodes are stacked up like meat for a shish kebab. The "skewer" itself in this case is not the hero, Soshnin, but the author's unchanging mood (248).

33. Igor' Zolotusskii, "Otchet o puti," *Znamia*, no. 1 (1987): 221. Trans. by J. L. Hellie as "A Progress Report" in *SSL* 24:3 (Summer 1988): 58. I have made slight corrections in this translation.

34. Kariakin et al.,"Khudozhnik ili publitsist—kto prav?" 2; L. Lavlinskii, "Zakon miloserdiia (Po stranitsam novykh proizvedenii Viktora Astaf'eva)," *Literaturnoe obozrenie*, no. 8 (1986): 19. Several reviewers noted that while it was pretty heavy going as detective story, the discomfort the reader felt was good for the soul: Oleg Shevchenko, "Neizbezhnost' Dostoevskogo," *Pod''em*, no. 11 (1986): 131; Evgenii Prigozhin, "Bol' i nadezhda," *Neva*, no. 4 (1987): 162.

35. "'Pechal'nyi detektiv' V. Astaf'eva. (Mnenie chitatelia, otkliki kritikov)," *VL*, no. 11 (1986): 73–112: A. Kucherskii, "Pechal'nyi negativ," 80; E. Starikova, "Kolokol trevogi," 87; Vadim Sokolov, "Moi drug Soshnin," 108–9. Trans. as "Viktor Astaf'ev's *A Sad Detective Story*: A Reader's Opinion and Two Critics' Replies," in *SSL* 24:4 (Fall 1988): Aleksandr Kucherskii, "The Sad Negative," 12; Ekaterina Starikova, "The Alarm Bell," 18–19; Vadim Sokolov, "My Friend Soshnin," 40. The narrator only mentions Jews once: as Soshnin remembers his literary studies, his fellow students are called *evreichat*, a derogatory reference that has been translated as 'Jew-kids'. This showed up in some editions of the work as the innocuous *veichata* 'residents of Veisk' but was restored in subsequent editions; see Sheila Kunkle, "Nationalism, Chauvinism and Viktor Astaf'ev's *Pechal'nyi Detektiv*," in *Graduate Essays on Slavic Languages and Literatures* (University of Pittsburgh, Department of Slavic Languages and Literatures) 2 (1989): 96–97. Lanshchikov does not mention this passage but instead notes that Astaf'ev himself was accused of denigrating the Russian character in this story: Lanshchikov, "Sem'ia," 267. On Astaf'ev's treatment of female characters, see Natal'ia Ivanova, "Ispytanie pravdoi," *Znamia*, no. 1 (1987): 198–220. Trans. as "Trial by Truth" by Jean Laves Hellie, in *SSL* 24:3 (Summer 1988): 5–57.

36. Zolotusskii, "Otchet," 222.

37. The one critic who briefly mentioned the Lipatov work in connection with *A Sad Detective* noted that the two heroes have only a minimal resemblance. Aleksei Gorshenin, "Ukhodiashchee i nastaiushchee," *Sibirskie ogni,* no. 6 (1987): 151.

38. Gerald Mikkelson and Margaret Winchell, "Valentin Rasputin and His Siberia," introduction to *Siberia on Fire: Stories and Essays by Valentin Rasputin* (De Kalb: Northern Illinois University Press, 1989), xvii.

39. Valentin Rasputin, "Pozhar," *NS,* no. 7 (1985); separate edition, *Vek zhivi-vek liubi* (Moscow: Izvestiia, 1985); "The Fire," trans. Alex Miller, *Soviet Literature,* no. 7 (1986), and by Gerald Mikkelson and Margaret Winchell in *Siberia on Fire.* Vasilii Belov, "Vse vperedi," *NS,* nos. 7–8 (1986); separate edition, *Vse vperedi* (Moscow: Sovetskii pisatel', 1987); *The Best Is Yet to Come,* trans. P. O. Gromm (Moscow: Raduga, 1989). A more literal translation of the title of Belov's novel is "Everything Lies Ahead."

40. Only one critic saw detective-story elements in *The Best Is Yet to Come.* "Belov's plot is structured subtly, parodistically on the detective-adventure novel." The critic has in mind Ivanov's following Liuba through a French hotel to see if she is having an affair: Viacheslav Gorbachev, "Chto vperedi? (O romane Vasiliia Belova *Vse vperedi*)," *Molodaia gvardiia,* no. 3 (1987): 253.

41. D. Ustiuzhanin, "Kasaetsia vsekh (Razdum'ia nad stranitsami novoi povesti V. Rasputina 'Pozhar')," *Literatura v shkole,* no. 2 (1986): 25.

42. The use of an impersonal construction emphasizes that the force making the villagers move is a combination of history, progress, and the government, all beyond the powers of mere mortals to challenge: "ne on reshal, a za nego reshilos' " (329); "he had not decided, it had been decided for him" (17).

43. Lanshchikov, *Ishchu sobesednika,* 6.

44. Viacheslav Lobodov, "Uroki pravdy," *Pod"em,* no. 11 (1986): 134.

45. David Gillespie, "Valentin Rasputin's 'Pozhar,'" *Quinquereme: New Studies in Modern Languages* 9:2 (July 1986): 212. The genre has been called a *povest'-predosterezhenie* 'story-warning' and a *povest'-prizyv* 'story-appeal' by F. Chapchakhov, "Dom ili pribezhishche? (Zametki o povesti Valentina Rasputina 'Pozhar')," *LG,* Aug. 7, 1985: 4.

46. Zolotusskii, "Otchet," 222.

47. Ivanova, "Ispytanie pravdoi," 202–3. See also V. Lakshin, "Po pravdu govoria: Romany, o kotorykh sporiat," *Izvestiia,* Dec. 3, 1986: 3, continued on Dec. 4, 1986: 3; trans. as "To Tell the Truth: Novels That Are Being Debated," *CDSP* 38:51 (Jan. 21, 1987): 9.

48. Belov, *Vse vperedi,* 128.

49. Zolotusskii, "Otchet," 226.

50. Lakshin, "Po pravde govoria"; Dmitrii Ivanov, "Chto vperedi?" *Ogonek,* no. 2 (1987): 12; "Chitateli o romane V. Belova 'Vse vperedi,'" *NS,* no. 8 (1987): 176–81.

51. Gorbachev, "Chto vperedi?" 250–77; "Chitateli o romane V. Belova"; Irina Spiridonova, "'Bezoblachnoe sirotstvo' (O romane V. Belova, *Vse vperedi*)," *Sever,* no. 4 (1987): 110–17. Spiridonova does fault Belov on his

female characters, who are presented only from a male point of view and have no voice of their own in this work.

52. Lavlinskii, "Zakon miloserdiia," 18. Valentin Rasputin stated that if literature seemed to be changing it is because "we're too upset to be writing epics": "Interv'iu," *Literaturnoe obozrenie*, no. 9 (1985); quoted in Spiridonova, "Bezoblachnoe sirotstvo,'" 111.

53. Zolotusskii, "Otchet," 224.

54. N. Leiderman, "Pochemu ne smolkaet kolokol?" *Ural*, no. 2 (1988): 158–59.

55. Burnashov, the hero of Vladimir Lichutin's novel *Liubostai* (The demon) (Moscow: Sovetskii pisatel', 1987), and the stepfather in Viktor Astaf'ev's "Liudochka" (*NM*, no. 9 [1989]) should also be included in this group.

56. Aleksandr Solzhenitsyn, "Matrenin dvor," *NM*, no. 1 (1963); trans. H. T. Willetts, in *The Portable Twentieth-Century Russian Reader*, ed. Clarence Brown (New York: Penguin, 1985), 464. The "spiritual similarity" between Darya and Matryona was noted by a number of Western critics, including David Gillespie, *Valentin Rasputin and Soviet Russian Village Prose* (London: Modern Humanities Research Association, 1986), pp. 68–69; I. Corten, "Solženicyn's Matrena and Rasputin's Dar'ja: Two Studies in Russian Peasant Spirituality," *Russian Language Journal* 33 (Winter 1979): 85–98; Teresa Polowy, *The Novellas of Valentin Rasputin: Genre, Language, and Style* (New York: Peter Lang, 1989), 236 n. 10. David Gillespie hears echoes of Solzhenitsyn's *The Gulag Archipelago* in the second part of Mozhaev's *Peasant Men and Women*: "History, Politics, and the Russian Peasant: Boris Mozhaev and the Collectivization of Agriculture," *SEER* 67:2 (April 1989): 205.

57. When one keeps in mind Solzhenitsyn's comments on such topics as Western mass culture and the role of Jews in the Revolution, the affinities between him and these writers (both in their fiction and in their public pronouncements) are even clearer. Spiridonova, "'Bezoblachnoe sirotstvo,'" 114, uses the term "moral maximalism." The term "monologic" is used by a number of critics in reference to works of this period; see, for example, Ivanova, "Ispytanie pravdoi," 201. It is implied in Spiridonova (115).

58. Quoted by F. Gilis, "'My pochemu takie-to?'" *Neva*, no. 5 (1986): 162.

59. Gorshenin, "Ukhodiashchee," 154.

60. Ivanova, "Ispytanie pravdoi," 199. See also Zolotusskii, "Otchet," 223.

CHAPTER EIGHT
REWRITING AND REREADING LITERARY HISTORY

1. "A Postcard from the Volcano."

2. Starikova wrote in 1989 about the emergence of manuscripts from the drawer and from samizdat: "We're not going to pretend that we didn't know anything at all about these pages. Much of what is only being published now was read much earlier and was secretly a part of the preservation and maturing of our consciousness. There was a lot that had an unspoken influence on what we have come to call ... the 'literary process.'" E. Starikova, "Shagi komandora. O rasskazakh Vladimira Tendriakova," *Znamia*, no. 9 (1988): 223.

3. Vladimir Tendriakov, "Den' na rodine," *Nauka i religiia*, no. 11 (1964); there were numerous lyrical essays and stories on this theme, e.g., Leonid Ivanov's "Rodnye mesta" (*NM*, no. 3 [1963]).

4. Tendriakov, "Den'," 47. For enother example of this "double view" in Tendriakov, see Katerina Clark, "The Centrality of Rural Themes in Postwar Soviet Fiction," in *Perspectives on Literature and Society in Eastern and Western Europe*, ed. Geoffrey Hosking and George Cushing (London: Macmillan, 1989), 81.

5. Abram Tertz (Andrei Sinyavsky), *The Trial Begins and On Socialist Realism*, trans. George Dennis (New York: Vintage, 1960), 215.

6. Tendriakov, "Den'," 43.

7. Ibid., 46.

8. Makarov calls this a *svetlyi mir* 'radiant world'; A. Makarov, *Romany S. Babaevskogo "Kavaler zolotoi zvezdy" i "Svet nad zemlei"* (Moscow: Znanie, 1952), 7.

9. Tendriakov, "Den'," 48.

10. Ibid., 50.

11. On Tendriakov, see Geoffrey Hosking, *Beyond Socialist Realism: Soviet Fiction since "Ivan Denisovich"* (New York: Holmes and Meier: 1980), 84–100.

12. Sinyavsky/Tertz, *On Socialist Realism*, 199.

13. Vladimir Tendriakov, "Para gnedykh," *NM*, no. 3 (1988): 9.

14. Ibid., 19.

15. Ibid., 22.

16. A few months after the Tendriakov stories appeared, "Proshchanie s mirom," Vasilii Subbotin's somewhat similar narrative of a rural child's view of collectivization and the purge years was published in *Oktiabr'* (no. 6 [1988]); there is no indication as to whether this is a newly written or a "delayed" work, but it appears to be the latter. Subbotin was born in 1921 and Tendriakov in 1923.

17. A. Turkov, "Srashchennyi provod. O rasskazakh Vladimira Tendriakova," *LG*, June 1, 1988: 4. The image of "spliced wires" comes from "Donna Anna," the fourth Tendriakov story in the March 1988 *Novyi mir*, whose setting is a frontline communications unit during World War II.

18. See, for instance, the clearly derivative story by K. Lavrent'ev, "Iz zhizni Glafiry Semenovny," *Sever*, no. 2 (1987); discussed in Sviatoslav Pedenko, "Chuvstvo puti. Po stranitsam zhurnala *Sever* v 1987 godu," *LR*, March 11, 1988: 3–4. For a survey of rural writing after 1985, see Evgenii Potupov, "Khoziaeva ili gosti? Eshche raz o tak nazyvaemoi 'derevenskoi proze,'" *LG*, Nov. 16, 1988: 4.

19. Vladimir Krupin, "Sorokovoi den'," *NS*, no. 11 (1981). Krupin also gained a wide audience for his allegorical "Zhivaia voda" (The water of life, 1980). The ruling conservative faction of the RSFSR Writers' Union was able to have him appointed editor of the journal *Moskva* in 1990.

20. Ibid., 93.

21. Boris Mozhaev has said that the same factors are going to change the nature of "war literature," which will be quite different when it is written by people who were not even old enough to experience the war as children. Boris Mozhaev, remarks made at the "Topicality of Contemporary Soviet Literature" conference, University of Amsterdam, May 31–June 2, 1988.

22. The reasons for this "quiet period" were the natural end of Village Prose as a literary movement; the deaths of Kazakov, Abramov, and Tendriakov (Shukshin, Ovechkin, Dorosh, and the rural poet Rubtsov had died earlier); and the vicious physical attack on Rasputin that left him unable to write for several years.

23. Lichutin's story was published in 1987: Vladimir Lichutin, *Liubostai* (Moscow: Sovetskii pisatel', 1987). Another example is Viktor Astaf'ev's story "Liudochka" (*NM*, no. 9 [1989]) in which a young girl leaves her "dying village" to go to a provincial city, where a series of tragic events leads to her suicide. A translation of the Astaf'ev story by David Gillespie appeared in *Soviet Literature*, no. 8 (1990).

24. Vasilii Belov, "Nezazhivaiushchaia rana," *NS*, no. 11 (1989).

25. A. Khvatov, "Znaki podlinnosti. Zametki o sovremennoi literature," *Zvezda*, no. 3 (1987): 186.

26. "Delayed" rural works by Yashin, Shukshin, and Prishvin have also appeared since 1985; see Pedenko, "Chuvstvo puti," 3.

27. Vladimir Soloukhin, "Idti po svoei trope. Interv'iu pered publikatsiei," *LG*, May 30, 1990: 4. If this trend catches on among other Russian writers and their literary executors, the literary glut—and paper shortage—is almost beyond imagining.

28. Marietta Chudakova observed in 1972, "It is obvious that 'one and the same' rural old man can be regarded in different literary periods and by different writers as an amusing exhibit at whom the author looks with laughter, or as a complex human character whom the author seeks to capture 'as an equal,' or again as a sage and prophet before whom the author hastens to do reverence with childlike meekness." See M. Chudakova, "Zametki o iazyke sovremennoi prozy," *NM*, no. 1 (1972): 228; trans. as "Notes on the Language of Contemporary Prose," *SSL* 9:1 (Winter 1972–1973): 73.

29. One could propose a third Platonov-Sokolov type of literature with rural themes, settings, or characters. A review of Sasha Sokolov's work described the novel *Between Dog and Wolf* as a "surrealist variation on 'village prose'"; Alexander Zholkovsky, "Starring Joe Stalin as Himself," *Los Angeles Times Book Review*, Feb. 11, 1990.

30. Iurii Davydov and Nikolai Anastas'ev, "Chto takoe russkaia literatura?" *LG*, March 1, 1989: 2. Viktor Astaf'ev had maintained for years that "we all came out of 'Matryona's Home,'" while Solzhenitsyn himself had always given Village Prose writers the most prominent place in contemporary Soviet Russian literature. See L. Polukhina, "Sozidat' miloserdiiu i bratstvo. V gostiakh u Viktora Astaf'eva," *LG*, Sept. 26, 1990: 4. See also Alexandr Solzhenitsyn, *The Oak and the Calf*, trans. Harry Willetts (New York: Harper and Row, 1980), 521.

31. Nikolai Anastas'ev and Iurii Davydov, "Liubov' k 'blizhnemu' ili 'dal'nemu'?" *LG*, Feb. 22, 1989: 2.

32. I. Tolstoi, "Literaturnaia voina v Leningrade," *Russkaia Mysl'*, May 11, 1990: 10.

33. Viktor Erofeev, "Pominki po sovetskoi literature," *LG*, July 4, 1990: 8; "A Funeral Feast for Soviet Literature," *SSL* 26:4 (Fall 1990): 10–18.

34. David Gillespie, "Ironies and Legacies: Village Prose and Glasnost'," *Forum for Modern Language Studies* 27:1 (1991): 73.

35. For a post-1985 example of this process, see Mikhail Lobanov, "Puti preobrazheniia," *Molodaia gvardiia*, no. 6 (1989): 257. Lobanov praises Village Prose—which he dates from Solzhenitsyn's "Matryona's Home"—for giving Russians their own artistic *tip myshleniia* 'mode of thought'.

36. A 1988 article by the Literary Department of *Ogonek* saw in the division of literature into such schools as "Village Prose" and "Urban Prose" a profoundly ideological maneuver that they blame on the conservative journal *Molodaia gvardiia*; the *Ogonek* critics see this kind of division leading to a further—and in their view harmful—segmentation of literature, into, for instance, "intelligentsia" and "popular," and into "national" and "foreign" types; "Anekdoty," *Ogonek*, no. 51 (1988): 14.

37. Astaf'ev and others point out that they did not speak out *against* Solzhenitsyn, as did a number of prominent literary figures. Boris Mozhaev is said to have defended Solzhenitsyn's right to a fair hearing at the Writers' Union in 1969; see Lily Daetz, "Die bäuerliche Literatur und ihre Tradition," in *Sowjetliteratur heute* (Munich: Beck, 1979), 111. Mozhaev also organized a group letter in defense of Alexander Tvardovsky on the eve of the latter's forced resignation from the editor's position at *Novyi mir*; see Solzhenitsyn, *The Oak and the Calf*, 275. On the other hand, at least one rural writer—Vladimir Soloukhin—supported the attack on Boris Pasternak (over the publication abroad of *Doctor Zhivago*) in the late 1950s; see Walter Laqueur, *Stalin: The Glasnost Revelations* (New York: Charles Scribner's Sons, 1990), 273.

38. Alexander Zholkovsky, "Dreaming Right and Reading Right: Five Keys to One of Il'f and Petrov's Ridiculous Men," *SR* 48:1 (Spring 1989): 36.

39. Vladimir Soloukhin, "Eto byl boets, voin, rytsar'. . . k 70-letiiu so dnia rozhdeniia Fedora Abramova," *Moskva*, no. 2 (1990): 167–68. In December 1989 the journal *Voprosy literatury* began a series of articles taking a new look at the literature of the Thaw; the first in this series is Sergei Chuprinin's "Neproshedshee vremia."

40. Igor' Zolotusskii, "Tropa Fedora Abramova. K 70-letiiu so dnia rozhdeniia," *LG*, Feb. 28, 1990: 5.

41. Gillespie, "Ironies and Legacies," 78.

42. Galina Belaia, "Pereput'e," *VL*, no. 12 (1987): 75.

43. Anastas'ev and Davydov, "Liubov'," 2. Donald Treadgold described the Village Prose writers clinging to their "artistic integrity"; *Twentieth Century Russia*, 7th ed. (Boulder: Westview Press, 1990), 492.

44. S. Frederick Starr, "The Road to Reform," in Abraham Brumberg, ed., *Chronicle of a Revolution: A Western-Soviet Inquiry into Perestroika* (New York: Pantheon, 1990), 25. Edward Brown called Village Prose "some of the best writing of the twentieth century," but it was "in no sense a protest literature"; *Russian Literature since the Revolution*, rev. ed. (Cambridge: Harvard University Press, 1982), 292–312. Deming Brown sees these writers as having made the best of what was permitted in literature during the years of stagnation; *Soviet Russian Literature since Stalin* (Cambridge: Cambridge University Press, 1978), 221.

45. Naum Korzhavin, in "Rezonans. Na anketu *IL* otvechaiut pisateli russkogo zarubezh'ia," *Inostrannaia literatura*, no. 2 (1989): 249. These sentiments are echoed in remarks summing up the survey of émigré writers' opinions by D. Zatonskii, "Vynos krivykh zerkal," *Inostrannaia Literatura*, no. 3 (1989): 248–49.

APPENDIX II
"KONDYR": A PARAMETRIC ANALYSIS

1. While the use of *legok* in this particular situation connects the newcomer to the devilish events at hand, the phrase *legok na pomine* in general has lost any diabolical implication.

2. The phrase "carnivalistic overtones" appears in Mikhail Bakhtin, *Problems of Dostoevsky's Poetics*, ed. and trans. Caryl Emerson (Minneapolis: University of Minnesota Press, 1984), 134. This list is based on the materials on "carnival" in Mikhail Bakhtin, *Rabelais and His World*, trans. Helene Iswolsky (Cambridge: MIT Press, 1968); Mikhail Bakhtin, *Problems of Dostoevsky's Poetics*; Mikhail Bakhtin, "Rable i Gogol' (Iskusstvo slova i narodnaia smekhovaia kul'tura)," in *Voprosy literatury i estetiki* (Moscow: Khudozhestvennaia literatura, 1975), 484–95; Katerina Clark and Michael Holquist, *Mikhail Bakhtin* (Cambridge: Harvard University Press, 1984).

3. Caryl Emerson, letter to the author, June 26, 1989.

4. Bakhtin, *Rabelais and His World*, 47.

5. Ibid., 51; Clark and Holquist, *Mikhail Bakhtin*, 299–302; Iu. M. Lotman and B. A. Uspenskii, "New Aspects in the Study of Early Russian Literature," trans. N.F.C. Owen, *The Semiotics of Russian Culture*, ed. Ann Shukman (Ann Arbor: University of Michigan Press, 1984), 46.

6. Emerson, letter to the author.

7. Lotman and Uspenskii, "New Aspects," 36–52; Ewa Thompson, "D. S. Likhachev and the Study of Old Russian Literature," *Russian Literature and Criticism*, Selected Papers from the Second World Congress for Soviet and East European Studies, Garmisch-Partenkirchen, Sept. 30–Oct. 4, 1980, ed. Evelyn Bristol (Berkeley: Berkeley Slavic Specialties, 1982), 245–54. These two articles criticize Likhachev and Panchenko for assuming in *Smekh v drevnei Rusi* that carnival laughter functions the same way in both contexts.

8. Linda J. Ivanits, *Russian Folk Belief* (Armonk, NY: M. E. Sharpe, 1989), 105; chapter 7, "'Spoiling' and Healing," 103–24.

9. D. S. Likhachev, A. M. Panchenko, and N. V. Ponyrko, *Smekh v drevnei Rusi* (Leningrad: Nauka, 1984), 175–202; G. A. Nosova, *Iazychestvo v pravoslavii* (Moscow: Nauka, 1975), 53–59; S. V. Maksimov, *Nechistaia, nevedomaia i krestnaia sila* (St. Petersburg: Golike and Vil'borg, 1903), 360–73.

10. Likhachev thinks that the emphasis on newlyweds at Shrovetide is also tied to a liturgical focus at the beginning of Lent on Adam and Eve and their fall from grace. Each young husband, says Likhachev, represents Adam, each young woman, Eve (*Smekh*, 183). Following this line of argument, one could see Kondyr and Alyona as "Adam" and "Eve" in their idyllic forest, and the whole story as Kondyr's attempt to return to Eden.

11. A. D. Leonov, "Kondyr'," in *Khodiat devki* (Moscow: Sovetskaia Rossiia, 1971), 150.

12. Valentin Rasputin, "Proshchanie s Materoi," in *Izbrannye proizvedeniia v dvukh tomakh* (Moscow: Molodaia gvardiia, 1984), vol. 2, 322.

13. For a discussion of the chronotope of rural childhood see chapter 2; for an explanation of "chronotope" see Mikhail Bakhtin, "Forms of Time and Chronotope in the Novel," in *The Dialogic Imagination*, trans. Caryl Emerson and Michael Holquist (Austin: University of Texas Press, 1981), 84–258, and Clark and Holquist, *Mikhail Bakhtin*, 275–88.

14. Aleksandr Logvinov, *Priokskie rodniki* (Moscow: Sovremennik, 1977), 155.

15. Ibid.

16. Ibid., 155–58.

17. Aleksandr Logvinov, "Istoki zhizni," review of *Khodiat devki*, by Aleksei Leonov, *NS*, Feb. 1973: 190–91. V. I. Protchenko agrees that Leonov's work does not represent an appeal for a return to the past even while recording the disappearance of thousand-year-old values; Protchenko, "Nekotorye voprosy razvitiia 'Derevenskoi prozy,'" *Problemy russkoi sovetskoi literatury 50–70-e gody*, ed. V. A. Kovalev (Leningrad: Nauka, 1976), 146.

18. Viacheslav Gorbachev, "Sud'by narodnye. Kogda mil belyi svet," *LR*, Aug. 25, 1972: 10.

19. In addition to the sources cited, information on Leonov comes from personal correspondence 1984–1989 and interviews in Leningrad in January 1986 and August 1987.

20. The only English translation of Leonov, other than "Kondyr," is "Deaf" ("Glukhaia"), trans. Alice Ingman, *Soviet Literature*, May 1972.

21. Evgenii Kutuzov, "Potrebnost' souchastiia," *Avrora*, May 1976: 68. Nancy Condee and Vladimir Padunov have spoken of a category of contemporary literature called *elektrichnaia* (lit. 'suburban train'), that is, light reading appropriate for commuters.

22. Nikolai Panteleimonov, "Aleksei Leonov i ego geroi," afterword to *I ostalis' zhit'*, by Aleksei Leonov (Leningrad: Lenizdat, 1984), 400. Leonard Babby reports that Leonov is a popular writer among older female collective-farm workers (i.e., people who know something of traditional village life) in the Kalinin/Tver' region.

23. Radii Pogodin, "Kto ty, vlastelin zemli?" *Avrora*, Oct. 1978: 154–59.

INDEX